PENGUIN BOOKS
CHANGEMAKERS

Gayatri Rangachari Shah is a journalist and columnist whose work has appeared in both national and international publications like the *New York Times*. She has a fortnightly column, 'Flight of Fancy', in *The Hindu*. She is a contributing editor at *Vogue* and *Architectural Digest* and India head at Tina Brown Live Media, which produces the globally renowned journalism summit Women in the World. Gayatri covers a variety of subjects, including culture, gender, design and education, and has profiled leading personalities around the world. She is a graduate of Mount Holyoke College and Columbia University's Graduate School of Journalism. She lives in Mumbai with her husband and two children.

Mallika Kapur is an international news journalist. She is currently a senior editor at Bloomberg Live, APAC. In her twenty-year career that spans three countries, she has been a producer, anchor and correspondent for CNN in London, Mumbai and Hong Kong. She has reported extensively on key economic, political, social and gender issues in India and covered some of Asia's biggest breaking news stories for the network. She has also anchored business news shows and hosted long-form feature programmes. Mallika attended Brown University and Columbia University's Graduate School of Journalism. She resides in Hong Kong with her husband and two children.

ADVANCE PRAISE FOR THE BOOK

'It's rare for a woman to make it in the man's world of films, even in Hollywood. The fact that *Changemakers* celebrates as many as twenty women who succeeded in bringing about fundamental changes in largely male-dominated Bollywood, speaks volumes about their courage, tenacity and grit. Here are a new set of role models for women everywhere'—Anand Mahindra, chairman, Mahindra Group

'This riveting look at the female powerhouses of Bollywood is long overdue. It brings alive the creativity and tenacity of the women behind India's entertainment juggernaut that shapes culture and mints money'—Tina Brown, award-winning journalist, editor, author and founder of the Women in the World Summit

CHANGE MAKERS

Twenty Women Transforming Bollywood Behind the Scenes

GAYATRI RANGACHARI SHAH | **MALLIKA KAPUR**

Foreword by Farah Khan

PENGUIN BOOKS

An imprint of Penguin Random House

PENGUIN BOOKS

USA | Canada | UK | Ireland | Australia
New Zealand | India | South Africa | China

Penguin Books is part of the Penguin Random House group of companies
whose addresses can be found at global.penguinrandomhouse.com

Published by Penguin Random House India Pvt. Ltd
7th Floor, Infinity Tower C, DLF Cyber City,
Gurgaon 122 002, Haryana, India

Penguin
Random House
India

First published in Penguin Books by Penguin Random House India 2018

ISBN 9780143441731

Typeset in Adobe Garamond Pro by Manipal Digital Systems, Manipal
Printed at Thomson Press India Ltd, New Delhi

www.penguin.co.in

MIX
Paper
FSC FSC® C010615

Contents

Foreword   vii

Introduction   ix

Charu Khurana: The Make-Up Artist   1

Juhi Chaturvedi: The Scriptwriter   13

Guneet Monga: The Producer   27

Anaita Shroff Adajania: The Stylist   41

Deepa Bhatia: The Editor   59

Gauri Shinde: The Director   71

Geeta Tandon: The Stunt Artist   85

Kiran Rao: The Multitasker   95

Anvita Dutt: The Lyricist   111

Anupama Chopra: The Journalist   125

Shanoo Sharma: The Casting Director   139

Priya Seth: The Cinematographer   155

Rohini Iyer: The Reputation Manager   169

Geeta Kapur: The Choreographer   183

Sneha Khanwalkar: The Music Director   195

Amrita Pandey: The Studio Executive   207

Shikha Kapur: The Marketing Executive   225

Amrita Mahal Nakai: The Production Designer   239

Shubha Ramachandra: The Script Supervisor   253
Hetal Dedhia: The Gaffer   265

Acknowledgements   277
Endnotes   280

FOREWORD

When I joined the Hindi film industry in the early 1990s, very few women worked behind the scenes. I started out as a fourth assistant director and was the only girl on set, apart from the stars. The few other women one saw were the hairdressers. Even the costume designers and make-up artists were men. People did not really want their daughters to work in the industry because it was largely male-dominated. We took a photo of the unit on the last day we filmed *Jo Jeeta Wohi Sikander,* for which I had done the choreography. That was in 1992. That picture is an accurate portrayal of the times. In a crew of seventy-five to eighty men, there is just one woman—me.

From the earliest days of Hindi cinema, when women were not allowed to act in movies—men wore wigs and dressed up as women to play female characters—to the present day, we have come a long way. Corporates have entered the business and there are many more educated people working in films now. That's brought in a new professionalism. The film industry is considered 'respectable' today, and because it is also lucrative, it is attracting talented men and women from across the country and around the world.

Things started changing in the early 2000s. I think *Main Hoon Na*[1] broke some kind of glass ceiling. I don't think that was acknowledged enough, though. It was unheard of for a woman to direct an action-packed, big-budget commercial Bollywood movie that went on to make crores of rupees. Till then, women were put into a niche—we were supposed to make 'sensitive' movies about 'sensitive' issues, that small movie about

---

[1] *Main Hoon Na* is a 2004 Indian film co-written and directed by Farah Khan, her directorial debut.

a couple that can't have children that would run as a morning show at a multiplex.

With *Main Hoon Na*, I became one of the few women to direct a mainstream entertainer. Today, there are several women directors. Perhaps not all are famous, but they are there. Now, units are full of women. In twenty-five years, the scene has changed dramatically.

On my films *Happy New Year* and *Om Shanti Om*, 50 per cent of my crew comprised women. I want to be clear that I do not choose a person because she is a woman, nor am I suggesting that anyone should get a job because of their gender. I choose the best person for the job; that they happen to be women is a great thing.

I would like men to read this book and realize that the women who work with them, and for them, go through a lot, and that they work much harder to get half the appreciation as men. Men take that for granted. I see male directors and I am amazed at their sense of entitlement and arrogance. Women tend to downplay their achievements. People would be surprised to know that even I have low self-esteem. I never talk about how many hits I have delivered and that nobody can push me around. Women don't speak like that.

I am delighted that Gayatri and Mallika have chosen to shine a light on the women who toil behind the scenes in this industry day in and day out. After reading their stories, I know you will applaud them. Gayatri and Mallika have profiled a solid list of women, many of whom I know and respect. Each one of them is an outstanding example of how hard work and living on your own terms pay off. I hope this book will inspire young women around the country to choose to work in films and make the industry even more dynamic.

What could be better?

—Farah Khan

INTRODUCTION

This book is about women in Bollywood. But it is not about those in the public gaze. The lives and loves, films and careers of actors are well chronicled. What about those women who work away from the limelight, behind the scenes of the Hindi film industry? You have most likely seen their work but often don't know it. And you probably aren't familiar with their names. They belong to a Bollywood we know little about.

Two decades into the twenty-first century, India is experiencing a seismic societal churn. Women have never been better educated, earned more or lived healthier lives. From boardrooms to courtrooms, factory floors to software centres, in sports, in the arts and in science, they have made great strides.

Yet, Indian women continue to encounter significant hurdles in the form of systemic oppression and deep-rooted cultural biases. The gender ratio is grossly imbalanced: India has 37 million more men than women, according to the 2011 census. Women remain physically vulnerable. The wage gap is a pressing problem. And despite a growing economy their numbers in the workforce are declining. A 2017 World Bank report says that only 27 per cent of Indian women are employed.

Against this paradox, one industry presents an intriguing picture: Bollywood.

Although the odds remain stacked against women in this field too—the gender ratio in India's film industry is 6.2 men to every woman, according to a report by the Geena Davis Institute on Gender in Media—the past two decades have seen a record number of women work behind the scenes of Hindi cinema.

While there is no data to track their numbers, there is strong anecdotal evidence. Actor Katrina Kaif says, 'I see more women on a film set for sure. Sometimes, you'll notice over 65 per cent of the people present are women.' Film star Vidya Balan concurs. 'Earlier, they were in the art and costume departments, but today, there are more women working as assistant directors and camera operators.'

Anil Kapoor, who has been acting for close to forty years, attributes this significant change to education, evolving mindsets, as well as the growing professionalism, discipline and corporate structure that defines the movie business today. 'There is no comparison with the earlier days,' he says. 'These days, some units I go to, there are mostly women.' This changing demographic is influencing what we see on screen. Karan Johar says, 'Women have made our films more edgy, more progressive, more relatable and much more accountable.'

This book pulls the curtain back on a group of women working in an industry that India is obsessed with. We profile twenty trailblazers who have cut through the ranks of a traditionally male-dominated field to establish themselves as undisputed leaders in their craft. They contribute to an art form that feeds the dreams and fuels the imagination of a billion people. Their journeys are nothing short of extraordinary.

These women are disruptors. Charu Khurana took her fight for women to work as make-up artists in Bollywood—a right they were denied for six decades—to India's Supreme Court. Priya Seth is a director of photography on commercial blockbusters. Anaita Shroff Adajania, who styles Bollywood stars, changed the way a generation of Indians dress. Geeta Tandon overcame years of sexual abuse to become one of the few women stunt artists in the industry. Anupama Chopra redefined film journalism. Kiran Rao resurrected a languishing film festival, and turned the spotlight on indie cinema. By placing female characters centre stage, Gauri Shinde's films make audiences rethink conventional wisdom and social norms. Juhi Chaturvedi's screenplays make sensitive subjects like sperm donation a topic of national conversation. Anvita Dutt conjures up haunting lyrics. Geeta Kapur puts the oomph in our dance moves. Shubha Ramachandra ensures our movies are seamless. Amrita Mahal Nakai designs beautiful sets that transport us, for a brief while, to another world. Deepa Bhatia toils silently, skilfully stitching stories together. Amrita Pandey helps run a global studio that takes Hindi films to key overseas markets like China. Shikha Kapur markets films so cleverly that we, the audience, rush to buy a theatre ticket. Shanoo Sharma's casting gives films authenticity. Guneet Monga's productions bridge the gap between East and West. Rohini Iyer, the ultimate reputation manager, is the go-to publicist for Bollywood A-listers. Hetal Dedhia mesmerizes us with the way she lights up a set. And Sneha Khanwalkar's unique music surprises India with a new sounds.

When we started our research, we found that very few of these women had a prior Bollywood connection. At a time when the Hindi movie industry is being accused of nepotism, the women in this book demonstrate that it *is* possible to make it in Hindi cinema through talent, persistence and tenacity. Most on our list do not come from film backgrounds. Even now, many are not known outside industry circles. They come from middle-class families and have not had lascivious godfathers or indulgent uncles to coax their careers along. They are where they are because of their determination and hard work.

It was incredibly hard to narrow our list down to just twenty. We made our choices after interviewing industry insiders, experts and academics. By no means is this a comprehensive, exhaustive list, and we would never claim it to be so. In the end, these were the women whose stories spoke to us. We found ourselves wanting to know more about them. Where did they come from? What attracted them to the film business? What made them persevere? What makes them thrive?

Our subjects made it clear they didn't want to be profiled simply because they are women. Their gender does not define them. We agree. But they recognize they have a responsibility that goes beyond their craft—a duty to share their stories so that young people across the country feel emboldened to pursue their passions. These women did. Others too can. We hope their stories will move and inspire you the way they have moved and inspired us.

Over the course of a year and a half, we conducted more than 120 interviews, many with industry stalwarts. The result, we hope, demonstrates that women are shattering Bollywood's glass ceiling through merit, resolve and talent. In an industry where on-screen glamour often eclipses the contribution of those who work behind the scenes, we believe these women deserve to be applauded and their journeys acknowledged. They are transforming the country's entertainment juggernaut, shaping

popular culture, and influencing social mores. Thanks to them, and the
many other women working in cinema, it's safe to say that Bollywood is
no longer the all boys' club it once was.

Around the world, the entertainment business is in the news. The
#MeToo movement, sparked in Hollywood by the Harvey Weinstein
scandal, unleashed a torrent of stories not just in the United States but
also in the UK, France and Australia. While India has not yet had its
#MeToo movement, it is encouraging to see more women speak out
about harassment, whether it's in the judiciary, in sports or in cinema.
There is a national outpouring of rage at heinous sexual crimes against
girls and women that will hopefully usher in the beginning of a zero-
tolerance movement against such criminality. We hope it continues to fuel
a growing confidence among the women of India, who are increasingly
bolder, stronger and less afraid.

In 1951, Pandit Jawaharlal Nehru said, 'To awaken the people, it is
the woman who must be awakened; once she is on the move, the family
moves, the village moves, the nation moves.'[1] By telling these stories, we
hope to provide a record of a particular time in India's historic journey
towards gender equality. We hope that these women will act as role models
for future generations. They are part of a new Bollywood, a new India.

---

[1] Cited from, Ashu Pasricha, 'Multidisciplinary Study of Maidservants'
     Lives', *Tribune*, 17 March 2002.

CHARU KHURANA
THE MAKE-UP ARTIST

haru Khurana stood inside the Supreme Court of India. It was 14 November 2014. The crisp Delhi winter was just setting in. There was a nip in the air, but Charu was hot and out of breath. She had driven herself to Tilak Marg in her silver Maruti Esteem, waited in a slow-moving queue before climbing seventy steep steps to reach the courtroom. Her back was sore and she was thirsty. She was six months pregnant. But there was no time to think about any of that.

Standing under the whirring fans, she held her breath as Justice Dipak Misra read out his verdict in *Charu Khurana v. The Union of India and Others*.[1] Unaware she was about to witness a watershed moment for women in India, Charu inhaled deeply. It was the culmination of a long journey—one that began many years earlier with a box of colourful, sparkling items.

In the Khurana household in New Delhi, that plain, beige box is a treasured family heirloom. Inside, a kaleidoscope of compartments hold an assortment of shiny bottles, pots of glitter and colourful plastic tubes. It is a vanity case that used to belong to Neelam Khurana, a former beautician, who passed it on to her daughter, Charu. Every now and then, Charu opens it and inhales a whiff of nostalgia. It is packed with memories of a happy, contented childhood, much of it spent playing with this box.

'There were little bottles of Christian Dior, Estee Lauder, Chanel!' the thirty-five-year-old exclaims. None of these brands were available in the pre-liberalization domestic Indian market in the 1980s. The contents of the box, out of reach for most people in the country, were prized valuables. A young Charu found them mesmerizing.

Charu is a celebrated make-up artist, admired for her creativity, respected for her grit. She has worked on some of India's biggest films and with the country's leading actors, including Kamal Haasan, Abhishek Bachchan and Anushka Shetty.

Her background is in the razzle-dazzle world of films and commercials—who doesn't remember the pointy-eared, double-horned monster in the iconic Onida ad with the 'neighbour's envy, owner's pride'

---

[1] *Charu Khurana v. Union of India and Ors.*, (2015) 1 SCC 192.

tag line? Or Mani Ratnam's *Raavan* and S.S. Rajamouli's *Baahubali?* That's Charu's work. But her skill often takes her beyond big-ticket films and entertainment. When CNN required a make-up artist for the network's interviews with Prime Minister Narendra Modi and with US President Barack Obama during his visit to New Delhi, it hired Charu. When the legendary editor Tina Brown brought her power-packed 'Women in the World Summit' to Asia for the first time, she chose Charu to be the make-up artist at the event.

Why Charu?

Perhaps it is because the girl who dreamed of a career as a make-up artist also unwittingly became something else—a crusader for gender equality in her country.

Sitting on a couch in her living room in Delhi's Lajpat Nagar early one morning, Charu remains focused even as her son climbs all over her. She recounts her lengthy struggle to end a decades-long discriminatory practice that banned women from working as make-up artists in the movie industry, allegedly because men needed the jobs.

You read that right.

Till 2014, women in India were not allowed to work as make-up artists in films. Sexism was rampant. When Charu, an ordinary girl with an extraordinarily deep-seated sense of justice, was denied work, she took matters into her own hands. After a lengthy battle, women were given the right to do make-up in the movies, because Charu decided to put up a hell of a fight for it.

Charu was born on 20 May 1982 in Kaithal, a small, sleepy district in northern Haryana. 'It's where my roots are,' she explains. 'I feel connected to it.' It's the kind of place where no one draws their curtains and everyone knows everyone. As was the case in many parts of India, Friday evenings were special. Families gathered in front of a television set as black-and-white images and lilting melodies from Hindi films filled their living rooms with dreams and their hearts with cheer. The weekly viewing of *Chitrahaar* on Doordarshan was not to be missed. The Khurana family never did.

Against this simple, middle-class backdrop, Charu's parents, businessman Ashok and his young wife Neelam, began their lives as Mr and Mrs Khurana. Ashok ran a textile business selling fabric through the family store, Khurana Cloth House. Neelam converted a room in the family house into Kaithal's first beauty parlour. Business flourished. The family beamed as they watched Neelam prosper. Life was good.

Ashok and Neelam had two children. A son, Rohit, was born in 1976. Six years later, they had a daughter. She was a delightful baby, Neelam gushes. They named her Charu. It means 'beautiful'. Holding the baby in her arms, Neelam could never have guessed she was cradling a future activist.

Mother and daughter share a close bond. Neelam stood by her daughter through her legal fight, accompanying her to court, helping out with the paperwork and offering moral support. 'Whenever I gave up hope, my mother would say, "No, it's going to happen,"' Charu says. They have a casual, friendly rapport that is evident in the way they complete each other's sentences. Their passion for make-up binds them. Neelam often chips in at the salon Charu now runs in New Delhi and is a hands-on grandmother who looks after Charu's two young sons, Dhariya and Maahir, when her daughter travels. Charu is married to her childhood sweetheart, Ashutosh. 'I dated him for almost sixteen years before getting married to him,' she laughs. He runs his own business, a footwear outlet, and like Charu's parents, is a huge source of support.

'My husband has been a big motivating factor,' she says. 'It's not about physical and financial support, it's about mental support. It's about saying, I'm here, don't worry, pursue your dreams.'

In the late 1980s, the Khuranas moved to Delhi after their business in Haryana went through a rough patch. Charu studied at Green Fields School. Ashok shifted to Dubai to work in the jewellery business and Neelam remained in Delhi with the kids. She gave up her work because 'the children were my future, the business was not,' she says. School holidays were spent in Dubai where Neelam would pick up cosmetics—lipsticks, mascaras, astringents, toners, and eyeliners—which eventually made their way into that trusted vanity case. Though her parents didn't allow her to wear make-up till she was in the twelfth grade, it didn't stop Charu from playing with her mother's cosmetics. She would mix colours, experiment with eyeliners, try on lipsticks, spritz herself with fragrance.

It was 19 January 1999 when Charu decided she would become a make-up artist. It was the day her brother got married. Charu, who was seventeen then, booked a beautician from a local salon to do her make-up. It went horribly wrong. 'She made me look awful!' Charu remembers between peals of laughter. 'When you are young, you are supposed to play with fresh colours. But she used dark colours on me—dark contours, dark lips, dark eyes. I was wearing such an expensive outfit, but I looked terrible!' she says. That is one family album she does not look at very often.

The make-up debacle had a silver lining. It convinced Charu to become a professional make-up artist herself. Though her mother had taught her some tricks of the trade (when using a foundation brush, count the number of strokes on each side of the face for even coverage), she decided to sign up for a workshop conducted by Vidya Tikari, a leading Delhi-based beautician. She was a quick learner. 'Very bright, very eager to learn and very hard-working,' Tikari recalls. Soon, Charu was shuttling between Mumbai and Delhi, doing make-up for fashion shows, weddings, parties and television commercials.

By 2003, she had earned enough to open her own studio in Delhi. Between running the salon and her freelance assignments, Charu was content, though completely unprepared for the blow that was to come in the form of the sealing drive. It was 2006, and the Municipal Corporation of Delhi was shutting down commercial establishments in residential areas. That included Lajpat Nagar, where Charu ran her salon in a family-owned apartment.

Charu weighed her options. She could relocate her salon—but rentals were steep. Unable to invest that kind of money, she shut shop.

It was a major setback. But Charu says failure pushed her forward. 'Life is always a challenge. I had to accept it,' she says. She also knew she had to do something to earn her bread and butter. The question was, what next?

Run a salon? She had done that. TV commercials? Check. Bridal makeup? Done. Fashion shows? Tick. Films? Yes, films were uncharted territory. Charu found herself thinking that perhaps this was where her future lay. She decided she would do make-up for the movies.

She did a quick check and discovered no one was focusing on special effects make-up in India. There was a big gap in the market and in that lay an opportunity. She enrolled in a postgraduate diploma course in special effects at the Cinema Makeup School in Los Angeles in 2008. It was a prestigious course, and it was expensive. The Khuranas, who place a premium on any form of learning, took a personal loan of Rs 32 lakh to fund it.

'Both my parents sacrificed a lot for me to be able to pursue this. We didn't have liquid cash. Mom parted with all the gold assets she had and sold them off for me. I've seen mothers do this for their sons, but when I saw my mom believing in me and helping me pursue my dreams, I was like, hats off to my mom,' Charu says.

The learning curve in LA was steep. Charu learnt how to make prosthetics, wigs, moustaches; how to make a wound appear when someone is shot on screen. It exposed her to a whole new world. Make-up was so much more than lipstick and eyeshadow and the techniques she was familiar with. Diploma in hand, she returned to India full of promise and enthusiasm.

Mumbai, India's financial capital and home to the world's most prolific movie industry, is a dream destination for hundreds of thousands of hopefuls who arrive every day looking for work, nurturing dreams of prosperity, stardom and success. Charu was no different. She had shut her salon in Delhi and had a loan to repay. She needed money. India's city of dreams was where she would earn it.

She was wrong. Almost each time she started a new project, she says filming would be disrupted by a group of men who would barge in and demand a fine from Charu. According to her, they were members of the Cine Costume, Make-Up Artists and Hairdressers Association (CCMAA), an industry body, and said Charu could not work because she was violating their rules.

Which rules? Sometimes, they complained Charu was not a resident of Maharashtra. On other days, they blamed her for not being a member of their union, Charu says. According to the by-laws, make-up artists and hairdressers were required to register themselves with their respective unions—those who didn't register, didn't have the right to work.

That's simple enough, thought Charu. She would join the union.

She applied to the CCMAA, not once, but several times. Each time, she was rejected. 'They simply said, "We don't accept women members." It came as such a shock. How can such unconstitutional things happen in India?' Charu asks.

The CCMAA told her to apply for a hairdressing card instead. The association would allow women to work as hairdressers—but make-up? No, that was for men only. The rule had been in place since the CCMAA's inception in 1955. According to the union, if it allowed women to do make-up, male make-up artists would lose their jobs.

The ban remained.

The bullying was rampant, deep and entrenched. Sought-after make-up artist Namrata Soni, who has worked on some of the biggest Bollywood box-office hits, including *Main Hoon Na, Om Shanti Om* and *Kabhi Alvida Na Kehna*, says she was threatened 'many, many times'.

During the shooting of a song sequence in Filmistan, a popular film studio outside Mumbai, Namrata was overseeing a team of twenty hair and make-up artists. All of a sudden, she says, members of the CCMAA barged in and disrupted filming. 'Someone grabbed my hand and tried to drag me out,' Namrata says. She called the police and told them she was being manhandled. According to Namrata, the union folks replied they had only touched her hand. This was not an isolated incident. 'The union guys used to come and disrupt filming on the sets on a regular basis,' Soni says.

Under duress, many production houses would pay the union a fine so that they could complete filming. On principle, Namrata never paid a fine. She never hid in the vanity van. And she never walked off a set. 'Because we live in a free country and we don't need permission to work in the film industry, or any industry,' she says vehemently. 'But it did make a lot of production houses uncomfortable about using women make-up artists.'

Thousands of livelihoods were affected as a result. Women who wanted to work in the movies as make-up artists, for the money, for the prestige, could not fulfil their dreams. They were restricted to doing make-up for weddings, private parties and fashion shows.

Charu was not going to give up. She couldn't—she had loans to repay. She resorted to hiring a male assistant to be her public face. After doing an actor's make-up, she would cool her heels in the vanity van while her assistant, a man, would go on set to do the final touches. She paid him 40 per cent of her salary and watched helplessly as he took credit for her hard work.

The Khuranas fretted. The loan weighed heavily on their shoulders. 'Where would we get that kind of money back from? We had invested so much. I was only a make-up artist. I could not go back to college and do an MBA and start all over again,' Charu says.

Frustrated, Charu went to the Dadar police station to file a first information report (FIR) against the CCMAA, but was turned away after being told not to pick a fight with such a powerful union. 'Madam, you are a woman, go home,' they said.

'I had an idea things were bad in Mumbai, but I had no idea *how* bad,' Charu recalls.

Deflated but not defeated, Charu filed a written complaint with the Federation of Western India Cine Employees (FWICE), the parent body of the CCMAA. FWICE demanded an explanation from the union. It got one. The CCMAA wrote back, saying:

> Make-up artist cards are issued only to male members from the date of formation of the Association, no make-up artist card has been issued to female members till date. This is done to ensure that male members are not deprived of working as make-up artists. If the female members are given make-up artist card then it will become impossible for the male members to get work as make-up artists and they will lose their sources of livelihood and will be deprived of their earnings to support themselves and their families because no one would be interested to engage the services of a male make-up artist if the female make-up artists are available, looking to the human tendency.[2]

---

[2] Letter dated 1 August 2009 to the Honourable General Secretary, Federation of Western India Cine Employees, Andheri (West), Mumbai, bearing Ref. No. FWICE/CCMA/670/2009 from the Cine Costume Make-up Artists and Hairdressers Association.

It wasn't just Mumbai—the discrimination extended to other parts of India too.

In 2009, Charu started work on the Tamil remake of the popular Hindi thriller *A Wednesday!* Titled *Unnaipol Oruvan*, it was filmed in Chennai and starred Kamal Haasan, one of the biggest names in Tamil cinema. Thirty days into the shoot, members of a local make-up union raided the set. They singled Charu out and told her she could not continue working because she didn't have a union card. Hassan intervened, instructing the union to give her a membership card. They couldn't do that, union members said, because Charu didn't live in Chennai.

In Chennai, it was allegedly an issue of domicile. In Mumbai, it was about gender as well as domicile. According to Charu, the unions, interlinked to one another, were looking for any excuse to keep her from working. 'The unions would put pressure on each other not to allow women to work as make-up artists,' Charu says. She was eventually allowed to complete her work on *Unnaipol Oruvan*, but only after shelling out Rs 46,000 as a fine.

For Charu, this was a turning point.

'She always had a strong sense of what is right and what is wrong,' says Neelam, sitting in Charu's salon in Delhi, the sound of hairdryers humming in the background. For this, Neelam credits her husband.

Ashok, wearing a white kurta, sits behind the cashier's desk. He is a man of few words and has a strong, silent personality. 'He is my driving force,' Charu says.

From him, she learned an important lesson: everyone has a responsibility towards others.

Charu was thirteen. She had gone with a cousin to work as an usher at an auto fair at Pragati Maidan, a convention ground in New Delhi. The money was indulgent—$200 for a day. Cash in hand, Charu raced to the shops and returned home that night, dripping with bags. Excited, she showed her father what she had bought—it included an expensive salwar-kameez for herself It was beige, with *chikankari* embroidery. Ashok responded gently, 'Charu, the next time I earn money, I am going to buy things for myself.' To which Charu replied, 'Wow! What will you get for me, Papa?'

'Nothing,' Ashok replied, leaving Charu speechless.

He went on: 'When you went out, you thought of yourself only. You didn't think of your family or anyone else. When I work, I think of everyone in the family, including you.'

It was a simple message. 'In a very polite manner, he taught me that you have to be responsible for the people around you,' Charu says. When she fought for the right to work, it wasn't just for herself, but for every female make-up artist denied her constitutional right.

Frustrated with the constant run-ins with aggressive unions, Charu considered legal recourse. The problem was, she had no idea how to go about it. She approached the National Commission for Women (NCW) in New Delhi, which describes itself as 'an apex national level organization in India with the mandate of protecting and promoting the interests of women'. Set up in 1992, part of its remit is to review the constitutional and legal safeguards for women.

The NCW introduced her to Jyotika Kalra, a New Delhi–based lawyer. Sitting in her tastefully decorated living room, she says, 'Wherever I find gender biases, I agitate.' Charu, who had saved all her documents, handed them over to Kalra. There was correspondence with the NWC, the Maharashtra Women's Commission, the Chennai Commission. 'I had gone to each and every doorstep to see how I could find justice for myself,' Charu recalls. When Kalra heard Charu's story, she immediately took on the case pro bono.

'She is a gem of a person,' Charu says. 'She did not charge me, not even a single penny. Jyotika Ma'am understood how critical the situation is.'

Kalra wasted no time in contacting the CCMAA. When she inquired about its discriminatory rule, she got a response similar to the one it had sent FWICE. It said the rule was intended to protect a man's livelihood because if women were allowed to do make-up, no actor would choose a man to do it.

'This is the mindset with which society works—if a woman works, she will be working at the cost of a man and ruining livelihoods. That always disturbs me,' says Kalra.

In January 2013, Kalra formally filed a writ petition on behalf of Charu and eight other make-up artists in the Supreme Court of India against unions in Maharashtra, Tamil Nadu, Karnataka, Kerala and Andhra Pradesh.

Charu followed the case closely, keeping in touch with Kalra at every step of the lengthy and tedious legal process. It took a lot longer than she had anticipated. In this environment, 'the next day' comes only after two months, Charu says. There was a lot of waiting around and a lot of legal jargon that wasn't easy to decode. 'It took me so much time to understand what they were trying to argue. It took time to understand legal lingo. I used to think justice delayed was justice denied.' But Charu kept up with the case.

'She is an intelligent, bold and good human being,' Kalra says of Charu. 'There is perseverance in what she does. She was present in court on each and every day.'

Finally, the day of reckoning arrived. Charu stood in the courtroom. Judge Dipak Misra spoke:

'How can this discrimination continue?' he is widely reported to have said in the courtroom.[3] 'We will not permit this. It cannot be allowed under our constitution. Why should only a male artist be allowed to put make-up?' He reportedly added, 'We are in 2014, not in 1935. Such things cannot continue even for a day.'

The judgement in Charu's case on the Supreme Court website reads:

The discrimination done by the Association, a trade union registered under the Act, whose rules have been accepted, cannot take the route of the discrimination solely on the basis of sex. It really plays foul of the statutory provisions. It is absolutely violative of constitutional values and norms. If a female artist does not get an opportunity to enter into the arena of being a member of the Association, she cannot work as a female artist. It is inconceivable. The likes of the

---

[3] www.livemint.com/Consumer/l5aJI4usA6Vl0MWNTphXUK/One-womans-fight-against-gender-bias-in-Bollywood.html; http://www.bbc.com/news/world-asia-india-28934239; https://www.theguardian.com/film/2014/nov/07/bollywood-ban-female-makeup-artists-india-supreme-court-illegal

petitioners are given membership as hair dressers, but not as make-up artist. There is no fathomable reason for the same. It is gender bias writ large. It is totally impermissible and wholly unacceptable.[4]

The judge instructed the unions to immediately scrap the by-laws that did not allow women to work as make-up artists and also struck down a regulation that people had to live in a particular city or town for five years to become a member of the association.

Charu hugged her mother and her lawyer before stepping out of the court to the flash of camera bulbs and TV crews. Charu, the little girl who used to play with the family vanity case, had helped remove a fifty-nine-year-old patriarchal ban.

The entire process had taken almost six years, but the fight was worth it. Charu became the first Indian woman to become a member of the CCMAA. Her victory made headlines in the Indian media, and stars and citizens took to social media to congratulate her. Superstar Hrithik Roshan tweeted his support: *Charu Khurana has been inducted as d 1st female make up artist in d film industry! About time this prehistoric gender battle was won!bravo![5]*

Today, Charu runs the Charu Khurana Make-Up Hair and Beauty Academy in New Delhi, from where she offers beauty services and teaches a professional make-up and hairstyling course. She is highly sought after and is free to work on a movie set, as is any other Indian woman who wants to.

Charu says she feels good she made a 'small difference' in India's struggle for gender equality. She fought to change the system in the world of make-up and movies, but the real difference, she says, will come when the next generation of Indian men learns to respect women. And there's one more thing. 'Women must believe in themselves,' she says.

Luckily, Charu did.

---

4   Judgment available on the website of the Supreme Court of India: http://www.supremecourtofindia.nic.in/jonew/bosir/orderpdfold/2096928.pdf
5   @iHrithik tweet on 21 April 2015.

JUHI CHATURVEDI
THE SCRIPTWRITER

In the early 1980s, Lucknow, the capital of India's most populous state, Uttar Pradesh, was a sleepy town. Monuments and ruins littered the city, a throwback to a period when it was a satrapy of the sultanate and Mughal Empire, and later, the cultural heart of the affluent kingdom of Awadh. In the summers, the electricity would go off for hours. Winters, though, were different. And winter mornings in Mahanagar Extension, the neighbourhood where the Chaturvedis lived in a sprawling home called Champakunj, were special.

A young girl would run into the garden, place a sheet under the blooming bushes, stand beside her grandfather and brother and shake the plants to capture falling flowers. She would then string them into a garland to be offered to God. The tactile, simple ritual is emblazoned in scriptwriter Juhi Chaturvedi's mind. She channelled a version of this memory into her most recent film, *October*, where the fragrant jasmine is a metaphor for one of the lead characters.

Gathering flowers is one of the many recollections that form the bedrock of Juhi's childhood, one filled with great joy but also heartache. This, and other visually moving memories inform the powerful, authentic stories Juhi writes, which have made her one of the country's most significant cinematic writers.

Juhi's work has taken audiences by storm. With three screenplays under her belt—for *Vicky Donor* (2012), *Piku* (2016) and *October* (2018)—as well as dialogues for *Shoebite* (2008 but unreleased), *Madras Cafe* (2013), *Song of the Scorpions* (2017), and *The Sky Is Pink* (2019), Juhi is highly sought after.

She has won multiple awards—the prestigious National Film Award for best screenplay and dialogue for *Piku*, Filmfare awards for best story and best screenplay for *Vicky Donor* and International Indian Film Academy (IIFA) awards in the same categories for both films. Director Shoojit Sircar, Juhi's close collaborator and the man behind *Shoebite*, *Madras Cafe*, *Vicky Donor*, *Piku* and *October*, says, 'She is one of the most talented writers in our industry. She is rare.'

All of Juhi's movies have been produced by Rising Sun Films. At its helm is producer Ronnie Lahiri, who says Juhi's storytelling has heart and soul. 'There is a realism in the characters she creates, which people can relate to,' he says. 'Thankfully, there is an absence of writerly technique; since she is not a trained scriptwriter, her writing doesn't follow a pattern. With Juhi's films, you never know where her story is going, which is exciting.'

At the trailer release of *October*, Sircar said that he considered the screenplay, story and dialogue the backbone of a film. He is right. After all, what is a film without a story? Audiences do respond (up to a point) to special effects, high-speed chases, beautiful locations, moving cinematography and high-profile movie stars, but they only take a movie so far. If we look back at the films India loves—whether it is *Mughal-e-Azam*, *Pyaasa*, *Mother India*, *Guide*, *Sholay*, *Deewar*, *Jaane Bhi Do Yaaro*, *Lagaan*, *Dil Chahta Hai*, or any of the others that have stood the test of time—they tell stories that grip us, haunt us, stay with us.

Juhi's stories revolve around unusual subjects—sperm donation, constipation, unconditional love. She made them topics of national conversation. Who would have thought bowel movements would grip the public's imagination? Or that the land that worships fertility would discuss reproductive challenges? These are risqué subjects for Bollywood. Juhi brought them to the fore in a palatable and sensitive manner. Handled superbly by the award-winning Sircar, her screenplays are a game changer in Hindi cinema.

People call her a genius for coming up with such unusual subjects. Juhi thinks of herself as anything but. She does, however, concede that the idea for *Vicky Donor* was a eureka moment. 'I had tasted big-screen cinema writing after writing the dialogues for *Shoebite*, so that desire to write was there,' she admits. 'I was a new mum and I like to believe that maybe it was that motherly instinct. What if someone doesn't have a baby? So you sort of understand that world a bit more,' she says with a laugh. 'But mostly, I just spend a lot of time thinking about people, not about a film per se.'

This wordsmith captures the essence of urban daily life in India accurately and poetically. Her dialogues get under the character's skin. They drip with reality, whether it is the fast-paced Punjabi-inflected Hindi of *Vicky Donor* and *October* or the Bengali and Hinglish of *Piku*. How does an untrained writer do it? 'My basic premise when I write is to explore a simple human emotion—a virtue or a vice, it doesn't matter,' she explains. 'Vices are equally a part of human nature; the feeling could be negative or positive. As long as it's coming from inside a human being, it's valid.'

American screenwriter Peter Landesman, who wrote the 2017 film *Mark Felt: The Man Who Brought Down the White House*, says that 'movies are about an emotional tether to the audience'.[1] Juhi's writing provides that tether. She has an ear for how Indians speak and deep observation skills that allow her to invent characters that audiences find familiar. Viewers can relate to a crotchety, elderly family member obsessed with his health, like Amitabh Bachchan's character, Bhaskar *da*, in *Piku*. Who hasn't come across someone haranguing their child like Dolly Ahluwalia's character, Mrs Dolly Arora, does in *Vicky Donor*?

The more extraordinary the writing, the more amazing the film. Throughout the twentieth century, Hindi cinema has always had notable individuals writing great stories—Wajahat Mirza, Ismat Chughtai, K.A. Abbas, Mukhram Sharma, Gulzar, Salim Khan, Javed Akhtar and Sachin Bhaumik are just some in an amazing pool of talented writers.

As Shyam Benegal told author Mihir Bose, in the 1940s and 1950s, Bollywood functioned like Hollywood. Directors used bound scripts and adhered to a storyline. In the mid-1960s, when films began to be packaged with talent, whether they were actors or musical geniuses, things began to change. Stars triumphed over story. Scriptwriters hardly got any credit.[2]

The writing duo of Salim Khan and Javed Akhtar, of Salim–Javed fame, began to chip away at this trend in the early 1970s. They fought for credit and better pay, and moved away from writing stories just to suit a star.[3]

By the late 1980s, many Hindi movies were made in an ad hoc fashion. Stories were narrated verbally and scripts and dialogues were often written

---

[1]	http://niemanstoryboard.org/stories/what-journalists-need-to-know-about-writing-screenplays/

[2]	Mihir Bose, *Bollywood: A History*, New Delhi: Roli Books, 2007, p. 32.

[3]	Diptakirti Chaudhuri, *Written By Salim-Javed: The Story of Hindi Cinema's Greatest Screenwriters,* Gurgaon: Penguin Books, 2015, p. 10.

on set as a film rolled. It was a period in Hindi cinema when new ideas were failing at the box office, so producers and actors were unwilling to gamble with originality. Directors wrung their hands over the lack of good writers, while writers said that no one bought their scripts if they veered from the tried and tested masala formula.

Today, things are different. Bollywood is a much more professional industry and most reputed production houses work with bound scripts. A well-written story is considered essential to a film's success. Scriptwriters are paid better than before. The most successful ones can expect to make anywhere from Rs 1,00,000 to Rs 1,50,000 per film, although this can often be paid out between a year to two years. Writing contracts, while much more prevalent than before, tend to favour producers who bear the costs of a film, but a model writing contract that safeguards the interests of both writers and producers is being created under the guidance of actor Aamir Khan, writer Anjum Rajabali and producer Ritesh Sidhwani.

And while Javed Akhtar famously joked about the pitfalls of writing original stories in Bollywood ('I never wrote a story that has not come before,' he quipped),[4] the success of movies based on original screenplays like the ones Juhi writes indicate that Indian audiences are clamouring for well-told stories.

Juhi could be any middle-class working mother juggling multiple responsibilities. She describes herself as shy and says that when she is part of a group, she is the last person to speak. She prefers one-on-one conversations. She and her husband, Asheesh Malhotra, have a ten-year-old daughter, Radha, who helps mom by acting as a sounding board.

Juhi, who worked at Ogilvy & Mather, the advertising agency, for twelve years, now spends the bulk of her time writing. Her Bollywood success doesn't faze her. Walking with her friends at night is still one of the most important parts of her day. She's the kind of woman you want as your best friend—level-headed, easy-going and a great listener.

At the trailer preview for *October* in March 2017, she wore a long ankle-length white cotton polka-dot dress, accessorized with a red beaded cloth necklace, her long hair worn loose. Her calm demeanour was far removed

---

[4] Ibid., p. 21.

from the frenzy around the film's star, Varun Dhawan, and newcomer Banita Sandhu. She sat on stage quietly, replying only to questions posed to her. She projected a simple, reserved, no-nonsense aura, and seemed embarrassed by the attention.

The hullabaloo of the movie business is a far cry from the Lucknow of Juhi's childhood. She was born on 3 January 1975, to Mridula and Dhirendra Nath Chaturvedi, five years after her brother Vinay. Her mother was a housewife. Dhirendra Nath studied history at the Banaras Hindu University, taught briefly, and eventually worked in the state education department.

For anyone who has seen *Piku*, the sprawling home in Kolkata that Amitabh Bachchan's character longs for is modelled on Champakunj, Juhi's ancestral home. Built in 1961 by her paternal grandfather, Dina Nath Chaturvedi, it was an enormous nineteen-room home with huge gardens. Dina Nath was the deputy director of education for the Uttar Pradesh Board and by all accounts, a formidable man. Mridula was from Gwalior. Juhi's childhood was filled with trips to Shivpuri, Panna and the districts of Bhind and Morena in the Chambal region, once famous for its dacoits. 'Chambal *ka paani piya hua hai* so one can't be afraid,' Juhi jokes.

The days were slow, uneventful, carefree. 'The only life one looked forward to was to come home, quickly finish your homework, drink your milk and cornflakes and run out and play on the road till seven or seven-thirty,' Juhi reminisces. Juhi and her neighbourhood pals played cricket on the road, I-Spy, and climbed trees. It was an uninhibited childhood.

Champakunj was lush and full of trees. Monkeys ran amok. When Juhi was three years old, she chanced upon an open door and strolled outside. She spotted an old monkey in the kitchen garden, minding his own business. Juhi hit him with a *jhadu* (broom). The sapien didn't react, so she tried again. And again. Finally, he pounced on her and bit her right cheek, leaving a scar she still carries. She had to go to Balrampur hospital for several rabies shots. 'My parents had to bribe me with a Cadbury or 5-Star chocolate so that I would go,' she recalls with a smile.

The house had one of the only telephones in the colony and grandfather Dina Nath kept a meticulous log of all the calls made—who made it, to which number, for what purpose and for how long.

When the monthly bill arrived, he would tally it. If it didn't match his account, he would question everyone in the household and beyond. 'There were so many times we would cheat,' Juhi laughs. 'My mother would go to the letter box as soon as the bill arrived and not show it to him for a few days. She would quickly fix the record, match it roughly and give it to me to hand over. The phone and logbook were the funniest things in the house.'

Champakunj's atmosphere was rarefied. In typical Lucknow fashion, there were addas, or salons, at home. Family and friends would gather to discuss poetry, literature, politics and books. All the discussions were in Hindustani; English was reserved for school. Juhi soaked up the background chatter as she went about her business at home.

The family's idyll was shattered on 22 December 1983, when Juhi was eight years old. Mridula burst a nerve in her nose, a result of severe hypertension, and was admitted to the ICU. Her condition was critical. Juhi and Vinay held hands, crying inconsolably. They prayed. Thankfully, Mridula rallied, but from that moment onwards, the Chaturvedi household was never the same.

Juhi's mother was put on strong medication which resulted in innumerable side effects, including depression. There were days when Mridula would cry for hours. Juhi learnt to cope. By the age of eleven, she knew how to check her mother's blood pressure. Juhi and Vinay learnt that when mummy wasn't well, it meant no birthday party, and certainly no tantrums. But when Mridula was well, it was another house. 'In spite of all that, it was a house full of much love and joy,' Juhi says, her face softening.

With Mridula's chronic ill health, Juhi's aunt, Lekha Chaturvedi, played a significant role in her upbringing. 'The creditable, wonderful thing about Juhi is that she faced all these challenges positively,' says Mrs Chaturvedi, whom Juhi calls Badi Mummy (older mother).

Movies were not a big part of the Chaturvedi household. Juhi was not allowed to go to theatres. Back in the 1980s, the kind of movies—usually flashy entertainers—that came to cinema halls held little appeal for the family. Instead, they watched movies shown on TV, including films by Satyajit Ray or art house films by foreign film-makers.

At high school in Loreto Convent, she was active in dramatics, debates and drawing. Writing was not on the radar—she never even contributed to the school magazine. Juhi's father ensured that she entered every art competition in the city. She won a number of prizes, from first prize at the Camlin All India Arts Competition to the Gandhi Jayanti drawing award.

'Juhi has been full of creativity ever since she was a child,' recalls her Badi Mummy. 'Juhi's drawings were really good; she used to look at photographs and make absolutely identical sketches.' The two are exceptionally close. She describes her niece as a perfectionist. 'She would erase a drawing four times and redraw it four times—no matter what, it should be perfect. She'd never compromise, and even today, she's like this.'

Juhi always knew her mind. After finishing school, she was dead set on attending arts college. But Dhirendra Nath wanted none of it. He didn't want his daughter to study a subject that he believed offered her no future. Juhi had aced her subjects in grade 11 but wanted to study at the Government College of Art and Craft. She recalls her father saying: 'What will I tell everyone, that's she's just drawing?' It was a battle of wills between father and daughter as huge arguments—Juhi calls them 'Mahabharatas'—raged at home.

Juhi filled in the admission form quietly and was admitted. Then Dhirendra Nath played his trump card: he refused to pay the tuition fee. Luckily, Juhi topped the entrance exam and won a scholarship—an annual fee waiver.

Her Badi Mummy remembers that despite this hiccup between father and daughter, the entire family was supportive. 'Emotionally, because of her mother's illness, she had to bear so much, but she was never left alone,' she says.

Despite her constant illness, Mridula did the best she could for her children. Juhi says her mother kept trying to look after them. 'The day before her last cancer operation, she made me *atte ke laddoo* because she knew I enjoyed them,' Juhi says. 'Her determination gave me strength.'

Juhi was driven, however, and began freelancing as an illustrator for the Lucknow edition of the *Times of India*. Her drawings, with a byline, appeared once or twice a week. With the money she made, she would buy art materials. Although she had enrolled for a bachelor's degree in fine arts to study painting, at the encouragement of Professor P.C. Little, who was head of the department of advertising and photography, she studied those subjects instead. 'I took a big leap of faith and he just changed my trajectory,' she says. After Juhi graduated, she moved to Delhi at the age of twenty-one, and found a job at the ad agency Lintas. She was the first girl in her family to move out of the house to work in a big city.

Rati Bawa, today a partner at Integral Consulting, was at Lintas and had hired her. She was Juhi's first boss and an early mentor. 'There was a quiet determination about her,' Rati remembers. 'She didn't talk much, but she answered whatever I asked confidently. What I realized is that she had big dreams, and she was determined to learn.'

At Ogilvy, the young artist thrived. Soon after joining the firm, Juhi met Asheesh Malhotra, who was an ad executive there. The two started spending time together. 'I shouldn't be saying this, but I loved the dark circles under her eyes, which were pretty haunting,' Asheesh says with a laugh.

Asheesh and Juhi married on 17 October 1999, and later moved to Mumbai to work at Ogilvy. Her husband says it wasn't easy to work with her because unlike others, she never wasted time on something that wasn't going to work. 'She would clearly tell you if something wasn't headed in the right direction rather than give you all the hope in the world,' he says.

It was at Ogilvy that Juhi started to write. She is thankful to ad guru and Padma Shri awardee Piyush Pandey, executive chairman and creative director for South Asia of Ogilvy, for his tutelage. Pandey encouraged her. 'He said, when you have language with you, you should write,' she remembers. 'He said I had ideas and they don't need art or copy, they just need to be expressed. "The way you tell them to me, write them exactly like that."' That's how she began writing ads. Juhi remained with Ogilvy till 2008, when she quit the firm to concentrate on writing full-time.

Juhi credits advertising with honing her writing. 'The thirty-second format chisels your thinking mind,' she says. 'It pushes you to value every second of the ad film, because you have such a short time to tell the story.

The idea has to be differentiated, it has to be big, it has to break the clutter. Advertising makes you sharper.'

One of her colleagues at Ogilvy was Shoojit, who later approached her to write dialogues for his film. She first wrote dialogues for *Shoebite,* which was eventually shelved, before taking the screenplay plunge with *Vicky Donor.*

An artistic background helps Juhi visualize her characters and settings. She instinctively knows what each character's home looks like in a film. 'I know what each one wears, eats, drinks, whatever,' she says. 'So I do poke my nose in costume and in production design, but only to explain the world I have created.' Given her artistic prowess, Juhi also does the publicity design for her films.

Juhi lives with Asheesh, Radha and her father in central Mumbai's Worli area. Unlike her more outgoing husband, she doesn't have too many close friends. Among the ones she has, Sonia Sen is special. A mainstay in Juhi's life, the two speak every weekday for an hour, sometimes longer. They discuss everything. 'Juhi was an epiphany for me,' says Sonia of her friend. 'She's fiercely feminist and liberated. But she's not strident. She's a strange mix, extremely soulful and very funny. She is a fabulous mimic. When she mimics someone, you can't tell it's Juhi talking.'

Juhi writes in her bedroom, either on her study table or, when she's tired, in bed on a small breakfast tray on which she parks her laptop. She writes only on the laptop, never in a notebook. Her screenplays are written in English, but she writes dialogues in Hindi. She wrote *Piku*'s Bengali dialogues because it's a language she is familiar with. In Champakunj, the Chaturvedis had Bengali tenants, and Juhi picked up the language easily.

She has a set routine, describing the writing process as very regimented. 'It's not romantic at all, it's not flowery and creative and beautiful, but within that space, I have made a beautiful world.' Before sitting down to write, Juhi burns camphor, places some flowers in front of the computer and draws the curtains—because she doesn't want to know the time. She doesn't want to know that morning is turning to afternoon and then to evening. 'I need an absolute blackout when writing. It puts you in a cocoon, it's the only way to cut off.'

She's in front of her computer by 10 a.m., even if she is not writing. 'Asheesh says, "*dukaan chalu ho gayi*",' she says with a laugh. At 4.30 p.m., she stops and focuses on daily life. After the household retires at night, she returns to the laptop.

Writers are known to be escapists, but a woman writing in India cannot hope for a complete switch-off from reality. Juhi has found a balance between being in the world—running a household and doing chores—and being away from it as she weaves stories in her head. The daily interruptions that life in urban India brings are a given. The doorbell rings often, and she has to manage a household even as she writes. Finding that balance is tricky.

'Somehow, you learn to live with the parallel worlds,' she shrugs. 'When I am not writing, I am a regular housewife taking care of the home and my child, but the months I am writing, it is a dual existence. 'I have been working for almost eighteen years and I just love being at home. It is an absolute trade-off, but I don't want to lose my relationship with the house and its issues. This is most precious to me. A child growing up needs a certain environment at home.'

When Juhi writes, the process consumes her. Although she has learnt to manage her emotions, she says it is hard. Till a script is done, she lives with the characters in her head. 'It's very disturbing,' she admits. 'As a writer, you are stuck in that zone. I got rashes and alopecia when I was writing *Piku* because one is so emotionally involved.'

After Juhi finished writing *Piku*, after she wrote in Amitabh Bachchan's character's death, she couldn't go back to the script. 'She just wept and wept,' Sonia says. 'She is consumed by the writing, both physically and mentally.'

Is Juhi amazed by her success? She says it hasn't affected her in the least 'because I didn't aspire to be a writer or have this kind of ambition,' she explains. 'I have just done my bit given my limitations. Writing is important, it is cathartic and helps me deal with my emotions. You knock on the doors of your soul and life and keep scratching at it. But I don't do it to achieve success. I don't write for the box office or for Shoojit or for anyone else. I like the idea that my thoughts are being said by Mr Bachchan who is a phenomenon, but more importantly, that I believe in something and that it is out there in that form.'

Soon after *Vicky Donor* released in 2012, Juhi's mother Mridula died, after suffering from various ailments for thirty-two years. She was just sixty-four. 'I genuinely believe she is now free from illness and that she is now liberated,' Juhi says quietly. 'This was the only way she could be well again and so it's all right. Parents don't ever leave you, though.'

It was extremely hard.

In the last scene in *Piku*, Amitabh Bachchan's character too is set free because he finally passes the bowel movement he wanted. Juhi took vignettes from her own life and wove them in loosely, capturing the emotion subtly and evocatively. 'Losing a parent, the understanding of care, that was the life I am used to,' she says.

Her second film analyses all the complex emotions that grown-up children experience with elder care. Juhi says she couldn't have written *Piku* before her mother passed away. 'It was just my father and me left after she went, and the script got that much more depth,' she says.

In *Piku*, Bhaskar, Amitabh Bachchan's character, is based loosely on Juhi's grandfather Dina Nath, who would have long conversations with his friend, Dr Srivastav. He would describe, in great detail, everything going on in his body.

'Of course you borrow from your life, but you don't borrow everything,' she points out. 'It's about every child dealing with ageing parents. I am over forty, and I am still answerable to my father. He will ask me what time I am going and when I will be back. Isn't art about our experiences? What you write comes from the experiences you go through. A hint of that always remains.'

Today, writers in Bollywood are in a much better place than they were even a few years ago. 'I definitely believe we are in that space where people are recognizing writers and valuing our thoughts. But I don't write for recognition, and the starting point should not be about that. I am using cinema as a medium to speak to people, perhaps in a way that someone who writes a book speaks to an audience. For me, the starting point is, what is my contribution to society?

Juhi doesn't put much stock in gender. 'I have never interacted with people based on whether they are men or women. It just doesn't matter.' She has had one female and three male mentors in her life—Professor

Little in college, Rati Bawa when she first started her career, Piyush Pandey in advertising, and, of course, Shoojit Sircar in film. If Pandey hadn't seen her gift for language and encouraged her to write ads, perhaps she wouldn't have taken the plunge. If Sircar hadn't prodded her to write dialogues for his film, would she have done so? All these people saw Juhi's potential. 'I was and continue to be a person with zero ambition,' she says, laughing.

As to her writing prowess, she can't explain it, saying simply, 'Maybe it is something God gave me. It is still early days, absolutely early days, and if this is what it is, I would like to believe there are many more films ahead. Somewhere, I feel the path will automatically open. Each film is another step in the journey.'

GUNEET MONGA
THE PRODUCER

G uneet Amarpreet Kaur Monga believes in miracles. There is no other way she can make sense of her journey so far. Given the knocks life has dealt her, it is hard to believe that this thirty-four-year-old film producer, with closely cropped hair and large, sparkling eyes framed by a pair of dark-rimmed spectacles, is not bitter. She is serene—so serene, in fact, that it feels like Mumbai, with its frenzied energy and high-decibel noise levels, slows down when Guneet speaks.

Guneet lives by the sea. Outside her window, palm trees sway gently and the Arabian Sea laps at the shore. Gazing at the ocean and breathing the fresh, salty air are important to her— 'It's calming, peaceful and it balances your energy.' Guneet's ocean-front flat in upscale Juhu is a far cry from a humble childhood spent in an apartment in Surajkund, near Faridabad, which her family rented for Rs 5,000 a month. Each morning, the chants of '*Om namah shivay*' fill her Mumbai home. 'When I wake up in this apartment, I thank the universe,' Guneet says. 'I give thanks every day.'

According to *Variety*, the widely read American film magazine, Guneet is one of fifty women from the entertainment industry doing 'extraordinary things on the worldwide stage.' In March 2018, the magazine published its first International Women's Impact Report, and Guneet was one of only two women from India in it. The other was actor Deepika Padukone.

The introduction to the report said, 'Let's face it: It's not always easy to be a woman in this world, let alone a showbiz leader that happens to be one. There are the usual leadership obstacles to overcome, plus downright sexism and resistance in certain pockets of the planet. Yet, these women persist.'[1]

Guneet is on the list for her work as a path-breaking female producer in Bollywood, part of a new wave of Indian film-makers making a global impact. Known for backing strong, independent content that sits comfortably between commercial entertainers and the art house world, Guneet has more than thirty films to her name, which include some of the most critically acclaimed movies in contemporary India, such as *The Lunchbox*, *Gangs of Wasseypur* and *Masaan*. Typically, these are low-

---

[1] Diane Garrett, 'Showbiz Women Prevail (and Persist) Around the Globe', Variety.com, 7 March 2018.

budget films with strong scripts that focus on edgy, alternative themes. Fundamentally Indian at heart, these indies have universal appeal.

The Lunchbox is Guneet's jewel in the crown. Simply put, it's the film that got her noticed and earned her and her co-producers a British Academy of Film and Television Arts (BAFTA) nomination in 2015. The poignant love story, which revolves around a box of food that gets delivered to the wrong person in a Mumbai office, premiered at the Cannes Film Festival in 2013 to a standing ovation. It went on to achieve unprecedented success worldwide—a rare Indian crossover hit. The *Guardian* gave it four out of five stars and said, '*The Lunchbox* is perfectly handled and beautifully acted; a quiet storm of banked emotions.'[2] Made on a low budget of Rs 10 crore, or $1.5 million, it became one of the highest-grossing foreign films in the US in 2014, earning $4.2 million.

Of *The Lunchbox*, Guneet says, 'That was the dream—of that one Indian film that goes and sells around the world.' It created history, but that is hardly surprising. Very little about Guneet is formulaic. She is not one to stick to tradition. She breaks it.

'I am a disruptor,' she says, a quiet confidence in her deep voice. It's hard to find an area in her personal or professional life where she has followed the tried and tested path. 'You have to be in the corner and do the work that nobody is doing and make enough noise so that you are noticed,' she insists. The trick is to keep at it.

Born in New Delhi on 21 November 1983, Guneet's life has been peppered with loss, depression and death. As a young child, she witnessed domestic violence within her home. Her first film bombed spectacularly. Both her parents died within six months of each other. Yet, the head of Sikhya Entertainment, a company she founded in 2008, is not bitter. You won't hear Guneet complain life has been unfair. She says she has a lot to be grateful for.

That includes no one showing up to watch her first film.

Brimming with ambition, Guneet dreamt of moving to Mumbai after studying mass communication in Delhi. She wanted to make films and tell stories. Her first brush with movies—as an intern on the French-

---

2   Xan Brooks, 'A Quiet Storm of Banked Emotions', *Guardian*, 13 April 2014.

German-Indian independent film *Valley of Flowers*—had her hooked.
Her job involved photocopying and scanning documents, entering
phone numbers into a database and doing odd jobs for the production
team. It was grunt work, but she loved every minute of it. This stint came
after she had tried her hand at umpteen other jobs. By the time she was
twenty-one, Guneet had been a DJ, an insurance agent, a sales agent for
Laughing Cow cheese, an event planner, a rally car driver and a property
saleswoman for her late father. Once she found herself on a movie set,
however, she knew there was no going back. Guneet wanted to make a
film herself.

Mumbai beckoned. But she needed capital to make the move and
a movie. Her neighbour in Delhi, Kamlesh Agarwal, offered to help by
investing Rs 50 lakh in her film project. In turn, he suggested Guneet
make 'cute cute films for children'. Guneet heard him out patiently, then
replied, 'Uncle, I think it is a very bad idea.' Boldly, she proposed another
one instead: why not give her the money so she could move to Mumbai
and make a film—on a topic of *her* choice. It was a big ask. Agarwal
relented. He gave her the capital.

'I never doubted her integrity,' he says years later, speaking
affectionately and admiringly of Guneet, whom he has known since she
was a teenager. 'She was honest and sincere in her approach, and it is
probably only because of that that I invested money in her. I knew she
would never cheat me.'

The aspiring film-maker arrived in India's heaving film capital with
money in her pocket, fire in her belly, but not a clue about where to
start. The only thing she knew was that she was going to make a movie.
Nothing was going to stop her. She networked and met as many people
as she could, convinced someone would have a story worth telling. 'I
used to meet people in food courts, in malls and say, *"Mere paas 50 lakh
hain, aapke paas story hai?"*' She was twenty-one, naive and daring at the
same time.

Her persistence paid off. She found a script that excited her. It told
the story of four boys with limited resources but an unrivalled passion for
cricket. She decided to buy into it through the first production company
she founded, Speaking Tree Films. The movie, titled *Say Salaam India*,

released in 2007. It was the kind of film that should have had cricket-mad India going ga-ga.

But fate had a different plan. A few days after the film released, India's cricket team crashed out of the World Cup in the West Indies. No one foresaw this debacle. Cricket fans were angry. They pelted stones at cricketers' homes and the media went on the offensive. A feel-good movie about cricket was not going to draw an audience, so cinemas sent the film reels back to Guneet. Her first film had tanked and she was shattered.

That she had let Agarwal down weighed heavily on the producer's conscience. Guneet had taken his money and watched it go down the drain. Somehow or the other, she would repay him. 'I used to keep telling him, if I don't give your money back, I should not be in this business.'

Agarwal didn't expect to recover the loss. 'I invested the money and she was a partner. It was to be shared—profit and loss. I never pushed Guneet to cover her part of the loss.'

But Guneet was already working on plan B. She was sure that someone, somewhere, would want to see the film. She decided to take the movie to a group of people who always get excited by cricket: students. Travelling across small cities and towns in north India, she arranged private screenings in schools, for which she charged a nominal fee. It wasn't a conventional strategy, but then Guneet is an out-of-the-box thinker. In nine months, she earned enough to pay Agarwal back in full. 'I just was so driven to make that money back that I went to the moon and back to try and make that happen.'

Looking back, Guneet says this setback taught her the single most important lesson a film producer needs to learn—that there is an audience for every film. 'You just have to find it.' There are ups and downs in business, which Guneet had learnt from her dad, a property consultant. 'My dad was always saying, *"Business mein yeh hota hai,"'* says Guneet. But her parents had also instilled a deep sense of honesty in her. 'My mother used to say, "Whatever you do, you are answerable to your own conscience."' Those lessons, of being honest and having a clear conscience, drove her to pay Agarwal back.

Guneet slows down when talking about her parents. It brings back painful memories of her mother suffering years of abuse and domestic violence at the hands of her father's family.

Witnessing that violence as a young child left Guneet with a fear of loud voices and a deep intolerance for injustice. She cannot bear to listen to anyone scream and she rarely raises her voice. Loud sounds transport her back to her childhood, when the Mongas lived in a sprawling family home in New Delhi's Greater Kailash where she saw her mother being verbally and physically abused. One night, when Guneet was twelve, the violence almost claimed her mother's life. 'They tried to set fire to my mom in front of me. There was police in the house, people holding me. It was crazy,' she shudders. That night, her parents fled and moved into a small rented apartment in what was then far-off Surajkund in south Delhi.

Guneet has refrained from speaking publicly about her childhood trauma. Sadly, her mother passed away in 2008 from cancer, and within a few months, her father succumbed to a kidney disease. Guneet was twenty-four. Barring one paternal aunt, she has no extended family and no siblings. This void is filled by her friends.

'She savours friendships and likes to keep her friends close,' says Mayank Jha, who lived in the same township, Charmwood Village in Surajkund, where Guneet spent her teenage years. The gated community lives up to its cheery name—it has a few villas, a high-rise, a pond and lots of parks. After moving there, Guneet felt safe and peaceful for the first time. She was surrounded by friends her age and was part of a community. She says they were the best years of her life.

'Looking back, I can connect the dots now,' Mayank says. 'Guneet was a really good storyteller. She was always very animated and talkative, and would get emotionally involved when telling a story. Let's just say, she was dramatic!' Despite her flair for drama, none of her friends guessed she would end up with a career in films. Today, a group of her school, college and Surajkund friends are her most loyal supporters. She considers them her family.

'It's a two-way street. Guneet gives as much as she takes from her relationships,' says her childhood friend, Prerna Saigal. Both girls were together from nursery through grade 12 at Blue Bells School in Delhi. 'She's very loyal,' Prerna says. 'Once, we were playing a basketball match in school and I got badly bruised. Guneet came running from the other side of the court, snatched the ball, handed it to me and said, "Prerna, *yeh leh.* '" She did that so her friend could have a go at dunking the ball into the basket. 'At that moment, something clicked,' Prerna says. 'I knew she was in my corner, I knew we would be friends for a long, long time.'

She was right. Prerna and Guneet developed such a close bond that Prerna says Guneet's parents were like a second mother and father to her. When they passed away, it was brutal. 'I remember that phone call at 3 a.m. when Uncle died. It was the worst phone call to get. I cried it out. But Guneet did not. I kept telling my other friends, she's not crying, she's not crying. She was so young but grew up overnight.'

For the next five years, Guneet battled her emotions and endured many dark days before she was introduced to the teachings of Nirmal Singhji Maharaj, better known as Guruji, a spiritual leader. Though he passed away in 2007, millions of devout followers around the world continue to worship him. They believe, as Guneet does, that he delivers miracles. He is said to have cured people of diseases, eliminated pain and shown devotees a way out of suffering. He quickly became an important part of Guneet's life. She says he transformed her.

A large portrait of Guruji sits on a table in her home in a sea-facing room which has been converted into a temple. Fairy lights are strung across the windows. At night, the little bulbs make the room glow. The focus of the room is a large, plush chair, enveloped by a decorative cream tent suspended from the ceiling. A pair of *juttis*, bedecked with flowers, is placed at the foot of the chair. No one sits on it—this is how the faithful mark Guruji's presence. 'It is his durbar,' Guneet says. Any of Guruji's followers can drop in and pray. Satsangs are held here. Guruji's disciples do *seva* in this space—they once sat on the floor with bowls and knives and peeled 16 kilograms of carrots to prepare halwa. For Guruji's worshippers, this room is a sanctuary.

'We all know there is some higher energy and we define it in different forms. I feel very blessed that I found a face to put to that energy,' Guneet says. She wears a locket with Guruji's picture at all times.

Faith is a central pillar of Guneet's life. Born a Sikh, her earliest memories revolve around family visits to a gurudwara in Delhi. That's where the Mongas would usher in the new year, every year. Guneet would look forward to it and savour the 31 December service at the Gurudwara Bangla Sahib in Connaught Place.

The festivities would start at 11.30 p.m. with music—dholaks, tablas and 10,000 people chanting *Wahe Guru,* a Sikh mantra to invoke the Almighty. As it approached midnight, the musicians would drop an instrument from the orchestra, one at a time, till the only sound left was that of voices chanting *Wahe Guru, Wahe Guru.* It created an intense, emotional vibration in the hall. 'It was magical. I didn't know how to define it but as a young child, I felt extremely elevated, extremely connected. I was overwhelmed and I would be crying.'

Years later, she found herself desperate to feel that way again.

It was 2014. Following the success of *The Lunchbox,* which she co-produced with her mentor and boss Anurag Kashyap and entrepreneur Arun Rangachari, Guneet hit rock bottom. 'Outwardly, the world was congratulating me for the success of *The Lunchbox.* Inwardly, I was dying.'

She had lost her parents, had not given herself a chance to grieve, had five unreleased films under her name and was out of a job—a job she had thrown herself into. Guneet had been the CEO of Anurag Kashyap Films Pvt. Ltd (AKFPL) for four years when Kashyap took a sudden decision to shut it down.

That decision felt personal. 'I was so invested in it, it was like taking something away from me. It did hurt me deeply.' Guneet, who used to work till 4 a.m. and return to office at 9 a.m., was left with a gaping hole in her life. She felt lonely. 'Because of Anurag, I did not really address the loss of my parents because he took that position. He was the protector, the father, the mentor.' Losing her job and her role model left her feeling bereft. Guneet says she felt like a failure. 'I felt like I was not good enough. It was one-and-a-half years of complete disillusionment. I wasn't ready to start my own venture and I didn't know how it would fare.'

Distraught, she visited several gurudwaras in search of one that had the same spiritual energy she would experience during her childhood New Year's Eves. Nothing came close, till her aunt took her to a satsang in Guruji's ashram in New Delhi. At once, it felt right.

Guneet asked Guruji for help. She asked him to help her get out of debt for a loan she had taken for a film she was working on, called

Tigers. It was sorted out within a week. It felt like a miracle. 'But it's not transactional,' she explains of her relationship with the divine power. 'I attribute it to the simple *funda* of asking the universe, and it shall be done. We have to ask. I have been able to do a lot because I have been fearless in asking. And as you keep asking, your needs keep reducing. I have learnt to ask for the right things.' Her face cracks into a smile. 'Initially, you start when you want material things and then you ask for other things, and the evolution of life happens.'

Guneet felt a strong, spiritual connection with Guruji and a deep belief he would look after her. In the months that followed, she travelled across the world looking for answers. 'It was like, why me? All my friends have normal lives, a structure, parents.' She was lonely and missed her parents. 'You just want those eyes to look at you and say I am happy for you.' She visited ashrams, tried Ayurveda to address health issues, learnt the martial art of *Kalaripayattu* in Pondicherry and even shaved her head. 'I was super depressed and was totally disillusioned. I used to have suicidal thoughts—I hated myself, I hated the way I looked and I specifically hated my hair.' Going bald was her way of running away from her identity.

'Depression is how you feel about yourself. You don't have control over it.' She believes Guruji nursed her back to health. She began visiting his ashram regularly and engaged with his followers. Over a period of time, she started to feel she was regaining a family. She developed a sense of belonging. The darkness began to lift. And slowly, very slowly, she clawed her way out of the illness. 'It was a slow process of self-empowerment,' she says, describing it as a huge personal victory.

Today, Guneet is at peace and appears content. She is working on multiple film projects under her own banner, Sikhya Entertainment. *Sikhya* is a Punjabi word that means 'to keep learning', and Guneet is invigorated by her work. 'I missed that. I missed being inspired. And now I pray: "Keep me inspired every day."'

Guneet's goal is to produce content that can find an audience between India and the US. Specifically, English-language films set in India that resonate globally—along the lines of the biographical film *Lion* or Ang Lee's multiple Academy Award–winning *Life of Pi*. Most of the films she has produced under the Anurag Kashyap banner AKFPL or her own company, Sikhya, have had alternative content that challenge the song-and-dance stereotype typically associated with Bollywood.

That Girl in Yellow Boots (2011), for instance, is an Indian thriller that exposes corruption, incest and desperation within Mumbai's seedy underworld. *Gangs of Wasseypur* (2012) is a gritty, realistic crime movie based on the coal mafia. *Peddlers* (2012) tells the story of two young men who fall into Mumbai's drug trade. *Haraamkhor* (2015) tells a forbidden love story between a teacher and his student. *Masaan* (2015) is a powerful, dark film about caste, death, love and desire.

The sheer diversity of these stories reflects the churn taking place in modern, aspirational India. These films depict the underbelly of the slice of contemporary life stories which you don't see in commercial entertainers. Gripping storylines that are neatly packed, they are a refreshing antidote to the predictable glitz and glamour of star-led films Bollywood has dished out for decades.

Today, there are enough takers for the kind of content Guneet backs. Since the first multiplex arrived in India in 1997, it has allowed audiences to develop broader, more sophisticated tastes and given independent film-makers an outlet for their work, encouraging them to take greater risks with their plots.

'Multiplexes started the conversation about showing more films, yes,' Guneet says. 'They helped to create a larger market, but the problem is, films are not shown for long enough.' That's true for the big blockbusters as well as the small indies. There just aren't enough screens. According to the research firm ICRA, India currently has around 2,200 multiplex screens. But the country needs many more. Home to the world's most prolific movie industry and a gargantuan population, India currently only has six screens per million people, compared to 23 per million in China and 126 per million in the US.[3]

Is it necessary for Guneet's film to send a message? It is starting to feel important, she agrees, because she feels a responsibility towards the public

---

[3] According to the KPMG–FICCI report, India has more than 8,000 screens (including over 2,000 multiplex screens) with a screen density of six per million people.

that comes to the cinema, unconsciously looking for answers. Over a raw salad at her favourite Los Angeles restaurant during a business trip to the United States, she says, 'I almost feel like, what are we doing with people's time, people's money?' If they choose to spend their money on a movie, this avant-garde producer wants them to feel it was worth it.

She works on instinct. If a story moves her, she does what it takes to produce it, even if people warn her that it may not be financially viable. Funding for independent film-makers remains a challenge in India. The Central government does not provide any tax breaks or significant grants for Hindi cinema. *The Lunchbox* got half of its funding from India, the rest came from France and Germany.

Guneet's film *Monsoon Shootout* (2013), a cops-and-gangsters thriller, is another example of an international co-production. It was funded by money from France and the Netherlands. When it got held up due to a shortage of money, she sold the only property her family owned, which was a house in Delhi she had built for her mother. When she needed funds to make *Haraamkhor* (2012) and *Peddlers* (2011), she turned to social media and crowd-funded the projects via Facebook. She is an out-and-out doer.

When *That Girl in Yellow Boots* was selected for the Sixty-seventh Venice Film Festival in 2010, Guneet and team arrived in Italy with more than a hundred posters and 1,000 postcards that cost an arm and a leg in excess baggage. They were ready to make a splash. She had no idea that sites for posters had to be bought months in advance, were expensive and that there were no spots left. Guneet was perplexed. 'I said, "I come from India, where we put posters on a wall." I had come armed with scissors and tape to do the job!' she says with a laugh. She visited cafes, hot dog stalls, pizzerias and begged the managers: could you please put up my poster? She went to Venice's famous squares where people were eating and dropped a bunch of postcards there. She had a film to sell, she needed to publicize it. Guneet being Guneet, she ended up sticking the posters on the only free space she could find: her friends' and colleagues' T-shirts!

She was inexperienced and out of her depth. After the film was screened, Guneet stood in the theatre and waited for people to come up to her to buy the movie. No one did. 'Nobody spoke to me and I thought, what is going on?' Exasperated, she went to the then director of the festival, Marco Mueller, and asked him, 'Where are the buyers? Why are they not buying our film? We've been selected, right?'

Once again, she was reminded how unprepared she was. Mueller told her that producers were expected to set up meetings with buyers months before they met at a festival. 'I said, "You should have told me!"' Mueller gave her the market book—a massive tome of around 1,500 pages—that listed all the festival attendees. With that, he offered her a word of advice. 'Meet as many of these people as you can,' he said, 'and give yourself three years to do it.'

Guneet took that advice to heart. She travelled the world to understand the international market. She went to France, the UK, the US. She slept on people's couches. She met buyers, producers, sales agents, distributors, studios. She showed them her movies. She learnt how festivals work. She networked and made contacts. And in her trademark style, she took chances.

One day, as the sun shone over the New York skyline, she walked in, without an appointment, to the Manhattan offices of Sony Pictures Classics, which distributes, produces and acquires independent films globally. She pleaded with the executives there, 'Please can you see my film? Please can you see *Yellow Boots*?'

A month later, she got a call back. Executives had viewed it and were ready with their feedback. They apologized that they were not ready to buy it. Guneet didn't mind. She had made a contact and started a relationship. Years later, it bore fruit. When Guneet was shopping around for a US partner for *The Lunchbox,* Sony Pictures Classics acquired it.

This is not a woman who gives up, Prerna says of her childhood friend. She remembers when Guneet needed to get something signed by Irrfan Khan. Prerna teased her and said, what about signing Aamir Khan? To which Guneet replied, if I get a chance, I will! 'What if he says no?' Prerna asked her. Guneet replied. 'But what if he says yes?'

With that attitude and chutzpah, Guneet became a regular on the international film festival circuit, developing an enviable Rolodex of international sales contacts. She quickly gained a reputation as a link between the Indian and Western markets.

Noted author, editor and film critic Baradwaj Rangan of filmcompanion.com says, 'Most of the people who work inside India don't have that kind of network outside the country.' Because of her extensive networking, Guneet has made impressive contacts within film studios around the world. 'At the end of the day, festivals and other people latch on to one person and depend on that one person to provide the gateway to that particular film-making community because programmers cannot keep track of every single movement in every single country. Guneet helped to create the bridge between Indian independent films and foreign distributors.'

Gaining credibility did not come easily. Age and gender were not on Guneet's side. She has a youthful face. During the early years of her career, she would colour her hair grey and wear a sari to meetings. 'Otherwise, how would a twenty-six-year-old be taken seriously? I just had to fake it—that I know my shit.' She was often turned away by marketing heads, CEOs and CFOs of companies who had little patience to listen to a young woman peddling stories.

Would they have listened to her if she were a man? 'Maybe,' she says, but adds that the discrimination she faced was driven more by age than gender.

Is Bollywood still a boys' club? She pauses before answering, 'There are a lot of boys.' Then pauses again. 'I have grown to realize that it is a boys' club. I am not a man. I don't smoke. I have always envied people who go on smoking breaks—so many deals are closed out there.'

But she also believes that some men within the film industry are champions of gender equality. The fact that the number of women in the film industry is growing is partly because of supportive men, she says. 'Look at Anurag, he would put me in front of the line each time.'

Guneet says she often sees people get intimidated by a woman in a position of authority. 'I think there is a generation of boys that has grown up feeling entitled to their privilege. They are not ready for an independent Indian woman. They have seen women around them serving and being there for their needs. Suddenly, when they grow up and meet women who don't do that, they don't know how to deal with it.'

This independent film producer has her eyes firmly set on an Oscar. 'The universe is conspiring. I believe it will guide me to a path and make me work for it.' Could she become the first Indian producer to bring home the coveted golden statue? Guneet, the woman who believes in miracles, says, 'It's on its way.'

ANAITA SHROFF ADAJANIA
THE STYLIST

On the evening of 24 September 2017, all roads in Mumbai led to the Grand Hyatt hotel. Every A-list celebrity, from Shah Rukh Khan to Aishwarya Rai Bachchan, was there. The occasion? *Vogue* India's tenth anniversary celebration. The magazine, the country's fashion bible, had put together a glitzy affair. As giant goblets of champagne circulated amongst the beautifully turned out guests, *Vogue*'s fashion director and creative genius, Anaita Shroff Adajania, stood back and surveyed the scene. Dressed in a floor-length pink Temperley London dress, accessorized with a Jimmy Choo handbag, she knew this moment was special.

The party was a celebration to mark ten years of *Vogue*, but it was also an acknowledgement of Anaita's influence. She had worked with most of the stars in attendance and helped turn them into formidable fashion icons. A critical player in the publication's India journey, when it comes to fashion, Anaita's opinion matters. She is a leading voice in the fashion world and is responsible for the looks of many famous movie stars in a number of Hindi cinema's blockbusters. Remember Alia Bhat's easy, breezy, boho chic look in *Dear Zindagi*? Aishwarya's sexy bikini-esque blouses and miniskirts and Hrithik's bare-chested, tight-jeans look in *Dhoom 2*? Deepika's Aztec skirt and off-shoulder grey T-shirt in *Cocktail*? That was all Anaita's handiwork.

Few would disagree that Bollywood sets the tone and trends in Indian fashion. In movie-mad India, stars are worshipped. Fans follow their every move and scrutinize them to see what they are wearing. Naturally, how they dress influences the larger public. With twenty films to her credit, the award-winning fashion whiz has styled the who's who of Hindi cinema, including (but not limited to) Shah Rukh Khan, Kareena Kapoor Khan, Hrithik Roshan, Deepika Padukone, Aishwarya Rai Bachchan, Katrina Kaif, Siddharth Malhotra and Kangana Ranaut. Amongst the global celebrities she has worked with are Kim Kardashian West, Victoria Beckham, Naomi Campbell, Gisele Bundchen, Cindy Crawford and Natalia Vodianova.

Anaita wears multiple professional hats. In addition to her full-time day job as fashion director at *Vogue* India, she also owns and runs her own company, Style Cell, a fashion consultancy through which she works on costume design, film styling, personal styling and advertisements. Alongside Anaita, a team of six stylists advise a battery of clients, from Bollywood to Tollywood to corporate India. Team Anaita curates everything from red carpet looks to billboard hoardings to movie costumes to what stars wear when they enter or exit airports. Anaita initiated these 'airport looks', which are a huge part of the paparazzi culture today.

Since early 2018, she also beamed into our homes on Sunday evenings via the Colors TV show 'Top Model India', a version of the hit US show 'America's Next Top Model', where she served as a celebrity judge.

'I never question her vision,' says actor Deepika Padukone. 'She brought in a certain amount of newness and edge to the way I dress. She's brought in that sense of fashion. As a stylist it's so important to understand the person you are styling—to understand what they are comfortable with and yet still pull them out of their comfort zone given what their personality is. That's the level of trust and comfort we share.'

Nowadays, it is a given that films and fashion blend seamlessly but there was an in-between period in the 1990s when the thought would have made purists cringe. 'The integration of Bollywood and high fashion is what Anaita is all about,' notes Karan Johar, who has known Anaita since they were in college. 'Hers is a unique fashion voice.'

Anaita won Hrithik Roshan's trust early on and the actor is another avowed fan of her work. 'I have no qualms in confessing, and my chest-high pants were proof enough, that my pre-Anaita phase was a style and fashion disaster,' he admits candidly. When Anaita began styling the star, she told him he wore his trousers too high. Hrithik was not offended. He took her advice. 'Almost single-handedly, this gutsy woman has transformed, or rather educated and reformed, the fashion sense of millions in this country and parts of the world,' he says.

Katrina Kaif, who first met Anaita when she was seventeen, considers her a leader in fashion and styling in India and the one who brought sartorial flair to the movies. '*Dhoom 3* was such a stylized film and I remember we hired a rehearsal hall, maybe about 1,000 square feet, full of racks and racks of clothes,' the actor recalls. 'It had all the biggest international designers who weren't even sending too much to India then. She had a global vision and she really has changed the game.'

Priya Tanna, editor of *Vogue* India, credits Anaita with turning Bollywood's fashion sense on its head. In the 1980s and 1990s, film styling focused on the glamour of costumes and dramatic ensembles, she explains. 'These were clothes specifically made to create an impact on the big screen,' she says. 'Anaita has done the reverse, she has taken street style, put the sexy and glamour in it and put it on the screen. Without robbing it of its aspiration and appeal, she has made film styling more accessible.'

The two have worked closely for over a decade. Their cabins are next to each other and Priya jokes that they are office spouses. 'Anaita is formidable and fierce—demanding and exacting of her team to do more and do better,' she says. 'But truth is, she is equally demanding of herself, if not more.'

When it comes to movie fashion, Anaita pushes the envelope. As Hrithik says, 'She is a trailblazer and still the complete antithesis of what I thought a trailblazer should be. When we shot for *Dhoom*, she was unafraid to approach me while I was in the middle of a shot, and ever so lightly whisper in my ear, "Babe, I'm the audience, forget about how you are looking and focus on making love to me (the audience)." My embarrassed dumbstruck nice-guy mind went boom and "Aryan" took birth that very second.'

Now in her mid-forties, Anaita's rise from stylist to style guru is a testimony to talent and grit. Over two decades, she's parlayed an abiding devotion to fashion into an impressive career. Moviemakers clamour for her to dress talent, brands chase her to publicize their wares on social media, and corporations hire her to provide employees style tips. Each year since its inception, she has been on the influential and widely read fashion website Business of Fashion's index of 500 professionals shaping the global fashion industry. Her work has been recognized with numerous awards, including the International Indian Film Academy's (IIFA) Best Fashion Stylist of the Year award twice.

Not everyone works with Kim Kardashian West and Pharell Williams in the span of a few months, and certainly not many Indians. Yet Anaita is at ease, whether she's with the hottest Bollywood superstar or a major global fashion icon. Even though she's a big fashion player, her own attire is simple and dressed down. She loves jeans and boyfriend shirts that are three sizes too big. In a room, she is usually the most underdressed person. Dark, thick, long hair and large black Dior eyeglasses, which she converted from a favourite pair of sunglasses, frame her face when she's reading or looking at a screen. She gives off an air of friendliness and approachability, a far cry from the stereotype of an intimidating, dour fashion editor. Her shoes are always comfortable and padded in anticipation of the many hours she knows she's going to be on her feet.

That's not to say she never does edgy or sexy. She loves lacey slip dresses. Once she and Deepika Padukone went out dressed identically— in a black lace top and torn jeans. 'Of course Deepika looked 100 times better!' Anaita jokes.

Historically, stars have always impacted the public's clothing choices.[1] In the early days of Hindi cinema, costuming was dominated by tailors and *dresswalla*s, all of whom were men, writes Claire M. Wilkinson-Weber in her book, *Fashioning Bollywood*. 'Prior to the mid-twentieth century, costume design was the prerogative of dressmen, dresswalas and personal tailors, all of them men,' she explains.[2]

Later, women like the celebrated Bhanu Athaiya, who won an Oscar for her work in the movie *Gandhi*; Leena Daru, Shalini Shah and Mani Rabadi forged a new way in costume design.[3] As Wilkinson-Weber notes, these designers, who came to the fore in the 1960s, never aspired to head a costume department with a team under them. Instead, they worked for individual stars in a film that might have multiple designers. In fact, it was quite common for actors and actresses to wear their own clothes in films.

Prior to liberalization, things were different. Moviemakers didn't pay as much attention to the clothes their characters wore. Gaudy sequins and mismatched prints ruled the roost. Anyone who recalls 1980s costumes

---

[1] Mihir Bose, *Bollywood : A History*, New Delhi: Roli Books, 2007, p. 95.

[2] Claire M. Wilkinson-Weber, *Fashioning Bollywood: The Making and Meaning of Hindi Film Costume*, UK: Bloomsbury, 2014, p. 21.

[3] Ibid., p. 19.

will remember how flashy they could be.[4] In fact, the word *filmy* was used as a pejorative. There were notable exceptions, however. *Umrao Jaan*, a period film which tells the story of a Lucknow courtesan, caught the public's imagination with its lavish costumes and elaborate jewellery.

In the 1990s, films began to reflect a more contemporary, urban aesthetic. As advertising and fashion gained momentum, post-liberalization, India's fashion landscape underwent a sea change as multiple luxury and high-street brands, both domestic and foreign, invaded the market.

The country's tastes were evolving. People looked Westward in a way they never had before. Cable TV boomed and with that, a plethora of outside influences hit the nation's shores. The way films looked began to change as young film-makers like Aditya Chopra and Karan Johar burst on the scene. They made films about people they could relate to—young, urban, contemporary, affluent characters who were Indian at heart but global in their outlook. Their movies' costumes had to reflect trendy and cool dressing that was relatable to Gen Next.

Today, the importance of attire in the look, feel and mood of a film is a given.

As Deepika says, 'Styling is an equally important part of film-making. It is as important as your visual effects. It's as important as the sound and what your DoP brings to the table. For me, as an actor, 50 per cent of the battle is won when you look the part. You look at yourself every morning in the mirror before you give your shot and as much as it's important to feel the character, to go through the process emotionally, the physical transformation is the other half of the battle. I think we have done that very successfully in films like *Love Aaj Kal* or *Cocktail*.'

'Anaita's styling me in *Cocktail* was a huge turning point for cinema, not just for me and my career,' continues Deepika. 'From a fashion point of view, every now and then you will have that one film that will sort of set the benchmark. *Cocktail* was that. It was a combination of the character I was playing and the way she visualized and helped me bring Veronica to life. The look became aspirational. When clothes like that become available in the market from the tiniest stores to the biggest stores, when girls want

---

[4]   Ibid., p. 4.

to start looking and dressing like certain characters, you know you have created something iconic.'

Even as film directors started paying more attention to the look and feel of a film, very few films were adding stylists to their crew. Styling was still a nascent concept. It was pioneered by the late designer Rohit Khosla in the late eighties and nineties, when he notably worked on tasteful ads for the sari brand Garden Vareli. In 1995, designer Manish Malhotra memorably transformed actor Urmila Matondkar in *Rangeela*. At that time there were only two strong fashion voices in film, says Karan Johar. 'Manish changed the fashion game and Anaita brought in her own fashion syntax,' he says.

Audiences began to appreciate the difference costumes made to a film but working with a single designer had its limitations. As the distinguished fashion photographer Farrokh Chothia points out, 'Designers were not going to source generic looks,' meaning that they would want to use their own designs. What films needed was a stylist.

Anaita was the first woman to legitimize the profession. 'As a stylist, I work with the overall look and feel, but not the actual making of the clothes,' Anaita explains. 'Unlike a designer, I am not dependent on the story I am telling that fashion season. It's about the aesthetic the character needs.'

Bringing her south Mumbai insouciant style to the big screen, Anaita arrived on the scene at the right time. She was perfectly suited to meet the growing need for authentic style that reflected a polished, modern aesthetic. As *Vogue* editor Priya Tanna says, today Anaita can be credited for mentoring an entire generation of stylists who have all benefited from her rigour, experience and eye.

Obsessed with fashion since childhood, Anaita did not have a formal fashion education but was always artistically inclined, good at stitching, art and crafts, and doodled quite a bit. She could fashion headbands, accessories and clothes out of the most basic materials, a skill that stands her in good stead even now.

Anaita was born on 25 February 1972 to Roshan and Sarosh Shroff. Her parents later divorced. Roshan remarried and had two more daughters, Scherezade and Roxanne, whom Anaita adores.

Roshan bought all the film magazines—*Stardust, Cine Blitz, Movie*— and Sarosh, an Air India official, would bring back copies of *Harper's & Queen* and *Vogue* from his overseas trips. Anaita pored over them, tearing out pages and filing them in cheap paper files bought from the local general store. 'Back then, I never knew why I did that but even now, I follow this referencing process, except now it's on my iPad.'

Fashion was in her blood. Rivalling the complexity of a telenovela soap opera, Anaita had, thanks to multiple marriages and divorces in her family, about ten grandparents at one point. She credits all of them for being huge sartorial influences.

Her maternal grandmother, Mehroo Masani, an extremely tall, handsome woman, only wore black, had a sewing machine in her wardrobe and did the most exquisite hand embroidery. 'From her, I learned the value of listening to other people's opinions,' Anaita says, recalling one incident in particular from when she was twelve years old. There was a family wedding, and Mehroo had planned, along with her friend, Katy Cooper, the tailoring legend from Colaba, an elaborate pink dress with a pleated tulle overskirt and layers of petticoats for her granddaughter. But when young Anaita saw it, she was aghast, thinking it to be too childish. She threw a big fuss. After much cajoling and coaxing, she listened to her granny, wore the frou-frou dress and turned out to be the belle of the ball.

The incident stayed with her. 'Because of that experience, as a stylist, I always ask the people I work with what they think, however young or inexperienced they may be. That's my way of staying younger and fresher. I don't work in a dominating manner. Team effort is way better than what I can do individually.'

Her maternal grandfather, Dinshaw Kapadia, owned two well-regarded bespoke clothing stores, Aristocrat and Esquire, in south Mumbai. She recalls idling away many an afternoon at the stores.

'I remember as a little girl sitting there, sharing my opinions with the customers, drawing with chalk, and all that. My Nana had this massive rotating leather chair which I would sit in while these men would come and be measured, suited up, and I would give my opinion on colours and swatches. They must have thought who this precocious little child is!'

Her grandfather was married to a British woman called Rita Goodman who loved to wear wigs, fitted dresses with thin belts, flared pants, high heels, and carry matching handbags. Anaita's obsession with Pucci stems from Rita, who wore a jumpsuit from the brand accented with a link chain belt and hoop earrings. Remember Aishwarya Rai in *Dhoom 2,* when she walks down the stairs wearing a spaghetti strap long Pucci dress? That's inspired by Granny Rita.

And finally, it was her parents. In the 1970s, Anaita's mother sported forest green flared pants and retro shirts with the buttons undone, along with six inch heels. Her nails would be painted a metallic green. Her father wore corduroy cropped jackets, big sideburns and occasionally a handlebar mustache. But Anaita wasn't entirely removed from Indian aesthetics either. Her stepfather's mother only wore old-style saris and her Punjabi stepmother's family wore large, avant-garde kurtas.

'All these influences were going on like a spin dryer in my head,' Anaita says with a laugh. 'Which is why in film, I borrow so much from reality. Not necessarily only my family, but also from my friends and my husband. It helps me make my characters more real.'

Aware of fashion from a young age, she remembers the day she showed up at her school's fun fair wearing a yellow blazer with oversized roman numeral prints bought from a local Colaba store. She paired it with black pants and topped off the look with her favourite big, gold anchor-shaped earrings. She was confident that she was going to be coolest but was horrified to find everyone else dressed in jeans and T-shirts! The only saving grace was that there was no photographic evidence. Anaita describes the experience as an 'a-ha' moment where she realized that there are dress codes depending on the occasion. She took the learning to heart, deciding then that being underdressed is better than being overdressed. It is now her mantra.

After school, Anaita had ambitions to study fashion design or hairdressing in London, but her mother would have none of it, insisting that she enrol in a degree programme. So off it was to St Xavier's in Mumbai to study political science. Here, she met Karan Johar, a classmate who became a close friend. 'Anaita and I have a romance going on with each other for the past three decades,' jokes Karan. He remembers that when they joined college, everyone was talking about this really hot girl. 'I went to the corridors of Xavier's and spotted her from a distance and I was awestruck. She wore a tiny denim skirt and had this cool body language. She was edgy and fun and I was fascinated by her persona. We became really good friends.'

Karan bullied Anaita into a role in *Dilwale Dulhaniya Le Jayenge*. Remember Kajol's flirty friend Sheena? That was Anaita. And recall when SRK stopped to give a girl a lift on his bike during the song *'Mere Khwabon Mein Jo Aaye'*? That was Anaita too!

She also met Homi Adajania, her future husband, in college. They were eighteen, quickly became fast friends and subsequently began dating. Today, the two have two young boys, Zreh and Zane.

While still in college, she was spotted by ad film-makers and shot a few ads for Clearasil, Cadbury and Titan, at a salary of Rs 600 per shoot. But the thrill didn't come from being in front of the camera. She loved being on set but behind the scenes. 'I didn't even know what styling was,' Anaita says with a laugh. 'At the time, it meant putting together a few looks, it wasn't a constructive job.'

Mahesh Mathai, who founded the film production house Highlight Films, hired Anaita straight out of college. He remembers her as a pretty, hip, independent young girl who would zip around town in a scooter. Even then she stood out with her experimental dress sense, Mathai recalls.

At Highlight, she was a jack of all trades, doing everything from cooking eggs at 4 a.m. to sourcing decor and clothes to helping with film editing. 'It was at this point that I realized I didn't like any part of the process except the costume and set. I mean, people would've died to be in an edit room with Raju Hirani, which I did for two weeks, but I had no interest in learning any of it. The only part I liked was what will the person wear and how will they carry themselves off, what kind of decor was being used, what bed sheet and bedcover.'

Mathai remembers Anaita as hard-working and resourceful. Often operating on minuscule budgets, she would use her imagination to source props and other items for a shoot. 'She was completely focused and you could tell she wanted to dress people.'

It was around this time, in the mid-1990s, that foreign fashion publications began to take note of India and its aspiring middle class. Amongst the first to set up shop was *Elle*, the French fashion magazine, which began its India operations in 1996. At twenty, Anaita was hired as a junior fashion editor and by twenty-four, she was already fashion editor. She was the youngest person to hold this title across all editions of *Elle* worldwide.

Elle was the perfect training ground for the budding stylist. 'We did everything ourselves, there was no question of hiring production and catering services, for example. There was no previewing fashion collections. Whatever was in the stores is what we sourced.'

It was also about being a bit of a hustler, looking for free deals and bargains. Anaita prides herself on being a cost-cutting stylist. 'I'm not someone who runs to brands every time I'm styling someone. I believe you need to do the dog work, run around, see what's happening, go to every store before you pick something up. My husband Homi complains that I keep looking at stuff in the stores and buy nothing, and I say because I owe it to my client to say that I saw all the options and chose the most cost-effective one for them. And I can't get that out of me, maybe it's my middle-class upbringing. I can't spend other people's money without thinking about it.'

At *Elle*, Anaita relied on her instinct. She worked closely with photographer Farrokh Chothia, whom she considers a mentor. Farrokh did numerous cover shoots for *Elle* and immediately recognized Anaita's talent. Few photographers were shooting women the way Farrokh did. 'He was the only photographer in India who brought out the best in women,' Anaita says, adding, 'he was always very supportive of me.'

Farrokh liked her strong, 'can do' attitude. 'You have to remember there was no concept of a stylist. In those days, the roles weren't so defined. She took on a lot of peripheral duties that today a stylist would not do. She always got things done.'

In January 1999, Farrokh asked Anaita to style a print ad he was doing for Maybelline. It was Anaita's first commercial ad shoot. Unlike today, there were no stylists for ads then. Whoever was there from the ad agency was told to buy some clothes and choose what looked best.

Anaita credits Farrokh with kick-starting her career in commercials. 'I was an editorial stylist. In ads, there was no proper thought behind the look and Farrokh stood behind me and said I want her, someone who only looks at aesthetics, who brings in the clothes, so our styling is more than just the clothing. It's body language, mood, lighting, all of that. He fought very hard for that, and that was the turning point in my career. He took me under his wing.'

Farrokh believes that 'Anaita can see the picture in her head before it has been shot. That's a gift not everyone has. Style is subjective, but the visual reference library of understanding what a team is trying to do—she gets that instinctively. She gets the feeling we are striving for. Styling is not only tied to fashion, brands and trends. When the trend goes, the picture looks stale.'

In 2000, Anaita quit *Elle* because the magazine didn't allow employees to freelance. She had moved up the food chain and had a salary of Rs 12,000 but there was more money to be made in ads and also in films. The progression to commercial Hindi cinema was but natural. Even though Bollywood was not considered cool, it was lucrative. It held a certain attraction. Anaita always felt she was meant to work in films. She can't explain why since she had never been an avid movie watcher, but it was a tug. And things were changing. Scripts were read keeping styling in mind and props and costumes were sourced to suit the story.

In 2001, she stepped in to style the film, *Everybody Says I'm Fine*, written and directed by Rahul Bose. 'Budgets were non-existent. Brands were non-existent. You couldn't go to a designer and ask for a dress. We used personal connections and made some clothes. There was no method to the madness. The protagonist would wear simple shirts and pants. I recently saw the film on a TV channel and I loved it. I thought we were good.'

Two years later, *L'Officiel*, the French luxury fashion magazine, launched in India. Anaita joined as fashion editor. She put Indian supermodel Lakshmi Menon on the cover in a satin green Gaultier dress. For an Indian touch, she stacked silver bangles sourced from shops in Colaba market. The cover was a clutter breaker. In the pre-social media era, it drew critical praise and won Anaita plaudits. 'We helped spread the message of a beautiful, raw, dusky Indian girl on the cover and it was a good first message to send out,' says Anaita. '*L'Officiel* was where my energy and my influences started coming out in my work in a big way.'

It was around this time that Aditya Chopra approached her to style *Dhoom*. 'There were no budgets,' Anaita recalls, but she didn't have a problem with that. When it released in 2004, it gave Anaita recognition and established her credibility. From then on, there was no looking back for the young Parsi girl from south Mumbai for whom fashion was an obsession.

'I remember using leather jackets in that film,' she says. 'No one was wearing leather jackets in Mumbai then. I remember driving on Marine Drive after the film came out and seeing these biker gangs and they were all wearing leather jackets. I felt we had something to do with that.'

'Anaita brought in a new language, and spoke a language people hadn't heard in the fraternity,' points out Karan. 'She broke ground. She understood glamour without being garish. Her styling was New Age and it was everything that was filmy but yet it was not.'

Anaita styled all the *Dhoom* movies, which became known for their sexy, glossy aesthetic. She also styled *Being Cyrus, Cocktail* and *Finding Fanny*, her husband's films, as well as *Love Aaj Kal, Ra.One, Players, Race 2, Bang Bang, Hero, Tamasha, Fitoor, Ae Dil Hai Mushkil, Half Girlfriend* and *Raabta*, among others.

On shoots, she's a master in control, coordinating with the photographer, her team and the subject of the shoot. She has a gift for dealing with all sorts of people, from movie stars to spot boys. 'She is a woman of substance who means business and says it like it is, yet I have never seen her use her power to intimidate anyone,' notes Hrithik. 'That's called grace.'

Homi says Anaita is highly committed and totally dedicated to her job. 'When we are working together, she will never pull her "spouse-card" and we switch to an exclusively professional relationship,' he says. 'She is self-taught and relies a lot on her instinct. I remember during *Being Cyrus* she went to the houses of several elderly people and actually bought their old clothes for some of the characters. During *Cocktail,* she styled Deepika in a fashion-forward way and told me to trust her vision, that the character would be very trendy a year later, by the time the film released.'

She was right.

Anaita's process involves making endless mood boards with her team. Researching and referencing are a big part of her life. When she gets a script, she reads it thoroughly, comes back with her creative inputs, storyboards, colour palettes. She and her team sketch out every character. Actors are typically not involved at this point. After she and the producer and possibly the director discuss everything and are in agreement, that's when they speak to the actor. Some actors are more involved than others. Deepika, for example, completely trusts Anaita and never gets involved. She's all about the character, Anaita says. For *Finding Fanny* and *Cocktail*, she did each film's fittings with Deepika in two hours. It is her ideal way of working—taking quick decisions.

Unfortunately, when it comes to films, Anaita gets very little preparation time. Many things cause costuming to have a tight turnaround—the actor may not be signed or the scripting may not be finished. Costume budgets also vary hugely, from Rs 10 lakh to over one crore for a big-budget film. Anaita says she has spent most of her life working with tight budgets.

In 2007, *Vogue* hit India and no one was better suited to helm its fashion styling than Anaita. She loves editorial work and finds it the most satisfying aspect of her career. 'In the early days we shot still photography on film. You would do something and you would wait five or six days to see one image slowly on a negative transparency. There was something to it. Editorial is more controlled. What is the backdrop? What is the environment? What is the hair? What is the make-up? What is the person wearing? It's like I am the director. It's my game. It's my pieces. When I have an idea I have to run it by an editor. After I have convinced her, then I just run with it. Then it's about creating that dream in your mind's eye.'

Anaita is most proud of the October 2010 *Vogue* cover for the magazine's third anniversary issue, which featured Cindy Crawford. As a child of the 1980s she grew up watching *Chitrahaar* and loved the sequined dresses sported by Zeenat Aman and Parveen Babi, and was an avid reader of *Vogue* and *Harper's Bazaar*. The glamour of it all left an indelible mark. Then in the 1990s, when Anaita was in college, American supermodels like Cindy Crawford, Linda Evangelista and Naomi Campbell captured the global imagination. These pin-up girls of the nineties, as designer Michael

Kors famously described them, were wildly iconic. Anaita never imagined that she would one day work with one of them, except that she did—with both Naomi and Cindy.

Seven years ago, when she still considered herself a kid in the business, she shot with Mark Seliger, an American photographer renowned for his portraiture. The team photographed Cindy Crawford in Malibu. Anita put the top model in a gold Balmain dress. 'It was the coming together of so many of my influences,' she remembers. 'Here was a girl wearing an amazing dress which reminded me of the sequined sheath dresses Parveen Babi would wear, with beautiful hair and make-up, stark yet sexy and strong, and I had Indian *jadau* jewellery on her. That was definitely a true moment.'

Anaita walks seamlessly between Bollywood styling and high-fashion styling. Priya Tanna credits her time at *Vogue* for creating a synergy between runway and reality. 'This is exactly what Anaita does best—whether it's a fantastical couture shoot for the magazine or styling Alia Bhatt in shorts and *ganji*s, she treats both with the same filter of edge, sexiness and style. They may sound diametrically opposite, but under Anaita's vision, both transform beautifully into sartorial objects of desire.'

Given her hectic life, how does she do it all? She has her editorial day job that often includes travel, her film assignments, her commercial ad work, her celebrity styling and her family life to manage. She goes into the *Vogue* office almost every day and has a team of six people under her. The magazine takes up 80 per cent of her time. She receives 500 emails a day at *Vogue* and doesn't have an assistant. Add to that the calls and text messages she receives from film folk who do not operate on email. 'Anaita is never working, yet she is a workaholic,' notes Hrithik. 'What I like most is how she makes it all look so easy, it's always like "where's the problem?". She takes serious hard work and magically turns it into fun and games.'

A product of her generation, Anaita keeps a diary and writes everything down in it. It's her lifeline. She structures her life in slots. Her children's holidays are marked in fluorescent yellow and she never accepts assignments on those days. 'As a mother, I don't want to jeopardize my evenings. I avoid fittings that happen late in the day, because everyone knows I prioritize my family. I actually say no to most work that comes my way.'

Unlike others, Anaita doesn't charge fees based on a percentage of the overall costume budget. She charges an upfront fee and provides a budget estimate for clothes. If she comes in under budget, the producer benefits. She calculates everything on actuals. Although she won't disclose it, her fee has remained unchanged for the past twelve years.

These days the newer stylists are often seen being besties with their famous clients but Anaita has never felt the need to do so. She also doesn't stress about looking hyper fashionable. 'In the past, I did feel I needed to have great clothes, especially at fashion weeks,' she says candidly. 'The first time I wore flats at a fashion week was when I was pregnant with Zreh and I enjoyed myself so much more! Luckily the sneakers trend came in and life has been bliss!'

A note of seriousness creeps into her voice. 'At the end of the day, people are looking at what I do, not what I wear.' Whether it's a Kardashian or a major Bollywood star, Anaita has a way of connecting with people and making them feel at ease. She cites a quote from the Business of Fashion's Instagram account by designer Roksanda Ilincic—'It's not about who you know, it's about the work you do. I am not here for anything frivolous. I would much rather be with my close friends or family or by myself. There is a phase in your life where you go through that insecurity of "am I doing enough?", "am I in touch with enough people?" I wasn't and it all worked out regardless.'

Social media has transformed the fashion landscape. Anaita's work is appreciated by a wider audience thanks to Instagram, where she has 2,90,000 followers, Twitter (1,93,700 followers) and Facebook (close to 5,000 friends), not to mention the countless blogs and websites devoted to celebrity fashion. 'I was never the one writing, my opinion wasn't shared, my work was always visual, but now, finally, there are people who care about my choices. People want to pay me to pick my favourite pieces and share them. I never expected that.'

Hrithik believes Anaita represents the true qualities that one needs to be successful today. 'She has the power to be individualistic with a great sense of self-worth, which is completely independent yet tolerant to outside validation and criticism respectively. She is pure feminine power!'

Does Anaita see herself as a pioneer? 'I never dwell on the past, I'm always somebody who is living for tomorrow. In those days, I just felt I was doing new things. I love what I do, and the creative process. I never thought I would end up here. I didn't have a path. I just went with the flow. If you do good work and you dream big—it works out.

DEEPA BHATIA
THE EDITOR

Deepa Bhatia does not know how to make a chapatti. No one ever taught her. 'I wanted my daughters to focus on other things,' her mother, Mala Bhatia, a homemaker, says. Mala thought the kitchen was a distraction. 'Go work and fulfil your dreams,' she told her girls, as she cooked, cleaned and kept their family home running.

That's precisely what the Bhatia girls did. Mala's younger daughter Deepa is one of India's foremost film editors, part of a group of women editors turning out some of the most critically acclaimed films in Hindi cinema.

Deepa has worked on a number of hit films that include *Taare Zameen Par, My Name Is Khan, Stanley Ka Dabba, Ferrari Ki Sawaari, Student of the Year, Hawaa Hawaai, Raees,* and *Sachin: A Billion Dreams*. She is highly sought after. 'If you want what's best for your film you should take on someone you respect and Deepa is someone I respect,' says director Abhishek Kapoor of *Kai Po Che, Rock On!!* and *Fitoor* fame, all of which Deepa has edited.

Millions of people have seen Deepa's work on screen but don't know it. That's just the way she likes it. Seated in an airy office in Mumbai's Bandra neighbourhood decorated with pen-and-ink art by her film-maker husband Amole Gupte, forty-year-year-old Deepa says, 'You should not know if a film is well cut because you should not have noticed it.' So if you've seen her films but don't know her name, that's okay with her. 'I am not a person who enjoys too much attention and so am not bothered by the lack of it,' she laughs, before taking a sip of green tea.

There is a good reason that the enigmatic process of film editing is called an 'invisible art'. A film editor sifts through hours of raw footage, often alone in a dark room, chooses a shot from multiple takes, then stitches the shots together to make a scene. After that, he or she combines the scenes to build a sequence, then strings sequences together to make movie magic. But the work is far from mechanical. Choosing the *right* take is key. Whether an editor chooses to retain a close-up or wide shot, linger on a shot or cut it short, creates a different psychological feeling in the viewer and is the kernel of the film-viewing experience itself. There's no formula which tells an editor what to do. It's about instinct.

'So much hinges on the edit. You can make or break a film on the editing table. It is that important,' says Jeroo Mulla, a noted film critic and teacher who taught Deepa when she was a student at Mumbai's prestigious Sophia Polytechnic for women. She is responsible for Deepa falling in love with films.

The legendary head of Sophia's film department kicked off the course by playing an alternative Hungarian short film *You*, directed by Istvan Szabo. According to Mulla, the film, which is an ode to the director's girlfriend, is pure cinema. 'I guess I show films that I love and I try to instil that love in my students,' Mulla says.

The morning that Mulla showed the film to her class changed Deepa's life. The movie's beauty, simplicity and lack of narrative enthralled the young student. Having grown up on a diet of Hindi films which tend to be linear and story-driven, Deepa wondered: 'Can films really be like this?' That simple short film changed her entire perspective. 'The film didn't have that commitment to plot or storyline that I was used to. It was so liberating! I got really excited by the experience of watching *You* and I knew I had to do something in this world.'

Film appreciation was part of the wide-ranging one-year postgraduate Social Communications Media (SCM) course at Sophia that Deepa joined after finishing her BCom degree from Narsee Monjee College of Commerce in 1993. ('Don't ask me why I studied that!' she says, laughing at the memory). A creative person with a flair for good writing, she thought the SCM course would equip her for a career in advertising.

During her course, Deepa watched the French film, *The Rules of the Game*, by Jean Renoir, considered one of the greatest films ever made. She saw Satyajit Ray's iconic and eloquent *Pather Panchali*. 'The more I saw of this cinema, the more excited I became. It did not even take me three weeks to know this is what I want to do,' she says. Public relations or advertising didn't appeal to her any more. How could it, when it was film that was changing her world view in exciting new ways?

Editing, like almost all aspects of the film business remains male-dominated, but in this field, it isn't just about the numbers. Though the pool of women editors is small in India, as it is globally, many women have risen to the top of the profession, piecing together many great classics.

Lawrence of Arabia is the work of British editor Anne Coates, who also edited *Erin Brockovich* and *Fifty Shades of Grey*. Director Martin Scorsese had a long partnership with his editor, Thelma Schoonmaker, who is tied with American film editor Barbara McLean for the most Academy Award nominations for Best Film Editing (seven each). Schoonmaker won three times—for *Raging Bull, The Aviator* and *The Departed*. This category is still dominated by male winners, as is most of the film industry worldwide.

India boasts of some legendary female editors. Aruna Raje graduated from the Film and Television Institute of India (FTII) in Pune in 1969 with a gold medal, becoming the first trained woman technician in India. She edited *Masoom, Bhairavi* and *Tum: A Dangerous Obsession* among other films. Reena Mohan is an award-winning editor who focuses on documentary films. And then there was Renu Saluja, a towering personality who worked on both art house and commercial cinema for thirty years till her death in 2000. Also a graduate of FTII, the versatile editor worked on a range of films including *Dharavi, Jaane Bhi Do Yaaro, Parinda, Hyderabad Blues* and *Bandit Queen*. She won four National Awards for Best Editing and is considered the gold standard in India's editing landscape.

'When I started, the only woman editor was Renu Saluja, who was like a goddess for all of us. Not just because she was a woman but because she was the best editor there was at that time. I don't think there was an equivalent of Renu Saluja and I don't think there ever will be,' says Deepa.

Today, a younger generation of women editors, including Deepa, are proud heirs to a rich professional heritage created by Saluja. Namrata Rao is the editor of *Love Sex Aur Dhokha* and *Band Baaja Baaraat. Dev. D* and *Jab We Met* are Aarti Bajaj's work. *Peepli Live* and *English Vinglish* are edited by Hemanti Sarkar. Ask any director in India to pick an editor he or she would want to work with and there is a good chance they will list one of the names above.

A career in films was not a natural choice for Deepa. Born in Mumbai on 11 January 1973, to Mala and Kanayalal Bhatia, she grew up in a household where the focus was firmly on education. Her father was a businessman, so the family assumed she would become a chartered accountant or go into management. 'My husband and I both believed that if we gave our daughters an education, they would be able to achieve anything,' says her mother, Mala. Though Mala completed college, she never got a chance to fulfil her dream of studying further—a regret she still harbours. There was no way she was going to let anything come in the way of her children getting their degrees.

Deepa is the younger of two children. Her sister, Rakhi, lives in an apartment across the hall from her in Mumbai. They live in the same building where they grew up. Mala lives with Rakhi and her family and Deepa, with Amole, their teenage son Partho and her mother-in-law. Theirs is a tightly knit family whose central pillar is Deepa.

'We all depend on her to create our paths,' says Amole, her husband of twenty-one years. 'She runs my life, she runs our son's life. She's the one we go to before taking any decisions. She's the one up at 3.30 a.m. making backup papers for Partho's academics.' Her energy is relentless. 'She's wired for action,' laughs Amole. 'I get tired just looking at her.'

Growing up, Deepa experienced a simple, carefree childhood in a middle-class family. 'We were not wealthy, but we grew up in a house of privilege,' Deepa says. That privilege was love. 'I've yet to see a man love a woman so much,' she says of her father's relationship with her mother, 'and when there's that kind of a relationship, there's harmony in the house.' The girls basked in that warmth.

'We had friends who would have the latest video tapes; so we'd go over and watch movies at their homes. But these were the friends who'd go home to find their mothers napping. So they'd come to our place where our mother was always there—with snacks for hungry children.' Her mother, whom she lovingly calls 'Sush,' a shortened form of her maiden name Sushila, remains a huge influence in her life.

At night, the young Bhatia girls would curl up on a couch to read books while their mother did the dishes in the kitchen. 'We didn't have full-time help but our mother never asked us to help her. She never said hello, you are fifteen, get the fuck up and do your bit,' Deepa recalls. Mala says she did that intentionally, not to spoil her daughters but to empower them. If her daughters became adept in the kitchen, they would spend too much time in it. That's not where she wanted them to be.

An alumna of Bai Avabai Framji Petit Girls' High School in Pali Hill, Bandra, Deepa says her upbringing was as non-filmy as can be but somewhere along the way, she was influenced by her father, a businessman, whose heart lay not in his job but in his passion for films. As a young man in Bombay in the 1960s, Kanayalal would organize live musical shows and work as a lyric writer in the industry briefly under the pseudonym K.L. Pardesi. 'He was quite a cool guy at the time!' Deepa gushes.

Back then, the film business wasn't a reliable profession—being a lyric writer meant hanging around a studio for several hours, waiting for a break. There was no guarantee of regular income. Once Kanayalal got married and had two children, he realized a job in the industry wasn't conducive to raising a family. He gave up his passion and started a small business supplying electrical equipment to the Indian Railways. He named it after the most precious thing in his life—Deepa Enterprises. 'That's how pampered I was!' Deepa smiles.

Once a year, her father travelled to Haridwar to attend an annual retreat organized by Guru Parmanand. There, he would write songs and perform them. He became more spiritual. 'I think he turned to religion as his dreams of working in films remained unfulfilled,' Deepa says thoughtfully.

These yearly trips, two weeks long, were traumatic for a family that rarely spent time apart. 'I can still remember the choking sensation when he was away,' Deepa says. Phone calls were expensive and there was no way to stay in touch except through letters. Her father wrote beautiful letters to his girls, reminding them to 'be respectful to Mom, to study, and how much he missed us. There is so much love in them,' Deepa says. The letters are tucked away deep inside Deepa's cupboard. She can't bring herself to look at them very often.

For years after leaving the film business, Deepa's father would pick up copies of *Screen*, a weekly film magazine published since 1951. 'It was his way of remaining connected to a world he really wanted to be a part of but could not,' she says. 'But he had that love for film, my God!' Not just any films but those of quality.

Deepa recalls a time she sat down to prepare for school exams. As she took out her text books, Mahesh Bhatt's path-breaking marital drama, *Arth*, came on TV. Her father immediately told her to stop studying and watch the film instead. 'It's a masterpiece,' he told his daughter. Studying could wait.

When *Mughal-e-Azam*, another classic, aired, he made his daughters watch that too. They complained bitterly about watching such a 'boring film' but years later, when she watched it again, Deepa admits she was blown away. Somewhere along her journey, her father's passion for classic cinema rubbed off on her.

Deepa never got the chance to share her common interest with her father. Kanayalal passed away suddenly in 1991, while Deepa was in her first year of college. He died from medical negligence following a surgery, leaving Mala and her two daughters devastated. They were emotionally distraught and financially stretched. There were loans to repay. There was a business to run. There was no time to grieve.

Deepa, as she always does, soldiered on. She would attend college in the morning and then help her mother run the family business. This arrangement allowed Deepa's older sister Rakhi to continue studying. A few years later, the daughters switched roles. Rakhi pitched in to support the family so that Deepa could study. The Bhatia girls were not going to let their mother handle things alone. That's not what they are. They care.

Those who work with Deepa say that's what makes her a stand-out editor. 'I have worked with Deepa extensively,' says Aamir Khan. 'She has a very sharp mind, she has a strong personality which creative people should have but she is also collaborative. During the process of cutting *Taare Zameen Par*, she and I sat together on the edit for months. She was so committed and so clear in her approach.'

Abhishek Kapoor agrees. 'When my film gets to her, I know it is safe. She protects it and looks at it like it is her own baby,' he points out. 'Her instinct is that of a very nurturing person,' he says, and that's why he hired Deepa to edit multiple films. 'That's an amazing quality she has. She takes care of the film, but for me. She guards it like a hawk, but for me.' Kapoor was so enthused by Deepa's work on his 2013 film *Kai Po Che* that three days after it released, he tweeted: *Deepa Bhatia, working with you is always a delight and a lesson in film-craft. #kaipoche owes the finesse to your magical mind & editing.*[1]

The relationship between an editor and a director is paramount to the process of film-making. 'Because he knows what he has shot, he knows what he has given you and only he knows how much you have turned it

---

[1]   Abhishek Kapoor, 25 February 2013 on Twitter.

around,' Deepa says. 'So when a director repeats you, you know it's the best compliment you could get because that means you have done your job well.'

Since an editor plays such an integral part in shaping a film, it's no surprise that many go on to become directors. Deepa has directed one film so far: the award-winning and critically acclaimed *Nero's Guests* featuring renowned journalist P. Sainath. The film tells the story of the agrarian crisis and growing inequality in India. She also assisted her husband in writing one of India's favourite films, *Taare Zameen Par,* about a child with dyslexia. She's one of the few editors who is comfortable—and skilled—editing both commercial, candy floss entertainers and alternative cinema.

Deepa gets involved with a film from a very early stage. Usually, the director hands her a copy of the script when it's in its first draft. That gives her a chance to internalize the story, so when she sits at the edit table, she is familiar with the plot and the characters. She starts cutting as soon as shooting commences. A director sends her rushes after every two or three days and Deepa edits in parallel. Every now and then she asks the director to come in and see if she's interpreting his vision correctly. She wants to be sure—'Is this the right vibe? The right pace? The right groove? It's very much an aesthetic marriage,' she explains.

Though it's a partnership, she prefers to work independently. 'Editing is not shooting.' She does not need to work with a crew. 'If I want to come at six in the morning, no one is going to ask me why I am here. And if I want to leave at two in the afternoon, I can. I need that independence. I can't work with somebody hovering over my back. I am someone who needs my space when I work.' Her directors respect that. They pop in to see her work from time to time but don't sit with her while she edits. 'I would die!' Deepa says. 'I click best with those who respect the fact that everything needs independence.'

Editing gives her peace of mind. 'I find it very calming. It's very Zen. It's like being in a monastery or a temple. And if I am not doing that, I actually get grumpy or I develop a fever.'

She likes to work on one film at a time so that she can give it her undivided attention. That way, she can relish it and not have a cluttered mind. That's how most editors like to work but it isn't always feasible.

'That's because editors are not the best paid. So if you have a house to run, a family to support, you are going to need to do two to three films together and that dilutes your quality. You can't help it.'

'I've tried not to be greedy at any point of time, tried not to make that mistake. I tell my directors and producers, don't put me in a position where I have to take on more to earn more.'

For Deepa, it's important to enjoy her work. 'Every day is exciting and I keep telling myself, till I get that high, I will do it. The day I feel, fuck, it's so boring, I will stop it. So that's why I don't do so much work that will make me lose that excitement.'

Deepa's strength as an editor lies in her knack for pacing. Every cut in a film affects its flow and rhythm, every edit should take a story forward. 'Editing is all about timing,' says Raj Surve, president of the Association of Film and Video Editors (AFVE) Mumbai. 'The way Deepa edits makes a film so real, so believable. It's hard to beat Deepa at that. Different films need different pacing. For example, an emotional scene needs to breathe, a comedy needs faster cuts. Deepa gets that.'

Surve picks the 2008 musical drama *Rock On!!* to illustrate his point. 'The way she edited it was unique, she brought in a new pattern,' he says. The movie kicks off with the foot-tapping number '*Socha Hai*' in which a band of four young men perform with enthusiasm and abandonment. The cuts are jagged, at times they are jumpy, the camera zooms in and pull outs quickly—all this adds to the raw, funky, youthful energy of the scene. Towards the end of the film, when the boys, who are grown men now, reunite for an emotional performance, the cuts are more staid, the shots hold steady. It creates a different sense of time. This is the work of a skilled editor.

Remarkably, Deepa has had no formal training in editing. She is self-taught and got a break when she least expected it. After completing her course at Sophia, she worked as an assistant director for a leading figure in the world of Hindi movies—Govind Nihalani—widely considered a pioneer of Indian parallel cinema.

Those were the days of non-digital editing. A film editor would take long pieces of film, literally splice the raw film reel and piece it back together with glue, creating the final film reel.

In 1996, Nihalani started work on a film about women's empowerment for UNICEF. It was called *Sanshodhan* and it coincided with the arrival of digital editing technology in India. There would be no more cutting and sticking of film rolls. An editor would use a keyboard to create in and out points, allowing a computer to do the work instead. It was a revolution in film-making.

Excited by the new technology, Nihalani decided to edit *Sanshodhan* digitally—it is one of the first films in India to be cut in a digital format.

He hired an editor who knew how to use the new software. But when the editor realized what the film entails—a lot of hours over a lot of days over a lot of weeks and months—he stopped showing up. 'There was all this material put on the computer, waiting to be edited and there was no one to cut it,' Deepa remembers. It seemed like a colossal waste of time.

It was the best thing to happen to Deepa.

She looked at the machine lying in front of her. Not sure what to do with it, she called a technician and asked him to turn it on. Within seconds, the screen lit up and Deepa started tinkering with the footage that had been loaded. She pressed some buttons. She put images on the timeline. 'I just started. I didn't know anything but by constantly questioning the technician, I taught myself. Even now, I tell my team there is no ego in accepting that you don't know something.' Being in the edit room was a homecoming. It felt as if she was always meant to edit.

After three weeks, she nervously showed her work to her boss. Nihalani was taken aback. 'When I came back to see what she had done, she had cut it so nicely.' He was delighted. He recognized a talent in Deepa that she wasn't aware she had—a natural sense for editing. He told her she should pursue it. He wasn't joking.

Nihalani's next project was a much-hyped film called *Hazaar Chaurasi Ki Ma* and he turned to Deepa and said, 'Will you cut it?' 'I was like what?' Deepa remembers. 'He said yes, you cut it.' He gently teased her by saying if she messed it up, he would get Renu Saluja to fix it.

Deepa agreed. 'It did not occur to me what a big risk he took by giving me such an important film to edit. It was really magnanimous of him.' But she had nothing to lose. 'I thought, he is telling me to try it, I'll try it!'

She got to work and gave it her all. Deepa worked hard—all day, and most of the night. She would go home around 5.30 a.m., bathe, take a nap, and be back at the editing table a few hours later. She was living and breathing the film.

There was a lot riding on it but Nihalani insists he was not nervous handing the footage over to a rookie editor. 'I had no doubts,' he says. 'I was very confident of her honest and studious approach to the work apart from her intelligence and imagination. Deepa has the mind of a film director and the mind of a storyteller and that gives her work a very special quality. She edits as if the film belongs to her. Today, she is one of the best editors in the country and I am very proud of her.'

According to Nihalani, Deepa has a tremendous sense of rhythm. 'Normally we use the term rhythm in the context of music. But there is a certain quality to telling a story which you can't quantify. You can't look at the film and say "ah, this is how the rhythm is used". The editor has to feel it.'

He paid her Rs 25,000 for the film. It was a decent salary those days. Today, it can go up to Rs 40 lakh per film but few editors command that level of pay. Junior editors still struggle. Because of advances in technology, there is a lot more footage shot when a film is being made. That means an editor has that much footage to sift through. 'The work has increased but the pay has not,' Deepa says.

'In all the fields, whether it is editing, cinematography or scriptwriting, my students have made headway. It is much easier today than in my time,' says Jeroo Mulla. Technology has changed the landscape fundamentally. Digital platforms have made cameras lighter, for example. 'That's just evolution. My grandmother didn't go to school. My mother did. I did a master's.'

Do women editors influence a film because they approach it with a different sensibility? Deepa isn't sure if it has much to do with gender. 'There may be a man who is as sensitive as I am. And not all women think the same way. They all come from their own sensibilities.' But the one area where she admits being a woman does influence her work is songs. 'I absolutely love cutting songs. I love, love, love, I mean I just love cutting songs! But I will 100 per cent not put in something cheap.'

So-called item songs, meant to titillate, have been criticized for objectifying women and treating them as 'items' for the male gaze. When Deepa cuts one of these songs, she looks at it from her filter, 'which is that of a woman and a woman who understands what sort of a society I am living in. I am very anal about that.' Referring to the number in the crime action film *Raees* that featured former adult star Sunny Leone, she says, 'You won't find a deliberately low angle of her breast. I'll dodge it. I am not against sexuality but I don't want to make it vulgar. I have my own aesthetic boundary.'

Deepa has honed her craft and developed her aesthetic sense over the years. After having her son, she took a break from editing. A time of reflection, introspection and learning followed. She needed perspective. 'So I took time off and read books—everything that was ever published on editing. I read. I watched films with a different lens. I became more analytical.'

Having not learned editing at film school, this was her way of studying. 'I tell my son and I tell my assistants who come from the Film and Television Institute of India, "You have the privilege of education. I did not have that. I had to learn under pressure. I was always afraid that I should not fuck up."'

She has not. And after this period of learning, she has never felt that she comes up short.

The learning continues. A voracious reader who always has multiple books on her bedside table, she's currently reading *Film Form—Essays in Film Theory* by the Soviet film director Sergei Eisenstein, considered a pioneer in the use of montage, a specific use of film editing.

Deepa is always looking for ways to improve her craft and herself, except in one area. The kitchen. Amole, who makes a mean mutton curry, does the heavy lifting there. Deepa pitches in by making a salad or pasta every now and then.

She still hasn't learned how to make a chapatti.

GAURI SHINDE
THE DIRECTOR

It's 4 October 2012. A nervous Gauri Shinde waits in a movie theatre in Goregaon, Mumbai, after the Indian premiere of her directorial debut, *English Vinglish*. It is a huge affair, with tons of stars and industry stalwarts in attendance for the late actor Sridevi Kapoor's 'comeback'. As the lights come on afterwards, the celebrity audience is exuberant. They are blown away by the film.

Through all the mayhem and congratulatory hugs afterwards, Gauri looks for her parents. It's getting late and she is concerned about them. Finally, they appear in the crowd. The moment is overwhelming. Her mother, unable to express herself in the crush of people, goes home. Only later, after the initial excitement of the release died down, Vaishali Shinde put her hand on Gauri's hand. With tears in her eyes, she said in Marathi, *'Maalaa kiti chaan vatla'* ('this was meant for me'), referring to the film's dedication. It was meant for Vaishali. That's when Gauri knew her mother loved her film.

Every once in a while, a movie comes along that entertains, uplifts the spirit and illuminates an aspect of the complexity of the human condition. So it was with *English Vinglish*, the drama written and directed by Gauri Shinde. It turned into an unexpected blockbuster and created a buzz around the newcomer. Suddenly, this debutant director, not yet forty years old, was the toast of filmdom.

English Vinglish catapulted Gauri into the limelight. Her journey demonstrates that success is within reach if you have hope, work hard and aim high. That's what a young girl from Pune, with no film background, relied on to make a name for herself in the rough and tumble world of Hindi cinema. She belongs to the new Bollywood, one that is defined by talent, diligence, perseverance and professionalism.

English Vinglish, with its deft portrayal of a middle-class Indian family, tugged at our heart strings with its honest depiction of Indian family dynamics. It centred on a middle-aged woman called Shashi Godbole, who runs a laddoo business out of her home but is taken for granted by her family and mocked for her lack of English fluency. The actors, especially the late Sridevi, who appeared on screen after a gap of fifteen years, delivered fine performances. That is a testimony to their talent and to the director's skill. Gauri was able to elicit touching, realistic acting from her cast.

The movie premiered at the Toronto Film Festival in 2012 to a ten-minute standing ovation. As Gauri left the Roy Thompson Hall, she was stopped by an elderly Iranian woman who hugged her, cried and said, 'Thank you for making this film, it's my story!'

English Vinglish is the story of so many women around the world, some of whom, like Gauri's mother, struggle to speak English and are often taken for granted. Typically, they toil silently and selflessly for their families, without recognition and without respite, and become subjects of ridicule—harsh or soft. After the film's debut in India, the public was full of praise, as was the film industry.

It was the first time Sridevi had worked with a woman director. The two clicked immediately. Weeks before her tragic passing, the actor said, 'It was wonderful to begin my second innings with Gauri. She was absolutely marvellous to work with and I blindly followed her. She knows exactly what she wants and gets the best out of everyone. That is the best quality I have noticed in her. Though she has her own mind, she's very open to suggestions and ultimately she will take a call as to what she wants. She's chilled, and that puts actors and technicians at ease.'

Gauri followed up the success of *English Vinglish* with 2016's *Dear Zindagi*, headlined by Shah Rukh Khan and Alia Bhatt. Here, too, she dealt with a complex subject based on a female protagonist. The plot centred on a young cinematographer (Bhatt) who flounders as she deals with difficult family and career issues, and so she turns to a therapist.

Alia calls Gauri an instinctive director. 'It was one of my most expressive performances and that's because Gauri really pushes you to go deep within,' says the actor. 'Sometimes, we would just have conversations telepathically because she would instinctively connect with you. She's someone who believes in striving at every step, so every scene for me was a challenge.'

Dear Zindagi received critical acclaim for tackling mental health and therapy, did reasonably well at the box office, although not as well as *English Vinglish*, and cemented Gauri's reputation for exploring thorny subjects in an accessible manner.

Both Gauri's films tell the story of a woman trying to navigate her way through life. One does it through language, the other, through therapy.

Gauri describes *English Vinglish* as a story 'about a woman who is trying to work on her self-esteem, who is bored of her situation and wanting to break free. In *Dear Zindagi,* it's about a young girl feeling lost, despite being so confident and successful, and not being able to grapple with the dilemmas and confusions of life.'

Fame hasn't affected Gauri; being around big-ticket movie stars hasn't changed who she is. She loves making movies but remains grounded. This is no starry, larger-than-life director. She is approachable, not intimidating, and is quick to laugh, putting others at ease. Dressing like a typical creative professional in the Mumbai movie industry, she sports loose-fitting shirts, comfortable pants and sneakers on most days. Her mass of curls is usually pulled back into a bun and her glasses sit atop her head when they aren't required. The look is completed with a worn, brown-leather, cross-body sling bag that contains her phone, cigarettes and chewing gum.

Despite her easy-going manner, there's no doubt that Gauri is the boss lady on the sets. Often surrounded by ten men at a time as the camera rolls, she issues instructions calmly. Some directors scream and shout. Not Gauri. 'It was a very relaxed atmosphere,' recalls Alia about the *Dear Zindagi* set, adding, 'At the same time, it was a hard-working atmosphere. Like when she wants the work done, everyone is on their toes. Having said that, she likes to have fun—she would randomly play the film's music, and if there's a nice light scene, she'd be like "OK, now just dance!"' Alia says Gauri liked to chat about different subjects and that helped them get to know each other on set.

Gauri is seen as an actor's director—clear about her vision, true to her script, yet open and willing to listen. Sridevi had said, 'For actors, it is very important to have a good director—it becomes like a cakewalk, you don't have to worry about the script, or about the look, because the director is so clear. With Gauri, there's no confusion, no tension. *English Vinglish* was Gauri's baby, she created it, she gathered the character, the story and so I believed in her. That's the reason I just surrendered to her.'

Alia agrees. 'Her emotional quotient is very high, and she manages to bring that emotional quotient within you just by helping you explore it within yourself. It was almost like therapy . . . shooting with her.'

Gauri is also a writer, and her stories explore untidy emotions authentically. Her husband, film-maker R. Balakrishnan (Balki), says, 'As a writer, she is pure in her heart. She doesn't conveniently manipulate the screenplay for it to have an effect or an impact. That is her biggest strength. When she makes a film, she adheres to the feeling with which she wrote the script, which is a challenge for all film-makers.'

Taking inspiration loosely from her own life, Gauri doesn't shy away from tough subjects. Her point of view is seen as fresh and original. Her idiom is contemporary and based on the experiences of urban Indian women.

The lyricist and scriptwriter Kausar Munir says Gauri puts content above everything. Munir, who has worked closely with the director as dialogue supervisor for *English Vinglish* and as a lyricist for *Dear Zindagi*, says that Gauri never compromises on anything essential to the script. 'She is very authentic about taking decisions when it comes to what the film and script requires rather than any other frills and fancies that come with it,' Munir says.

She adds that Gauri is not one to be influenced by market forces or the glamour of the business. 'With a big star like Sridevi coming on-screen after so many years, it could have been so easy for her to cash in on that stardom. She could've had a dance number or song, but she didn't. It was about Shashi, the character. Sridevi did a fantabulous job of portraying Shashi. All her actors, technicians, producers, they serve the script and not the other way around.'

Gauri first established herself with ad films and continues to be much sought after in that field. She's directed over 100 TV commercials for well-known brands like Axis Bank, Havells and Tanishq. Early in her career, she also worked on documentaries on Kashmir, Leh and Ladakh, and made two short films, *Oh Man!* (2003) and *Y Not?* (2005), which were screened at international film festivals.

Directing a full-length feature seemed like a natural, if daunting, extension. Like Kaira, Alia's character, says in *Dear Zindagi*'s opening scenes, 'I want to shoot my own feature film, enough of this patchwork, I can't keep waiting for other cameramen to fall ill. No one will even know that I've just shot this entire scene, I want to shoot my own film.'

Film-making isn't for the faint-hearted. Creating and crafting a story that is put out into the world and judged as either good or bad requires passion and nerves of steel. 'Sometimes you think, I was quietly sitting in my room, doing my own thing, why did I have to put myself out there for criticism? Why be this vulnerable person?' She says this as she paces around her office in Mumbai's Bandra neighbourhood where she and Balki run the aptly named Hope Productions. In the driveway sits a black Hackney cab, brought back from London by Balki. Photos of actors and films made by Gauri and Balki adorn one wall of the reception area. Above a doorway is a framed photo of a silver chappal with the caption 'new steps, new directions' written underneath.

Born on 6 July 1973, Gauri grew up in Pune, which was, in the 1970s and '80s, still a small town with a blissfully bucolic atmosphere. Vijay and Vaishali Shinde raised their family in a small bungalow with a garden.

Gauri was the middle of three children. Her brother Indrajeet is five years older and Abhijeet is four-and-a-half years younger. Vaishali says her daughter was '*hoshiyar* (smart), sensitive, *ziddi* (stubborn) and bold'. Gauri cycled to St Joseph's High School Convent nearby. She played sports—basketball, badminton and table tennis—at the district and inter-college levels and hung out with friends. Being at an all-girls school fostered a strong sense of camaraderie between the students.

Movies were not an obsession. Gauri recalls watching progressive Marathi films and theatre. The first English movie she saw was *The Sound of Music*, with her father. She credits him with introducing her to different types of cinema. Another film that made an impact, albeit a negative one, was *The Deep*, a 1977 film made by Peter Yates. It heightened her fear of water. Like most Indian households in the 1980s, the Shindes watched the local language televised movie on Saturday evenings and the weekly Hindi movie on Sundays. At thirteen, Gauri fell in love with Jackie Shroff after watching the romantic action film *Hero*, in which he played the lead role.

In the pre-Internet, pre-cable TV era, Gauri spent her free time immersed in books and writing letters. She had ten pen pals, wrote poetry in school and college and read voraciously. She had to be told to put off the lights and go to sleep. Her father encouraged the children to go to libraries. The British Council Library was a favourite haunt. 'I used to be excited to go to the library and exchange books,' Gauri recalls.

Vaishali loved making things and when Vijay's factory, which manufactured geysers and taxi meters, floundered, she stepped up and started making and selling spices. She did so well that Vijay also joined the business. The brand sold both domestically and overseas under the name VV Products. Vaishali is renowned for her Kolhapuri masala, which adds a robust flavour to meats and vegetables. At home, the smell of cinnamon, cloves and red chilli would waft through the air. Gauri and her brothers would help their parents with the business and to this day, Gauri uses her mother's spices to cook. She told her mother, whom she affectionately calls the 'Mistress of Spices', 'I'll have to stop eating food once you're not there.'

Although Gauri didn't realize it at the time, her mother was a role model. Married at eighteen, running a business in her early twenties, and tending to the home and raising three children was no mean feat. In past interviews, Gauri has stated that she made her first film to say sorry and to thank her mother.[1]

For Vaishali, educating her only daughter was a mission. She herself had a diploma in home science and had wanted to come to Pune to attend the reputed SNDT college, but had not had the opportunity to do so before marriage. 'Gauri *hone ke baad hi maine socha tha ki mein usko bahut sikhaungi*,' Vaishali says. '*Baad mein uski bahut iccha thi ki woh Bombay mein jaayegi. Meri iccha puri nahin hui toh maine socha ki meri ladki ki hone dena chahiye.*' (After Gauri was born, I thought I would let her study a lot. Afterwards, she really wanted to go to Mumbai. My wishes were not fulfilled, so I wanted my daughter's to be.)

---

[1] Shashi Baliga, *The Hindu Business Line*, 11 October 2012, http://www.thehindubusinessline.com/news/variety/to-sri-with-love/article3985116.ece

Priya Gupta, Times News Network, 24 July 2014, https://timesofindia.indiatimes.com/entertainment/bollywood/news-interviews/I-am-a-better-director-than-Balki-Gauri-Shinde/articleshow/16697950.cms?referral=PM

Watching her parents run a business spurred Gauri to study commerce, since she thought that she would one day own a business herself. 'I thought I'm going to be this kick-ass businesswoman without knowing what I was going to do.' She calls that decision the biggest regret of her life, and often ends up hiding the fact that she studied the subject. 'For someone like me, it made no sense. I tell people I studied literature!' she jokes.

To distract herself, Gauri studied French at the Alliance Francaise and got a job as a trainee at Pratibha Advertising. Her days were packed. In the afternoons, she would work at the ad agency and in the evenings, she would play basketball. 'I had this restless streak where it's not OK to not do anything,' Gauri says of that time. 'My brain needed to be occupied, it was always working overtime.' It was while working at Pratibha and later at Notre Advertising as a trainee for Rs 700 in Pune that Gauri realized she wanted to be a copywriter.

She enrolled in a diploma course in Mass Communications at Symbiosis Institute while simultaneously pursuing a master's degree in English literature at Pune University. Zipping around in a Kinetic Honda two-wheeler, she would shuttle between the institutions.

Mumbai had always beckoned. She had visited with her parents and was attracted to its buzz. 'I had always had this sense of freedom—no matter how much freedom I had, I always wanted to feel freer.' Growing up, she had always been a bit of a rebel, even though she didn't need to be—her parents never stopped her from doing anything. In fact, they pushed and encouraged their only daughter. But, as Gauri says, 'I always wanted to push the boundaries.'

Vaishali would later say that her daughter showed her a new way of looking at things. Vaishali came from a traditional Maharashtrian background. Her father, Gauri's maternal grandfather, was a minister to the Maharaja of Kolhapur, and Vaishali did not watch a Hindi film till she was eighteen years old! But she encouraged her daughter to pursue multiple interests, including sports and studies. When Gauri wanted to move to Mumbai, her parents did not stand in her way. In 1995, Gauri moved into a two-bedroom flat in Andheri, which she shared with three other young women, splitting the Rs 15,000 monthly rent evenly.

After interning with film and TV personality Siddharth Kak, and working on *Surabhi*, a TV cultural magazine show, Gauri was still keen on advertising. To pay the bills, she worked at a production house and did other odd jobs for five months. But she was diligent about pursuing her goal, poring over trade magazines like *Advertising & Marketing*. She kept abreast of industry developments, and cold-called agencies to set up meetings. Wearing a printed, long, fitted skirt paired with either a blue or a white shirt, she would often take the local train to meetings and interviews.

Her perseverance paid off. She landed her first job as a copywriter at IB&W, an ad agency, where she remained for a year. Her colleagues thought of her as a cool, young writer who had a way with words. Employees were meant to sign a register upon reaching work, and Gauri was perpetually late. The commute from Andheri to Worli in the mornings was always rushed. She would take the 8.57 a.m. train from Andheri, get off at Mahalaxmi and take a cab, but that pesky 9.30 a.m. start time would always prove elusive. To explain her tardiness, Gauri would make up little stories and write them into the register. 'There was a knock on my door' is how one started. The stories developed their own following—people would ask her what she had written that day. Finally, she was told off by a senior manager. Much to the disappointment of her colleagues, the stories stopped.

After a year at IB&W, Gauri took some time off. She was twenty-three and unsure about where she was headed. A magazine job? Film production? As she was figuring things out, advertising drew her back. 'Advertising was always like this home I went back to after dabbling in other things,' she says. It was when she joined Bates Clarion, another ad agency, in the films department, that she saw the inner workings of how an ad film is made. It was a thrilling feeling.

Advertising was highly professionalized and responsibilities were clearly delineated. As India's economy opened up in the early 1990s, advertising went through a renaissance. Amer Jaleel, chairman and chief creative officer of Mullen Lintas, who was senior to Gauri at Clarion and later became a good friend, says, 'Advertising held a lure for her because it was also about coming up with creative ideas and slogans. She wanted to know how creative people think. She was quite restless and was wondering what to do because she was in a creative profession, but not in a creative capacity. I think her heart was in film, but she may not have known it completely.'

In 1999, she moved to Lowe Lintas to work in the films department, where she remained till 2003. 'My first impression of Gauri was that she seemed very intelligent and attractive and that she would do a good job,' says her then boss, Kavita Advani, who headed the films and TV department. Advani recalls Gauri as being very quiet but tremendously dedicated. 'I gave an entire portfolio to her, which she took care of to everyone's satisfaction,' recalls Advani, who thinks that even then, Gauri wanted to be a writer.

As a film executive, Gauri had to handle pre-production meetings, do post-production work, go for shoots, interact with the client-servicing people and the creative team. As a result, she got to see the creative side of conceptualizing and storyboarding an ad, as well as a chance to observe film production.

In 2001, Gauri took a break and went to New York to study film, obtaining a diploma in film-making from the New York Film Academy. She had thought of working in the US, but after 9/11, the American economy was in the doldrums. Six months later, she came back to India and got her first gig as an ad director, for Fair & Lovely under-eye dark circle remover cream. Gauri cringes at the memory. She admits to being terrified, of having sleepless nights and working really hard on the ad. She belaboured the shot breakdowns. 'You feel like a nervous wreck and you fake a bit of confidence in the beginning and then it sets in,' she recalls.

It was at this time that she met her future husband Balki, who was heading the agency. Gauri got consistent work there, but was sensitive to any perception that she was not deserving. 'I had this huge drive in me to prove that I could do it on my own and that only happened when I left the agency and was directing,' she says emphatically.

In 2003, she struck out on her own. That's when her ad film career really started. She is embarrassed of some of her early work, but remains proud of the first Havells ad and the Tanishq remarriage ad. Both were game changers because of their innovative approach to gender.

Havells India, an electrical equipment company, wanted to commission an ad that conveyed the message that their wires don't catch fire. Anil Gupta, chairman and managing director of the firm, recalls Gauri's pitch. She suggested the story of a poor woman on a construction site constantly getting burned picking up chapattis, so her young son creates a tong out of Havells electric wire. The concept was based on a story by Munshi Premchand. 'That ad became a trendsetter and still resonates a decade after it was made. I give Gauri credit for our journey of converting this electric company to a consumer brand.'

Gupta notes that Gauri 'is one of the easiest people to work with, unlike many of the directors and producers who come from Bollywood, who have their own airs. She has made successful films but she's not aggressive or rude, she convinces the client quickly that she'll take care of their brand, which is important for every corporate.' He thinks her demeanour is reflective of her upbringing.

Shikha Sharma, CEO of Axis Bank, was drawn to the originality and progressive attitude of the Havells ads and wanted to bring the same earthiness to Axis Bank campaigns. 'I wanted to know who had done it. We wanted to emote in a similar fashion,' Sharma says. Gauri was hired to do Axis ads. 'She delivers flawlessly. There's no rework required.'

When Gauri joined the ad industry, she had hardly watched cinema, but over the years, she gradually became a film buff. 'It opened my eyes and I realized there was this whole world out there. I became an avid film watcher, but I still never wanted to make films,' she says.

In 2007, Gauri and Balki got married. It was also the year that Balki debuted his film *Cheeni Kum*, starring Amitabh Bachchan and Tabu. By now, Gauri was exploring the idea of making a feature film herself. Balki says he had known years before she made *English Vinglish* that she was ready to do one. 'She had done a short film which was superbly written and beautifully done,' he says, and adds, 'It took me fourteen years to do my first feature and she did it so much faster.'

Gauri once again returned to New York to enrol in a screenwriting class, but quit after just two days because she thought it was rubbish. She decided to go back to India, but as she was crossing the road, an idea struck her—of a married woman who wants to do something, who is bored of her situation and wants to break free. That was the genesis of *English Vinglish*. She worked hard on the screenplay, writing at home even as she worked on her ad films. The script took two years to complete, yet Gauri wasn't satisfied. 'I'm a huge self-critic, I'd rather not make a film that is mediocre or bad,' she says.

Casting Sridevi was a master stroke. Although hugely popular, she had quit acting to focus on raising a family. She was remembered as a glamorous figure, certainly not the plain Jane housewife she ended up portraying in the film. Shooting commenced on 7 July 2011, a day after Gauri's thirty-eighth birthday.

Filming was fun. As Sridevi said, 'During most of the shoot, we were laughing, giggling, enjoying. It was a beautiful experience working with Gauri—there are only a few such directors you come across during your career who are talented and very sensitive. She has got the best qualities as a director. I am lucky that I got an opportunity to work with her.'

Providing an example of Gauri's empathy on set, Sridevi recalled how understanding she was of Shivansh Kotia, who played Sridevi's seven-year-old son Saagar in the film. 'As soon as his shot got over, he would go and look at the monitor and Gauri would let him happily watch and enjoy it,' Sridevi noted. 'She would ask the little boy, "*Theek ho gaya, accha hai?*" to make sure he was happy. These are small gestures that are very cool. Gauri is at heart a very sensitive person.'

Being married to a film-maker who understands the quirks of the industry helps. Balki is her principle reader, critic and adviser. The couple watches movies together and talks shop a lot. 'It's easier than being married to a dentist or a lawyer,' Gauri jokes. 'We're the nastiest to each other,' Balki says half-seriously. 'We de-motivate each other tremendously, we're ruthless critics. We can slam each other if we see each other's work that we don't like. It's almost like we've done something so awful we can't look at each other.'

Gauri jokes that her baseline for her debut film was that it shouldn't be embarrassing and make her cringe. But she was acutely concerned about what her mother would think. Eventually, after the film's release, and after her mom had seen it a few times, Gauri went to Pune to visit her folks. 'I had dedicated the film to my mother, kind of based it on her life,'

Gauri says emotionally. In the next minute, she adds with a laugh, 'Her only complaint was, "Where's the French guy?"'

The film wowed everyone. 'It felt nice, *kuch* decent *banaya*,' Gauri says in her trademark low-key manner.

With *Dear Zindagi*, Gauri once again tapped into emotions she had felt. The idea came to her in May 2014 and by the end of the year, she had written the script. She was perusing the Sunday edition of the *New York Times* while in New York, her go-to inspirational city. While reading a travel story on Paris, she chanced upon the word 'therapy'. That led to a screenplay about a young woman who goes to a therapist to sort herself out.

Even though the main character, Kaira, is closer in age to Gauri, it's not entirely based on her life but on feelings she's had. Candidly admitting that she's been to a series of counsellors and psychotherapists ('I'm a sucker for this stuff, I am curious about it,' she says) she based Shah Rukh Khan's character on an aspiring therapist.

Was it hard directing a big-name movie star? Gauri doesn't think so. The movies are a highly people-centric, emotional business, and 'you don't want to put your power out there just because you are the captain of the ship,' she says. 'You know how people say *tumko kuch pata nahin*, I'll figure it out? Shah Rukh never gave me that. It was always a collaboration. If he had a suggestion, he'd always ask politely, 'Gauri, shall we do this instead of . . .' and he'd always have good suggestions.

She takes the same approach with all actors. 'Even where Alia was concerned, just because she is younger than me, I didn't want to be the boss. We would just look at each other and I'd know she's thinking the same thing. The process becomes exciting when you're in sync. The other person doesn't even have to complete the sentence and you get it. So I think that's when there's space for magic to happen and that's exciting.'

Gauri is both a writer and a director. Which process does she enjoy more? She finds it hard to say. Writing, according to her, is easy since it's solitary and nobody knows what you are doing. It's also scary because that's where the ideas form.

Directing is an adrenaline rush, where a unit teeming with people works together for months at a time. When the shoot is over, they vanish.

'You find yourself sitting alone with one editor in the room,' Gauri says. She said she was depressed during the edit of *English Vinglish*. 'I missed shooting and the whole process and I was like, what the fuck happened? It's not like in an office where the same people are there. It is a psychotic experience. With *Dear Zindagi*, it wasn't as intense since I sort of knew what was coming.'

She is not sure she would ever direct a film she hasn't written, but believes in never saying never. As for being pegged as a director who does women-centric films, Gauri shrugs. 'These are media-created words,' she says. 'If something is successful, people are not afraid to try it. The industry is a boys' club, but it's not stupid in terms of the commercials—when it comes to that aspect, they are gender-agnostic!'

Does Gauri make it a point to hire women? 'I don't think like that,' she replies, although her unit had a number of women. 'For me, it is competency and talent over gender.' For her, being comfortable in a person's presence is important—to receive good, positive vibes from the people she works with. 'You need to be able to pick each other up if there's a slump,' she says.

Regarding the casting couch, thankfully, she says, she hasn't experienced it. 'Maybe it's to do with being a married person and slightly older when I entered the industry, but I am sure there are instances. No one has come to me saying I have had this happen and I need help. If that happened, I would speak up. Men have each other's backs, for sure. And women don't. There's no unofficial grievance cell in the industry. It would be nice to have that where someone can pick up the phone and lodge a complaint. There has to be some solidarity and unity among us. But there's also a reason, for women the opportunity has been so scarce and it's so new, you want to grab what you have. It's about somehow surviving.'

Is she overwhelmed by her career trajectory? After a pause, she simply says, 'You have to be careful what you wish for because it does come true.'

GEETA TANDON
THE STUNT ARTIST

Geeta Tandon sits on the floor of her modest one-room home in Malad, a working-class suburb in north Mumbai. Morning light streams in through a large window, creating shadows on the bare pink walls. Geeta rubs her calf vigorously. Still sore, she is massaging an injury she endured while riding a horse without a saddle and boots.

Geeta, India's foremost female Bollywood stunt artist and body double, isn't afraid of getting hurt. She is used to it. Her suffering started well before she embarked on her career and her body is testament to that. From stitch marks on her hairline to bruises on her feet, scar after scar tells a story—of injury, of accidents, of falls. Those are the ones you can see. Other, deeper wounds remain concealed. But this 'daredevil' as the local media calls the thirty-four-year-old, wears her wounds like a badge of honour. 'There is gain in pain,' she says.

The aroma of Maggi noodles and sweet, steaming masala chai fills her home. She is tired after filming a horse-riding sequence the previous night for a Hindi television serial *Chandra Nandini*, a period drama based on the life of Chandragupta Maurya. Tandon has never learned horse riding or taken a martial arts course. Yet, she wields a sword, brandishes a revolver, drives cars through hoops of fire, chases bad guys on bikes, crashes through glass, jumps off rooftops—and yes, rides horses. Every skill she has acquired, she has learned on the job.

'Do I feel scared? Everyone feels scared,' she laughs. 'But because I do this, I can run my house.'

While stunt artists usually remain invisible, lost behind the larger-than-life personae of the stars they fill in for, Geeta is one of the few women to make a name for herself through her work in commercial films. The cool stunts Deepika Padukone pulled off in *Chennai Express*? That's Geeta. The scene in which Kareena Kapoor falls off a bike in *Udta Punjab*? Geeta again. The thrilling car chase in the Aishwarya Rai starrer *Jazba*? That was Geeta too.

Stunt work is an unusual choice for an Indian woman. Of the 581 stunt artists registered with the Movie Stunt Artist Association (MSAA) in Mumbai, only twelve are women, according to Aejaz Gulab, the group's general secretary. Geeta is one of them. 'She's got guts,' Gulab says. She's also got one hell of a story about how she landed on a film set.

Geeta is slim and slight. She wears comfortable grey jersey shorts and a faded T-shirt, has highlights in her shoulder-length hair and wears an edgy septum ring that glints as it catches the light. It's hard to picture her in anything but these no-nonsense clothes. Yet, she insists she was a salwar-kameez–wearing girl next door who assumed that her innocent childhood, which revolved around her parents, three siblings, school and playing outdoors, would last forever.

Born in Kota, Rajasthan, in 1983, Geeta moved to Vashi, New Mumbai with her family when she was just a few months old. Her father, Shugli Maharaj, was a priest who earned money by conducting pujas and singing bhajans during festivals. Money was good during the festive season, otherwise it was erratic.

Her mother, Renu, showered the children with love. She would wake them up early in the morning, give them breakfast, prepare their tiffin boxes for school not with simple things like rotis, Geeta says, 'but with sandwiches'. After school, she would help the children study. 'She was a perfect mother,' Geeta says.

The idyllic family unit didn't last long. Geeta's parents developed differences and separated. The children were told that Renu had gone to their Nani's house. They waited, eagerly anticipating their mother's return, but she never came home.

Geeta was nine years old when she and her siblings learned that their mother had died. 'We cried a lot, my sisters and brothers, and that's it. No one realized that they must help the children understand what has happened.' They never found out the reason for their mother's death. She says it felt like someone had drilled a hole in her heart.

Her mother's untimely death put a huge burden on her father. Strapped for cash and unable to look after four children, he shunted the family between various relatives' homes. They would live in Delhi for a few months, Punjab for a few. Sometimes the siblings were separated, forced to live with different aunts and uncles who could not accommodate all the children together. Their schooling suffered. Shugli Maharaj tried to rent a small home in Delhi for his family, but money remained scarce. They would often go hungry. 'Forget two days at a stretch, I don't remember ever eating properly those days—we would eat bread once a day,' Geeta says.

The family soon returned to Mumbai where a new chapter awaited Geeta: marriage. She was fifteen years old.

Her father had hastily arranged her wedding to Vikram Chopra,[1] a man ten years older than Geeta. He owned a trucking business that brought in good income—enough to put food on the table at every meal, which is more than what Shugli Maharaj could provide his children. Geeta agreed, thinking marriage would usher in a new phase in her life. It would give her something she craved: stability. 'I thought I would get a house, a mother, relatives, food on time, a TV, that I would get to watch serials.' The wedding was a simple temple ceremony attended by a handful of relatives.

Within a matter of hours, Geeta's dreams were shattered. 'Things were bad from the first night. Who knew what a *suhaag raat* was?' She was a teenager whose ideas of relationships and sex were based on conservative Hindi TV serials and a few Bollywood films. In her mind, a wedding night ritual involved drinking a glass of milk and going to sleep.

Her husband assumed a motherless child would have lost her innocence, that she would be more sexually aware. 'These people made such a fuss over the suhaag raat. I told them, "I don't want to do it, I don't want to do it,"' she says. Her in-laws retaliated by beating her. They could not fathom why the teen bride would not want to consummate her marriage on the first night.

A pattern emerged—a day spent cooking and cleaning would give way to a night of violence and forced sex. Her husband was brazen in his abuse towards her. He would come home inebriated and smash a plate on the wall. He would pull her hair, punch and kick her. Once he hurled a gas cylinder at Geeta.

'My mother-in-law would tell him, "Go and tear her clothes, rape her. Are you not a man?"' Geeta says, emotional at the memory. Nobody intervened, not the neighbours, not the relatives who would be hanging around the house. 'If he beat me in front of them, they would continue to watch TV and ignore me, just like they show in the TV serials.' She yearned for the days before her marriage when she would go hungry. At least she wasn't abused then.

---

[1]   Name has been changed to protect the identity of this person.

She grit her teeth and endured the pain. A year later, she was pregnant. By the age of nineteen, she had two children, a son and a daughter, but the torture continued. Night after night, her husband would abuse her. Their daughter would jump on her father, pull his hair and beg, 'Don't hit her, don't hit her.' For years, Geeta's son had nightmares about the violence he witnessed and would wake up screaming in the middle of the night.

It is not uncommon for women to keep quiet about domestic violence or refrain from seeking help. Social conditioning from a young age encourages girls in India to accept their lot in life, to make sacrifices for the sake of the family, and to put a man first. In Geeta's case, there was one more issue holding her captive in her hell: she had nowhere to go.

Legal recourse was not an option. India does not consider marital rape a crime, citing factors such as social custom, illiteracy, poverty and a generally accepted view that marriage is sacred. Even though the country tightened its sexual violence laws after the gruesome gang rape of a young woman in Delhi in 2012, legislators are reluctant to touch the issue of marital rape. That subject continues to be a political and cultural hot potato. In twenty-first century India, a man retains the right to force himself on his wife.

One night, when Geeta was twenty, the cruelty got out of hand. Her husband banged her head hard against the wall five times. Dizzy and distraught, Geeta ran out of the house. She hailed an autorickshaw and made it to the local police station. She tried to lodge a complaint against her husband but the police turned her away, callously telling her to solve her domestic problems at home.

'What's the use of complaining?' Geeta asks rhetorically. 'The law is only for those who have money and power.' Her voice rises an octave. 'Just because you get married, does it mean you have bought a woman? What have you bought—a puppet? Whenever you want, you sleep with her? I am against that. Sex is something that should be done out of love and from your heart. Not by force.'

Something in Geeta snapped. She had had enough. Each kick and punch steadied her resolve. She was done with the abuse, she was done with the marriage, she was ready to start over. She took her children and walked out.

She found refuge at the one place she knew would not turn her away—Shri Guru Singh Sabha, a gurudwara in Vashi. It welcomes anyone in need, from any faith. The priests gave her and the children food, a place to bathe and a safe space to sleep. As she spread a sheet over a mattress in the verandah that night, she realized she had not had a full night's sleep in years.

Geeta woke up early the next morning. She desperately needed a job. She had no money and no educational qualifications. Unable to afford bus fare, she would walk for hours each day, looking for work. She was offered all sorts of petty jobs, including one in a massage parlour which turned out to be a front for a brothel.

Her prospects looked bleak but Geeta was not one to give up. She had to make it on her own. Geeta continued to look for work, eventually finding a job in a canteen in Vashi where bus drivers would stop by for lunch every afternoon. Geeta would start work at 8.30 a.m. By noon, she would have 500 rotis ready. That earned her Rs 1,200 a month and free lunch for herself and the children. That salary allowed her to rent a tiny room near the canteen. Geeta would leave the children at home, lock the door from outside and show up for work every morning. 'What else could I do? Who would look after them? They were better off and safer inside the room. It was the best option I had at that time.'

Next came a slightly better paying job as a dancer in a Bhangra troupe that would perform at weddings. Noticed for her energy and *bindas*, carefree, attitude, an acquaintance asked her if she wanted to try her hand at doing stunts in movies. Geeta didn't know what that involved—except that the applicant needed to be brave, have a high pain threshold, and that the money was good. Despite no training in stunt work, she gave it a shot—and landed up amidst the scenic hills of Ladakh for one of her first assignments. It was a television commercial for Bingo! chips.

The flavour was 'red chilli *bijli*' and the message was that the hot chips would set your taste buds ablaze. To make the point, the commercial depicted a woman dancing whose lehenga catches fire. That woman was Geeta. During the fourth take, a strong wind blew, which burned her face. She was singed so badly her eyebrows are scanty even today.

Geeta reacted like she always does to adversity—by bouncing back. 'What's the big deal? The doctor would fix my face. I had work at least!'

And, she had money. She received Rs 18,000 for this shoot. She bought herself one gram of gold to celebrate. 'Yes, a gold bracelet. I was very happy with that.' Later, she sold the piece of jewellery and used some of the funds to buy the room she now lives in.

In the spring of 2014, a friend who worked in the TV business suggested Geeta's name to a reality TV game show called *Khatron Ki Khiladi*, based on the American hit *Fear Factor*. She did not win but the upside is she got noticed and started getting more work as a stunt artist.

Geeta was now a member of the staunchly male-dominated world of action. Historically, very few women have performed stunts in Bollywood. In almost all other facets of film-making—producing, directing, scriptwriting, editing—the number of women working behind the scenes has increased dramatically since the 1970s. But the world of stunts remains heavily male-dominated.

India's original stunt queen, Fearless Nadia, burst on to the scene in the 1930s. Born Mary Ann Evans in Australia in 1908, she came to India as a little girl. Her father was a volunteer with the British army. Mary worked in the circus as a trapeze artist, travelled with a theatre group, and was a trained gymnast. In 1935, she made her Hindi film debut under the pseudonym Nadia in *Hunterwali* and stunned people with her acrobatic prowess. The audience loved her! Over the next decade, she starred in over fifty films and performed her own stunts in every one of them. She shot to stardom quickly but with time the legacy of the blonde, blue-eyed 'Fearless Nadia' faded.

Forty years later came the 1975 superhit drama *Sholay*, widely considered the most successful Hindi film of all time. Most movie buffs would probably draw a blank at the mention of the name Reshma Pathan. Mention Basanti though, and almost anyone will tell you she was the feisty female character played by actress Hema Malini. Basanti was depicted as a young woman who earned her living driving a horse cart. The role involved several cart chases and stunts—but few in the audience know that the stunts were performed by Pathan, a stunt artist, and not Hema Malini.

Pathan is now sixty-three and lives and work in Mumbai. 'I do roles of *buddhis* now, like a grandmother being thrown down the stairs. I don't do roles of young women any more,' she chuckles, adding, 'I like to work, it keeps me active.'

Like Geeta, Pathan's family struggled financially, so she got into the movie business to make ends meet. 'Some women become stunt artists because they want to, others because they have to,' says Pathan. She started working as a body double and stunt artist at the age of fourteen. She joined the stunt union in 1974, and was one of the first women to be given membership. Back then, as now, female stunt artists were an anomaly.

'It's a risky profession,' Pathan says. 'Some young girls worry, "If I break my leg or my hand, or my face gets scarred, who will marry me?"'

'Being an Indian woman has its limitations,' adds Gulab, the general secretary of the union and an action director himself. 'An Indian woman is expected to stay at home and devote time to her husband, her kids. We cannot push anyone to become a stunt artist.' Can they encourage women though? 'Yes, if they come forward, we tell them you can do it.'

Geeta says the union does not discriminate against women. She says there is no wage gap either and that payment is determined by the nature of the stunt, not by gender. Her work—which involves mostly car and bike chases, smashing through glass and free falls—gets her between Rs 5 and 6 lakhs a year. It is the kind of money she could never have dreamt of.

Sitting in the one-room home that she now owns, Geeta appears content. Having a roof over her head has given her a sense of security, though she never takes it for granted. In a rare moment of quiet reflection, between munching biscuits dunked in numerous cups of tea, she reveals why she agreed to share her story. 'If someone reads about me, she will realize that after going through so much, a woman can emerge from failure and become something. It is not necessary to belong to someone, to a man. A woman can achieve a lot alone.'

Her greatest pride, clearly, are her two well-mannered, educated, ambitious children. Geeta's son and daughter are strapping teenagers who are incredibly proud of their mother. Eighteen-year-old Harsha is in her first year of college, studying for a Bachelor of Commerce degree and Pratap, fifteen, is in grade 11. They haven't seen their father in years. And they don't want to. They know what he put their mother through. 'I hate him,' Pratap says.

The children often brag to their friends about the media coverage their mother receives. At the same time, they are aware her job has a dark side. Every time she takes on an assignment, they know Geeta risks her life for the high stakes multi-crore entertainment industry she works in.

'I feel scared when my mother goes out to work,' Harsha admits. 'She always comes back with some injury. Sometimes a bruise here, sometimes a bruise there.' She's lucky it has only been injuries so far.

Indeed, the job is risky. A spinal cord injury for a film in the early days of her career left Geeta bedridden for four months. She depleted her savings paying for her treatment. Her landlord at the time told Geeta she had to vacate the room despite paying the rent. He was concerned that she would never be well enough to work again. 'I felt really, really sad then,' Geeta says.

Across India, the film industry churns out around 1,000 films a year, making accidents inevitable that leaves injured stuntmen and stuntwomen penniless because they are not covered by insurance. Though there are no figures available for this, stunt artistes and technicians have died during film or television shoots. In 2016, two Kannada stuntmen jumped from a chopper into a reservoir during a film shoot. They drowned immediately. There were no rescue boats on standby and the men were not wearing life jackets. The film crew was later charged with culpable homicide. Actor Akshay Kumar, known for performing hair-raising stunts himself, has said that he saw a young stunt artist die in front of his eyes during a car stunt.[2]

While union laws make it compulsory for producers to bear medical expenses if a stunt artiste cannot return to work because of an injury suffered during a shoot, this law does not cover rehearsals, Geeta says. Stunt artists who get injured during practice sessions have to bear their own medical expenses.

But there are green shoots of change. Earlier, if you fell, you got hurt—that was part of the job. 'Today, stunt artistes can wear belts, put on a knee cap, add some padding. Those things were not available back then,' Geeta says. Action directors are demanding that film producers pay more

---

[2] 'Akshay Kumar: I Have Seen a Young Stuntman Die in Front of My Eyes', *Mid-day*, 24 November 2017, https://bit.ly/2LbkJk2

attention to safety but the standards in India are still a far cry from the norm on an international film set that typically has a safety officer on site.

Mumbai's stunt artists have found a champion in Akshay Kumar. Following the 2016 death of international stunt co-ordinator Scott Cosgrove who was due to work on a project with Kumar, the actor penned an open letter to stuntmen and stuntwomen. It was published in the Indian press. In it, he lauded their hard work and recognized the fact that the film fraternity barely acknowledged these men and women who made stars look like superheroes. 'My children still have their father in one piece because there is always someone prepared to take the fall that I may not be able to . . . You deserve so much more than a wage packet and I hope I live long enough to see a change. I know in my twenty-five-year-long career nothing much has changed. But it will, and I will try and make sure of that.'

Kumar put his money where his mouth is. He helped launch the first of its kind insurance scheme for the stunt artists of the Hindi film industry. In doing so, he is helping redefine the stunt industry. In her own way, Geeta too is. Her goal is to become Indian cinema's first female action director—the person who designs an action sequence. 'In India, that's the way to go down in history. When I say that to people in the union office, they laugh at me. No woman has dared to have that dream before. But, I am a fighter.' No one doubts that.

As she prepares to go and workout on the scorching sands of Marve Beach, Geeta steps out of her home on to Mumbai's congested streets. Squinting in the daylight, she says, 'God seriously saved me. Many times. I guess he wanted me to live to see today.'

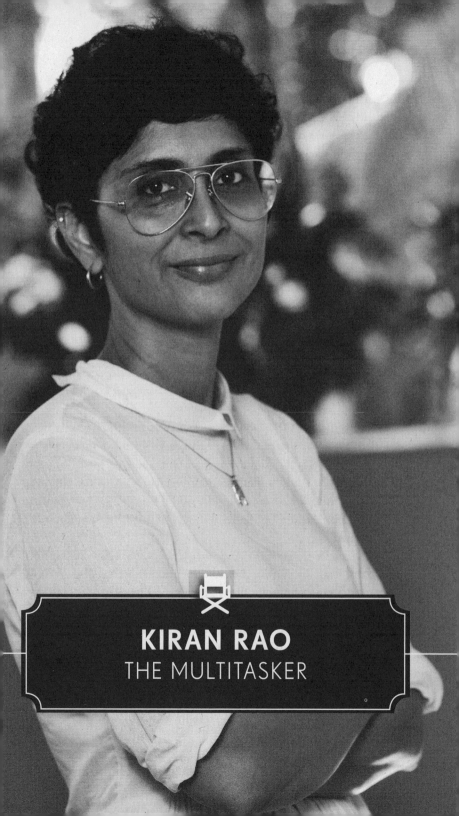

KIRAN RAO
THE MULTITASKER

Red carpeting and heavy drapes lend the Liberty Theatre in Mumbai's Marine Lines an old-world cinematic glamour. The hall was an apt setting for the nineteenth edition of the Mumbai Film Festival's opening night on 12 October 2017. The week-long extravaganza, called Jio MAMI, which stands for Mumbai Academy of the Moving Image, began with a bang as the film fraternity glided in to see director Anurag Kashyap's highly anticipated *Mukkabaaz*. As star after star traipsed in—among them Aamir Khan, Kangana Ranaut, Karan Johar and Konkona Sen Sharma—Kiran Rao, MAMI's chairperson, beamed. She had good reason.

It had been a long, hard road to get the film festival back on its feet since Kiran assumed its leadership in 2014. That was when MAMI was in danger of folding up because of a fund crunch. Corporate support had fizzled and the festival had lost its momentum. Kiran places a huge premium on having a special platform for cinema; so when she got an unexpected call from the festival's founder, award-winning film-maker Shyam Benegal, asking her to join the board, she says she couldn't say no. 'Mr Benegal is Mr Benegal, and of course you have to do anything he says.'

Resurrecting MAMI, which was launched in 1997, wasn't easy. 'For all of us, it was a steep learning curve,' says Kiran, who took over as chairperson in 2015. 'I've done events for films and large screenings, but the idea of screening 200 films and documentaries across the city over seven days, getting films from across the world, assembling a jury, putting up events and talks during the festival, and doing it year-round—well, that's intense.'

Kiran works closely with Anupama Chopra, the festival's director, and Smriti Kiran, its creative director. The triumvirate has made MAMI the country's most important film festival and a highly anticipated event in Mumbai's cultural calendar. Thanks to generous backing by Jio, a subsidiary of Reliance Industries, the festival is able to provide year-round programming and acts as a major platform for many film-makers, both aspiring and established. It offers film screenings, masterclasses, film appreciation classes, workshops and networking opportunities.

'There's nothing at MAMI that Kiran hasn't championed and shaped,' says Smriti. 'She's a force of nature. My first impression of Kiran

96

was this ball of energy that had come into the room and transformed it. She has an absolute hunger for life, which is why I think MAMI has got a lot of energy in the past four years.'

Kiran spearheads MAMI, but making films is her true calling. Lauded as a flag bearer for independent cinema in India, Kiran wears several hats and negotiates multiple worlds. She is a writer, a director and a producer. She plays an integral role at AKP Films, the film company founded by Aamir Khan in 1999, through which she has steered a number of films to success. Her roster includes *Taare Zameen Par, Jaane Tu . . . Ya Jaane Na, Peepli [Live], Delhi Belly, Dhobi Ghat, Dangal* and *Secret Superstar*, as well as three seasons of the transformative TV show *Satyamev Jayate*.

A storyteller herself, Kiran wrote and directed the critically acclaimed *Dhobi Ghat* (2011). Trade analyst Taran Adarsh called its script intensely intelligent.[1] Critics from magazines, newspapers and websites praised the film's sensitive character portrayals, unhurried tone and non-linear narrative. 'With *Dhobi Ghat*, you can feel the sensitive and artistic film-maker behind it,' says the lauded film-maker Vishal Bhardwaj, before adding, 'cinema is her pure passion.'

Kiran receives tons of scripts and is constantly solicited by aspiring film-makers. That's how the script of *Delhi Belly*, the hilarious black comedy, ended up on her desk. She found it so ridiculously funny that she pushed husband Aamir Khan to co-produce it.

'Film-makers from the independent world look to her for championing them because her word carries weight and because she can make a difference,' says Anupama Chopra. 'That position and power to empower narratives, because she has a great love for movies that are not mainstream, that are independent, eclectic and different, are wonderful.'

Kiran is one half of a power couple that has figured out the magic of telling interesting stories that go against the grain of the usual Bollywood fare and still win at the box office. Are Kiran and Aamir the secret ingredient that guarantees a film's success? Judging by the quality of films, and the box-office numbers, it appears so. They have leveraged their power

---

[1] https://blogs.wsj.com/indiarealtime/2011/01/21/review-round-up-dhobi-ghat-a-beautiful-ode-to-mumbai-impresses-critics/

to make films that stand apart. As an eighteen-year-old production house, AKP Films has produced eight movies, a low number with high hit rates. AKP is choosy and discerning. Few companies in Bollywood have as enviable a track record.

'I can't think of a more joyous thing to do than to make a film,' Kiran says with feeling. As a medium, cinema encapsulates all her passions—performance, music, language, imagery, mise en scène, space and setting. An ardent advocate of independent cinema, she wants to create a better environment for indies—films typically made on smaller budgets, which explore unconventional subjects and are usually made by film-makers outside the studio system.

When it comes to such cinema, her generosity of spirit is well known. Kiran's help in finding national distribution for the film *Ship of Theseus,* hailed as 'the most significant film to come out of India in a very long time',[2] demonstrated her commitment to championing unconventional stories. 'Kiran is an idealist. She feels that young, independent film-makers who don't have the backing of large corporations or studios should have a voice, and this has been something that has always been important to her,' explains Aamir.

She is also passionate about documentaries, helping the Indian Documentary Foundation (IDF) by moderating Good Pitch, an event that connects documentary film-makers to stakeholders like non-profits, activists, funders and the media. Sophy V. Sivaraman, co-founder and CEO of the IDF, says it was 'automatic that Kiran would be the one we would approach. She has a high level of focus, intelligence and she's a film-maker herself. Our process is about promoting film-makers and trying to get pledges from people for that. There's nobody else I can think of who would have the film-maker's back like Kiran would.'

Aamir points out that Kiran wants to bring art and culture from around the world to India. 'She loves art house cinema and unusual films on unusual topics,' he says. 'For her it's this whole new world which she wants to experience and wants Indians to experience—about different

---

[2] http://www.thehindu.com/todays-paper/tp-features/tp-cinemaplus/desi-ship-on-a-world-tour/article18510126.ece

lives and cultures and different forms of storytelling. It is a passion for her, and I think that more than half her time goes in doing things that actually don't involve her work personally or directly.'

Kiran's main aim is to build wider audiences for the kind of cinema that otherwise may not be seen, whether it is documentaries, shorts or features. She wants to develop an ecosystem that allows films to thrive. 'I want to showcase cinema as an art form,' she says. Then, with a laugh, she adds, 'I feel like I've taken on projects now that I should have taken up after retirement!'

Although she's married to an adored superstar whose stock rises with each year, Kiran has retained her own identity, rather than be subsumed or fused with her husband's. In the past, she was wary about being famous, but Kiran has struck a balance, retaining her individuality in the fishbowl existence movie folks often find themselves in.

'The smartest move Aamir made was marrying her,' says Srila Chatterjee, who hired Kiran early in her career and who is a friend. Chatterjee, who ran one of India's best production companies, Highlight Films, for twenty-five years, knows Kiran well. The two share a Kolkata connection from their childhood. 'She's very well read. She's smart. She is a beautiful thinking woman.'

Kiran's MAMI colleague, Smriti says, 'I don't even think about whom she is married to. I love the fact that Kiran is just a regular gal, regular teammate, who talks to everybody.' She cites the example of being on the road together in Berlin for the film festival. 'We were travelling in trains, eating falafel on the road.'

Talk to anyone who knows her, within and outside the industry, and they agree that Kiran is down-to-earth. As Vishal Bhardwaj says, 'She is married to this huge commercial star and yet she is keeping her identity, her sanctity, her purity, intact. She's a rare person who is connected with mainstream cinema and yet untouched by it.'

Kiran's mop of short, curly hair and trim figure make her seem much younger than someone in her mid-forties. Her appearance, atypical in an industry where long hair and overt feminine appeal hold sway, is enough for some to brand her a 'serious intellectual'. The truth is that Kiran does not fit into any stereotype. She is intelligent, easy-going and exuberant.

She giggles easily, uses her hands to gesticulate, and harbours no airs. And she is the only celebrity in filmdom who makes retro eyeglasses look cool.

'I am amazed at how *not* a princess she is,' marvels Anupama. 'Literally two hours before we had the 2015 MAMI opening ceremony at the Gateway of India, we were working on the seating plan and trying to do the menus for the closing ceremony at Taj Land's End. Kiran is sitting there with these menus spread out before her, asking, "Do you want paneer or do you want chicken?" In which world does the chairperson do this?'

Everyone she works with says Kiran is hands-on. When she decides to get involved with a project, she gets into the trenches. At MAMI, she goes to pitch meetings to raise funds. 'It's not, "I'll direct you from my ivory tower and you guys run this,"' Anupama says. Smriti says Kiran will not lend her name to something unless she believes in it. 'She's invested in what she does, and doesn't take anything for granted. She's thorough, she will roll up her sleeves, she has a different way of doing things and she makes them happen.'

IDF's Sivaraman agrees. 'Good Pitch is complicated,' she explains, referring to the documentary impact forum that Kiran moderates. 'It's not like she just comes in, picks up the mic and moderates. She's involved in the entire process, is constantly updated about the programme, and does her homework. She brings her whole self into it.'

Aamir jokes that he keeps complaining to her that she has more time for MAMI than she does for him. 'If I want to go for a film with her, she will say, "Oh I have a meeting for MAMI,"' he says with a laugh.

This dedication holds true for whatever Kiran pursues. Case in point: her work with the Paani Foundation, which she and Aamir founded alongside the team of *Satyamev Jayate* in 2016. Maharashtra had experienced one of its worst droughts that year. Kiran and Aamir set up the foundation which, according to its website, aims to harness the power of communication to mobilize, motivate and train people in the mission to eradicate drought by offering training in scientific watershed management, leadership and community building.[3] Kiran plays an integral role in the

---

[3] https://www.paanifoundation.in/

non-profit, touring the interiors of Maharashtra in blistering temperatures to spearhead the effort. Paani Foundation works in approximately 90 per cent of drought-hit Maharashtra.

But back to cinema. Kiran's pull to it began during her days at Sophia College in Mumbai and Jamia Millia Islamia in Delhi, where she studied film. It was the mid-1990s. Documentary film-makers like Lalit Vachani, Sanjay Kak and the Media Storm Group were part of the faculty at Jamia. 'We saw certain types of films, and since I was never really exposed to commercial cinema, television and popular culture in my life, I was automatically drawn to art house, independent cinema,' she explains. 'At Jamia, we saw all the greats, from Andrei Tarkovsky and Federico Fellini to Robert Bresson and Alain Resnais,' she says, referring to the celebrated twentieth-century European directors.

When Kiran was growing up in the 1970s and '80s, Hindi indie cinema was at its zenith. Directors like Shyam Benegal, Mrinal Sen, Saeed Mirza, Mani Kaul, Sai Paranjpye, Govind Nihalani, Kundan Shah and others were making movies that went against the grain of the typical *mirch masala* fare. Though indie cinema has been around since the dawn of film-making in India—the 1950s paved the way for Indian New Wave—these films, also called 'Parallel Cinema', were helped by institutions like the National School of Drama (NSD), set up in 1959, the Film and Television Institute of India (FTII) in 1960, and in funding and distribution by the National Film Development Corporation (NFDC) and the Films Division of the government.

Films were not a big part of Kiran's childhood in Kolkata. Books and music were. Uma and Satyanarayan Rao had three girls—Suman, born in 1965, Madhu, born in 1969, and the baby, Kiran, born in 1973. Satyanarayan worked for a steel company and whenever he travelled, he brought back books for his girls. The sisters never got toys as gifts, only books. Kiran maintains that reading 'has influenced me as a film-maker more than other films have. I find myself attracted to films that have the layering and sweep of literature rather than straightforward plot-driven ones.'

Kiran was more ebullient than the other children in the family, say her parents. She started speaking at a very early age and would observe and imitate people. She made friends easily. 'She was always fond of play-acting,' recalls Uma Rao. They describe their youngest daughter as communicative, assertive and sensitive.

The arts run in her family. Kiran's maternal great-grandfather was the celebrated Kannada poet and writer Panje Mangesh Rao. The Raos went to see movies (mostly English) on Friday evenings at The Saturday Club. As in most households of that era, Hindi movies were seen on Doordarshan on Sundays.

She remembers one particular foreign film, whose name escapes her now. 'It showed divers finding a sunken ship and discovering its inhabitants leading normal lives under the sea! I will never forget that, the magic in the realization that cinema could be completely different from reality and completely plausible at the same time.'

At the age of twelve, she entered a movie hall for the first time to see the classic *The Sound of Music*. It was thrilling. The second visit did not happen for another four years. This time, she went with her grandmother to see *National Velvet*. 'I remember looking at my granny in the darkened theatre and she would just be commenting on what nonsense it all was. "*Hain kalla hain!* (what is going on?)" and all this in Konkani. And that's the memory I have really not so much of the film as much as of her, of people's reactions. I literally went to the cinema a handful of times till I became an adult.'

Kiran studied at the prestigious Loreto House, an all-girls school, followed by La Martiniere in Kolkata. Shivani Bhasin Sachdeva, her best friend from nursery onwards, remembers Kiran as a bright, talented girl who was good at academics, sporty (a trait she inherits from her father), and creative. Kiran loved to act and always had a part in the school play. When they enacted *Cinderella* one year, Kiran had the lead role and Shivani was one of the mean stepsisters. Even outside of school, the girls would play-act. 'We used to play dress-up, and she dressed up as all sorts of characters, including a *rickshawalla*,' Shivani says with a laugh.

'I was the class clown,' Kiran says cheerfully. 'The teacher would say, "Kiran, come on stage and do something while I correct papers." And I was happy to oblige!' She was constantly playing the fool but she never let her grades suffer.

Loreto was special. The school played a big role in its students' lives, and that extended beyond the classroom. It instilled in Kiran a deep desire to contribute to society, which remains with her till today. Loreto taught her to have a sense of purpose that was higher than oneself. 'I used to think, "You can't do whatever you want, you have to give back." It was this leftie, good Samaritan in me.'

It was only in college that Kiran realized she could use art as a platform to give back. 'When I thought about it, I realized art is really a fundamental need that people have. It can be quite transformational. I had been so deeply touched by so many writers, musicians, poets, actors and film-makers who had changed my world view over time—why couldn't I do the same?'

Kiran first visited Mumbai after her eldest sister got married, and immediately knew that this city of dreams would eventually be her home. She enrolled at Sophia College to study economics and literature. She loved every moment there. Great literature teachers like Dr Margarida Colaco and Mrs Hira Stevens opened up the world of words for her.

At Sophia, Kiran was president of the Dramatics Society and the Nature Club. She pursued various interests, but showed no interest in economics. She didn't know enough about film to pursue it academically at an institution like FTII. Photography seemed like an interesting option. By asking around, she learned about Jamia's course in Delhi, which provides the academic fundamentals of radio, photography, media theory and film. It was also more affordable for her parents.

Being in the capital was wonderful. As usual, Kiran made lots of friends. Despite being broke, unable to afford autorickshaws and being harassed on buses, Kiran and her two roommates went to as many movie screenings as possible at different embassies, the India Habitat Centre and the India International Centre. By the end of the course, she knew she wanted to tell her own stories.

But her heart lay in Mumbai. She moved back in 1998, ready to make her own movie. She describes herself back then—'I was overconfident, thinking I would make my first film by 2000! You know how it is in college—you think you're the cat's whiskers. You've written a paper on Bresson and think you know everything about film-making, and not realizing that you're in the rarefied environment of a master's degree, where you are seeing wonderful films in a darkened room and discussing everything as if the world depended on your opinion! Then you come to Mumbai and you have no one here and no one gives a damn about you. Mumbai can be incredibly hostile. It is tough. But I had studied here and loved it, and it was my city from the first time I saw it. I knew I would figure things out.'

She needed a job. Kiran knew of Subhash Ghai, the celebrated film-maker of *Taal*. She sent him a fax saying, 'My name is Kiran Rao and I have just finished studying film and I am keen to work. So let me know if you have an opening.' Not surprisingly, she never heard back. Given the hundreds of similar emails she receives today, she understands why.

Her parents, who had always been supportive, didn't interfere. They knew their youngest child would make a success of whichever profession she chose. When she moved from Delhi to Mumbai, Kiran promised her parents that if she didn't land a job in ten days, she would move to Bengaluru to be with them.

She got one. Less than two weeks after arriving in Mumbai, she got an offer to join an ad film company run by Shamin Desai. It was an upcoming production company called Shot in the Dark Films. It paid decently, so she could afford to live in south Mumbai's Gamdevi neighbourhood. Kiran worked closely with Desai for a year and a half, and learnt the ropes of production as an assistant director. She did casting, costumes, production design—pretty much everything. 'It was a crash course in film-making and production,' she says. Yet, she remained clear about never wanting to make ad films, even though people told her it would be good practice before she made a movie. Advertising was more technically advanced than Hindi cinema back then. It also paid well. However, Kiran was insistent. She didn't want to 'push something that people didn't need and convince them that they needed it'.

The dawn of the millennium turned out to be a watershed for Kiran. By then, she had left advertising. Her friend Reema Kagti called and asked her if she wanted to be a third AD (assistant director) on a feature on which Reema herself was a second AD. Although it was not as lucrative as a job in advertising, Kiran immediately agreed.

That's how *Lagaan* came along. It was a film that changed the lives of almost everyone who worked on it, including Kiran. From a professional point of view, *Lagaan* was the first big Hindi film to employ production systems commonly used in Hollywood. It was schedule-driven. A first assistant director ran the set, people had clearly defined roles and worked off a completed script. It was also how she met her future husband, although the romance didn't blossom till four years after the film released. Kiran first saw Aamir Khan on the big screen, when she was a fourteen-year-old, and saw the star's breakout film, *Qayamat Se Qayamat Tak*, in 1988. She says she loved him in it but loved the film more![4]

Shot on a large scale, *Lagaan* was a massive production that included Indian and foreign actors and technicians. It was an extremely challenging work environment and so intense that it spurred a director, Satyajit Bhatkal, to make a documentary on the film's making. Called *Madness in the Desert (Chale Chalo: The Lunacy of Film Making)*, it won a national award in 2004.

Kiran and Aamir first crossed paths in late 1999, on a bus full of crew in Bhuj, where they had gone to do a recce. 'Aamir came up and introduced himself to all of us and I remember thinking, "Oh, for the huge star that he is, he is rather cool and unassuming," she recalls. Aamir says he got to know her well only a few years later, and he was struck by her 'very infectious, positive energy. She has a spontaneous, unadulterated joy within her.'

Kiran was in charge of make-up, hair and wardrobe, and was paid about Rs 13,000 a month while on set in Bhuj, Gujarat.[5] Ever practical, she gave up her Mumbai apartment to save on rent, packed up her things, which included a few posters, pictures and books, and set off for Bhuj. 'I was into simple living and lived light—maybe two suitcases, a table or chair and a mattress,' she says with a smile.

---

[4] Pradeep Chandra, *Aamir Khan: Actor, Activist, Achiever*, Delhi: Niyogi Books, 2014.

[5] In the film's credits, Kiran was credited as a third AD, but technically the hair, make-up and wardrobe job is done by what's called a second second AD.

As one of the four assistant directors, Kiran was responsible for getting the whole lot of actors ready, rousing them at the unearthly hour of 4 a.m. every day, a thankless task—which actor is going to be nice when they are woken up at that time? Since it was a period film, wardrobe was vital. Kiran had to supervise all aspects, including hairpieces and wigs. The process would take two hours or more. On any given day, there were 200 extras on set. It was a gruelling schedule. 'I learnt how to see a job through, how to work with people, which I think was the most valuable experience *Lagaan* gave me. And I also had the most fun I've ever had on a film.'

It was a supercharged, energetic atmosphere, with the Indian and overseas crew celebrating local festivals, playing cards and partying till the early hours after a full day of shooting. Javed Akhtar and A.R. Rahman would come and everyone would gather around to sing songs.

The film was a huge hit and was nominated for an Oscar for 'best foreign language film' at the 74th Academy Awards in 2002.

For a budding film-maker, *Lagaan* was the perfect training ground. After seeing an operation of that scale, Kiran gained significant skills. Soon after the film wrapped up, she began work on Mira Nair's *Monsoon Wedding*, where she was second assistant director. The film world is tricky, for work is unpredictable. For the next few years, Kiran worked on a few films and lots of commercials—many with Highlight Films.

In the late 1990s, around the time Kiran joined the industry, winds of change were beginning to sweep through it. Film-makers were targeting a growing urban market that was beginning to hunger for something other than the usual masala potboiler. She had been working on a script for a few years.

The result was *Dhobi Ghat*, named after Mumbai's iconic open-air laundromat. It traced the paths of four people from different walks of life whose lives intersect. A non-linear narrative, it was shot using a hand-held camera and sync sound. From the opening scene of raindrops falling on the quintessential Mumbai black-and-yellow taxi to various indoor and outdoor locations, the film portrayed the raw edginess of a city infused with infinite possibilities and characters with complex inner lives. Mumbai, Kiran says, was the fifth character in the film. Notably, there was no intermission, a gutsy move in a market where people are reluctant to tinker with a tried and tested formula. Thoughtful and subtle, *Dhobi Ghat* made people sit up and notice the young film-maker. It was released in 2011 and was lauded for its nuanced exploration of urban life.

'I am drawn to stories that say something about the world we live in, that give insight into people and the way things are,' Kiran explains. 'I am interested in people's experiences and struggles. Such films move me more. It could be a documentary about a cow farmer in Norway. I am not immediately drawn to what's called an "entertainer".'

Kiran believes India's commercial films can get better. 'We can't have this lopsided scenario where even though commercial films routinely flop at the box office, they get all the screens while art house films get no screens at all. The most important thing is to invest in building more cinemas— including a few speciality art house cinemas, in film infrastructure and in film education and technical training, which sorely lacks in our country. As an independent film-maker, I want to be able to put my film out there as widely as possible, and as a commercial film producer, I want to see good storytelling across the board.'

Good writing courses, better equipment and infrastructure, serious film studies, more screens and film festivals are ways to improve films and film culture in the country. MAMI is one way Kiran is trying to make that happen.

There is now a mind-boggling array of programmes instituted at the festival. These include Short Films, Restored Classics, World Cinema and After Dark, showing low-budget horror and action thrillers. Content Studio identifies digital content for talented young film-makers across India. There's an award for the best film on gender equality and an international competition section for first-time fiction and documentary features, among several others.

Kiran says that after four years of being part of MAMI, Anupama, Smriti and she are more confident of pulling the festival off. 'In my head, I always wanted to have a space in the city for independent cinema,' she notes. 'MAMI does that, with both the annual Mumbai Film Festival as well as a year-round programme of screenings, masterclasses and workshops.'

Kiran consumes theatre, music, dance and the visual arts in spades. You're as likely to find her at an offbeat music concert as you are at a play at Prithvi Theatre.

Her days are spent working on her various projects in a serene workspace surrounded by trees and birds in Bandra, walking distance from her sea-facing home. She renovated the studio space herself, using salvaged wood wherever she could, reverting to original casings, nuts, bolts and other touches. Design is an abiding passion and she's made the 'office' a refuge. It's where she holds meetings, and where she finds inspiration to work on her next screenplay. It's also where Azad, Kiran and Aamir's seven-year-old, comes to hang out with his mom after school.

What's it like to be married to a humongous movie star when you yourself have no celebrity trappings? Kiran says, 'For starters, Aamir lives his life really simply and there is no stardom in our routine lives. He's just incredibly driven and has a great passion for things that excite him— be it film-making or playing Settlers of Catan! He gives everything he does his fullest. He also is my anchor, my lodestone—he brings me back to being who I am.'

The two were friends before they became a couple. It was after his divorce that Kiran and Aamir realized that they had similar world views, and were intellectually and ideologically copacetic. 'Kiran is caring, sensitive and loving,' says Aamir. 'She's got a great sense of understanding the other person and she has a great ability to allow a person his or her individuality and independence, without feeling threatened in any way. That is remarkable.'

Kiran clearly adores her husband and describes him as unique and inspiring. 'I don't know anyone like him—someone who believes in fair play and being gentlemanly, not in the patriarchal sense but in terms of human decency. In his business and personal life, he is very caring.' Her parents, Uma and Satyanarayan, were initially taken aback when Kiran told them about her relationship with Aamir. 'He is very normal, a family man,' says her father fondly.

Is it hard to share someone she loves with a billion people? Kiran doesn't think so. She believes his being in a public place is a force of good, although she does mind the lack of time they get together. Aamir does not make it to PTA meetings and the daily routine of childcare falls on her shoulders. 'It used to bother me, but it doesn't any more. Aamir is a great sponge for me and Azad, a buffer for us, and he has a tremendous ability to not be negative. He gives reasoned, practical advice.'

Surrendering some aspect of one's privacy is difficult. Azad was born via surrogacy at a time when people were not open about using the method. Kiran and Aamir going public with it helped dissipate the stigma somewhat, but keeping the process under wraps till their son was born wasn't easy.

What she finds tough is the level of frenetic energy that is her life and her husband's. Things are always busy for both of them. As a producer at AKP Films, she works on current and future projects. Sometimes she wears a creative hat, at other times, she goes over budgets or meets distributors. She and Aamir take joint decisions on which projects to pursue and the couple constantly talk shop. Kiran is involved in finalizing scripts, casting, crew selection, location selection to the extent that the director needs it. 'I think she's got a great aesthetic.' Aamir notes that Kiran spent a lot of time as producer on set during the making of *Secret Superstar*.

Kiran has struck a balance between being a sought-after public figure and maintaining her privacy. People who know her say that she doesn't require external validation. Srila Chatterjee describes Kiran as someone who 'has no need for anyone to like or fawn over her. That's a huge strength, when you're not looking for appreciation because you have conviction. She may be at the centre of Bollywood, but she's clearly been able to use the best of it to further what she wants to do or thinks should be done.'

Kiran shrugs when asked about being a celebrity. 'I don't feel I am particularly deserving of it, but I do think we need a lot of women out there to show other girls that it's possible to be a film-maker, a cinematographer, a show-runner,' she says. In a country where a majority of women have little control over their lives, Kiran hopes that by being out there, she will motivate other women. 'I realize I am in the unique position of having a foot in both the mainstream and the fringes of cinema, and it's my privilege to be a part of both. I try to use this position to change the landscape for the better. But basically I am happy just being myself and doing my thing—perhaps differently than people expect!'

ANVITA DUTT
THE LYRICIST

nvita Dutt believes all stories start with 'once upon a time'. The words are tattooed on her right arm. One of Bollywood's leading lyricists says her own story was shaped by the library at Hindon Air Force Base in Uttar Pradesh. It had high ceilings and two large French windows through which soft sunlight streamed in, filling the room with a warm glow. Its walls were lined with mismatched cupboards. Some were tall, some short, some deep, some shallow. They were stuffed with books donated by families of air force officers lightening their load before moving on to the next posting. It was here, in her 'favouritest' library, which smelled of 'paper and ink and well-thumbed books,' that Anvita, who was passionate about stories, became a voracious reader.

'I lived with books, I didn't need people,' she says.

Take a moment to think of the most popular Hindi films of the last decade. *Rock On!!* will be on the list, as will *Dostana*, *Bachna Ae Haseeno*, *Student of the Year*, *Lipstick Under My Burkha* and *Queen*. Anvita has been involved with all of them—either as a dialogue writer or as lyricist.

The award-winning wordsmith has worked on over thirty films but insists her contribution to Hindi cinema is 'very small'. She appears embarrassed at the suggestion that it could be anything else. Yet, few can deny the tremendous impact Anvita made with the 2014 smash hit *Queen*, for which she wrote the lyrics and dialogues. The bitter-sweet tale of self-discovery was at once critically acclaimed and loved by audiences. The storyline has strong feminist undertones and retains a light touch, largely due to its songs, which were an instant success.

'She gets the situation,' says Amit Trivedi, the music director of *Queen*. 'Whatever brief the director gives her, she gets it bang on and she comes up with something that works within the film and takes the story forward, but it also has the power to work outside the film and become a stand-alone hit.' *Queen*'s 'London Thumakda', set to peppy Punjabi beats, raced to the top of the charts and has become a Bollywood classic. It's a staple on radio stations and if Anvita happens to catch it or any of her songs, she reacts the same way each time, 'Oh my God, I wrote this! I am still delighted that I wrote this song. I love it!'

It would be wrong to mistake her excitement for arrogance. Instead, her reaction comes from a place of gratitude. Anvita is humble to a fault. 'I look at songs as gifts,' she explains. Gifts that she has a deep respect for.

For Anvita, writing is sacred. She says sitting in front of a blank piece of paper is 'the most frightening thing in the world'. She is consumed by a nervous energy when she sits at her desk because, 'you are creating something from nothing. It's ether.' And when she's not writing for herself, she worries about living up to the expectations of the person who has hired her to write. She asks herself, 'What if it doesn't happen this time?'

When it does, she says it feels like magic.

'I always imagine that there are words, like dust particles, all around me. So when I breathe, I move, they bounce off me,' she says, her voice becoming softer. 'I feel if I am still and I don't really do anything, the right words follow and they just kind of sit.' Suddenly, she laughs. 'It sounds like mumbo-jumbo, I don't know if I am making sense?'

Anvita feels things deeply, be it joy or pain. So it's not surprising that she has made a name for herself as a sensitive writer. 'Everything she writes is very real to her. Even though it is usually about other people in a film script, she feels every word she writes. She personalizes it,' says Vishal Dadlani, the well known music composer who has worked with Anvita on films like *Student of the Year*, *Dostana*, *Bachna Ae Haseeno* and *RA.One*.

'We, the audience, are the people who listen to stories that have nothing to do with us and we cry, just from the truth of those stories. And Anvita is one of those people who makes this happen,' Dadlani says.

Anvita is part of a small crew of new-age female dialogue and songwriters making an impact in a space historically dominated by men. For years, directors and producers turned to Gulzar, Javed Akhtar or Prasoon Joshi to write dialogues and lyrics for their films. Only a handful of women had done this job before.

They include Saroj Mohini Nayyar, wife of late composer O.P. Nayyar, who wrote '*Pritam Aan Milo*' in 1955 for the film, *Mr. and Mrs. 55* by Guru Dutt. Poet Maya Govind carried the baton forward, writing for 450 films including M.F. Hussain's *Gaja Gamini* and *Main Khiladi Tu Anari* among others. Folk singer Ila Arun has written songs too and recently, rapper Hard Kaur has brought female 'swag' into the industry.

Born in Delhi on 20 February, 1972, Anvita's father Mike Dutt was an Indian Air Force pilot and her mother, Annu, was a homemaker. Anvita grew up in military cantonments in twelve cities across India. She describes her family as 'typically middle class'. She is the oldest of three children. Brother Mayank came along when she was four and her sister, Meghna, is nine years younger. Mayank lives in Singapore but shares a close and easy relationship with his older sister. They laugh a lot when they are together. 'We are more friends than siblings and that's the reason why we joke around a lot,' he says. 'There's no "big sister, younger brother" kind of feeling. We see ourselves as equals and that makes the relationship far more comfortable.'

She doesn't share such an easy relationship with most people. Anvita is a self-confessed loner but says she has 'trained' herself to be a people's person, at least in her professional life. Being in the movie business helps. How else does one tell a story?

'She has a deeply creative and inwardly turned side and can sometimes appear inaccessible to a lot of people,' says her neighbour Gauri Dhanalakshmi or 'Dhanu' as Anvita affectionately calls her. 'Anvita is not the brooding sort. She is very anchored in herself. When I think of her in the chaos and business of my day, that space is still. With Anvita, there's a coffee, there's a chat, there's a smoke. It's a very quiet space.'

The two women hit it off instantly when they first met in 2012. They talk a lot. But other times, they sit quietly, each hammering away at their laptops, writing. Dhanu is a business psychologist but shares Anvita's passion for words. They often share poetry. One of them will say, 'Have you read this? Look at what they've done with this line! And we will both look at it, mesmerized,' Dhanu laughs.

Inside Anvita's beautiful garden apartment, the shadows of large champa, chiku, parijat and neem plants provide a welcoming shade and coolness during summer. In her home it feels like Anvita belongs to another world—an older, gentler one where time moves slowly.

A four-poster wooden bed sits in the middle of the living room. It serves as a place to sit, sleep, eat or lounge. There's no couch and no dining table either. A limestone block from Raja Ravi Varma's printing press stands on top of a wooden cabinet. One side has a stencil of Sita, Ram and

Lakshman, the other depicts Shiva riding Nandi. A handful of marigolds lie in front of it. A tealight burns in a diffuser with neroli oil, filling her home with a citrusy, floral fragrance. On summer days she chooses khus, which reminds her of her childhood summers in north India.

Anvita usually wears saris—soft, *mulmul* ones. Her blouses are loose and she often wears her saris on top of a pajama. When rushed, it's a pair of baggy trousers with an oversized shirt. Sleeves rolled up, they reveal tattooed arms. Each one of Anvita's eleven tattoos tells a story.

On her left hand is the word, 'Aparajita', which means 'she who cannot be defeated'. Anvita got it just before she wrote *Queen*. She had 'once upon a time' tattooed on her right arm after completing her first film, *Bachna Ae Haseeno*. There's also a tattoo of a hummingbird, the only bird that can fly backwards, defying expectations. She got this when she decided she would direct films. There's a tattoo of a rose. Anvita says that is 'a gentler, love message for myself.' A tattoo of a dragonfly on her right wrist was got because 'she flies, hovers, is magical and almost a bit of an introvert. It's not the one everyone will notice immediately.' Her mother would point to a dragonfly when Anvita was a child and the little girl would say 'helicopter, papa'—because the buzzing gossamer wings would remind her of her father who flew choppers while in the air force.

Anvita's home, the tattoos and her attire reflect a personality that is a blurring of contradictions. She is at once traditional and modern, passionate yet detached, a dreamer and a realist.

Though becoming a writer was low on her list of childhood ambitions—after 'engine driver, prime minister, Helen and a chef,' she says with a grin, by the time Anvita was in college, it had moved up the list.

She has her grade 11 English teacher, Mrs Raghubir, to thank for that. After handing out a set of examination results, Mrs Raghubir pulled Anvita aside and asked her what she wanted to become when she grew up. The young student was quick to reply—'a chef'. Her teacher responded, 'You do know that you are a writer, right? You don't answer questions, you tell stories.'

With those words, Mrs Raghubir influenced Anvita's path. She set aside aspirations of becoming a chef. 'In my head, I didn't even know that writing was a profession. But Mrs Raghubir told me to think about it: "That is your calling."'

In 1993, Anvita decided to move to Mumbai to look for a job. She had begun to think about a career in advertising since it involved writing. But the move was going to be expensive. So the skinny, young girl went door to door in New Delhi, carrying a heavy black backpack, trying to sell encyclopedias to earn money. She didn't want to ask her parents to fund her, she wanted to do it on her own.

The moment she saved Rs 10,000, she bought herself a train ticket to India's city of dreams. In Mumbai, she stayed with her parents' friends while she hunted for a job. Her father gave her a month to find employment. If she didn't, she had to return home.

The first night in Mumbai was bleak. Though the family she was staying with was hospitable, they lived in a small apartment with barely enough space to accommodate a house guest. Anvita felt awkward. The next day she travelled the length of Mumbai, starting from the southern tip of the city, looking for a hostel that would have her.

Exhausted by sunset, she stopped to eat noodles at a Chinese street food cart in Shivaji Park. The sky grew dark. Before she knew it, she was standing by the side of the road, sobbing uncontrollably. Her parents had given her a month to prove herself. She felt she was failing. It was just day one.

A group of teenagers was hanging around the food cart. Anvita asked if they knew of a hostel close by. They pointed to a house and said the lady who lived there accepted paying guests. It was run by a widow called Munim Aunty. Anvita knocked on her door. Munim Aunty said her accommodation was full. Anvita begged for a place on her couch. Finally, Aunty relented and Anvita moved in. She hasn't left Mumbai since.

'Someone was looking out for me that night,' she says with a smile.

A few days later, Anvita landed herself a job as a trainee copywriter at Everest Advertising. She was paid Rs 2,000 a month. Anvita was thrilled. Her perseverance was paying off.

Fast forward fourteen years. After a career in copywriting, Anvita was ready to try something different. She longed to tell stories. She was fortunate to get a job as a dialogue writer at Yash Raj Films, one of India's leading film studios. But she came into her own when she began to write lyrics. That happened by chance.

One day, she bumped into the studio head Aditya Chopra when she had come to collect a cheque. He asked her to write dummy lyrics for a song since the musicians were jamming and needed some words to play around with. Anvita obliged.

'The next day, I walked into his office and that sheet was lying in front of him,' Anvita recalls. 'He said, "You've written these?" I said yes. He said, "These aren't dummy lyrics." My first thought was, "Oh fuck, I can't even write dummy lyrics!" He said, "These are called lyrics. Lyrics."'

That was the first song she wrote. It was for *Bachna Ae Haseeno*.

Anvita writes in her living room. Behind a towering bookshelf sits an imposing wooden desk that holds neatly stacked papers, a bunch of pencils and a silver laptop. Blue and cream wallpaper depicting dancing peacocks forms the backdrop to this setting which looks like a scene from a still life. This is her sanctuary.

If she's working on a song, she can write it anywhere, any time—in a studio, in a car, in her home. She puts on her headphones, listens to the melody she's been given and usually, the words just flow. They rolled out when she heard the melody for *Queen*. She was in Goa with music director Amit Trivedi. They went for walks, drank, went to the beach and got foot massages. One morning, Trivedi played a tune on his synthesizer and she wrote, '*Tu ghanti Big Ben di, poora London thumakda*', which loosely translates to, '*You are Big Ben, the whole of London dances to your tune*'.

'Her choice of words is unique, it's refreshing,' Trivedi says. They jammed, and she wrote. By lunchtime, '*London Thumakda*' was done. Within five days, they had completed all the eight songs for *Queen*. 'We had so much fun doing it, that's why the work is so good,' Anvita says, smiling.

Writing dialogues for a film requires a different level of commitment, Anvita explains. So she is more disciplined about how she goes about that process. 'I can't force the writing, but what I can do is show up.' Because she works from home, she has created a ritual around the simple act of showing up at her desk.

Her day begins early, around 5 a.m., because she likes the silence. She wakes up before the newspaper man does his rounds, before the milkman cycles through the colony, before her pet dog, Clio, a golden brown boxer, comes to lick her face because, 'even that can move you away from the process'.

'I get up, wash my face, brush my teeth and on hard days, I will bathe and dress up, like I am going for work. I make my coffee and I walk to my desk. Till then, I am not even trying to think about my work. I am almost floating. I eat something light, I sit down, I roll a cigarette. I smoke that first cigarette without doing anything else.'

She puts on her headphones, goes to iTunes and puts her music on shuffle. 'I don't like shuffle. It bothers me. But on that day, I put it on shuffle. It's kind of a meditative thing. I am not really thinking about anything much and I'll have my coffee, smoke my cigarette and at some point of time I'll pick up my pencil because, oh fuck, suddenly there's an idea.'

At that moment, Anvita grabs a pencil and hits the pause button. Then she puts the song on loop. And that song becomes a soundtrack in her mind to the film she writes. The fantasy film *Phillauri* was written to Beethoven's *Moonlight Sonata*. *Queen* was written with Coldplay's albums on loop. Soon, the writing and the soundtrack get intertwined in a strange way that only she understands.

The first film she wrote for herself, *Bulbul*—a period film set in Bengal—was written in 2013 to Bhimsen Joshi's Raga Puriya. The film lay dormant for four years until Anvita returned to it in 2017. Before pitching it to producers, she didn't open the script. She put on her headphones, shut her eyes and played Raga Puriya. 'And it's like, I knew the entire film. All the nuances, what I was thinking then and how I was seeing the characters and what my plan was on how to shoot my film, the treatment . . . everything came back,' she says, a faraway glimmer in her large eyes. Anvita is now directing *Bulbul*.

It's an unconventional approach but then, she has never been a conformist. As a child, she says she was 'violently introverted'. Books were her best friends. She would spend hours in the airy libraries at the cantonments she lived in, returning home only when they shut—annoying her mother who had instructed her to come home before it grew dark.

At the library, she would read everything she could get her hands on, whether it was appropriate for the age or not. 'It was only later, when I grew up and read literature, I suddenly realized oh, I read Dickens when I was in the grade 5.' This made her even more socially awkward around her peers because while she was reading Dickens, they were reading Noddy books. She didn't understand the significance of her own bookish hunger back then.

Her parents, in turn, didn't understand their firstborn. Her mother would complain that Anvita spent all her time with her nose buried in storybooks instead of focusing on schoolwork. 'From her point of view, I was wasting my time.'

'You have to understand, it's got nothing to do with my family. It's to do with me. I was an odd child. I would not talk. My voice would become hoarse because I would not have talked in days. I would not talk in school, I would not talk at home. I was quiet. I would read and I would write. When I was sad, or when I felt I did not belong, the only way I would deal with it was by writing poetry and stories.' She would fill thick registers with her writing.

Stories are central to her existence and she can't resist them—which explains her obsession with books. When she was in London on a recce trip with *Queen*'s unit, she found herself at a bookstore. She picked up a book. Then another. Then a few more. When she was done, she realized she had filled eight shopping baskets with books. She had to step out of the store to buy a cheap suitcase that she could stuff the books in.

'That's not the bad part of the story,' she laughs. 'At the airport I had to pay £3,000 for excess baggage. I emptied my bank account buying a suitcase full of books. I don't have money—I am a fucking writer!'

The thought of leaving those books behind in the London bookstore never occurred to her. 'How can you let go of a new story?' she asks, bewildered at the suggestion. 'You walk around and there is something about a book that calls to you. You pick it up, you look at the back of the book, you look at the front, you read the first line and it hooks you. It's tugging away at you and if you move away, it hurts.'

The passionate reader is drawn to fantasy writing. Her favourite authors are Neil Gaiman, Stephen King, Philip Pullman and Ursula K Le Guin. Do they inspire her? 'I am sure they do. Of course, craft gives the structure. But the fantastical leap comes from other writers having done it. There is no better teacher than an excellent writer.'

Her best works are packed with emotion. She picks two of them in particular, and calls them bookends to a part her life. One is called 'Kyun Main Jagoon', a slow, soft song from the film *Patiala House*. She wrote it the day her marriage broke.

Anvita was married to her first love—a young man she met in college. He was her first crush, the first boy she kissed. They got married when they were twenty-three. But heady love wasn't enough to sustain a lifelong partnership. 'What happened is, we grew up,' and their relationship changed. They've been divorced for eight years but remain friends and catch up for a coffee once in a while.

The day her marriage ended, she sat with a friend and cried her heart out. She didn't say a word. Nor did her friend. He simply handed Anvita a piece of paper and a pencil and said, 'It's the only thing that will help.'

She wrote a few lines.

Later that day, she had a recording with well-known music composers Shankar–Ehsaan–Loy. They gave her a melody and asked to write to it. The words she had written earlier that day fit the music perfectly. It's closing lines are:

Kyun main jagoon aur voh sapney bo raha hai
Kyun mera rab yun aankhein kholey so raha hai.
(Why does He scatter dreams into my waking world/ Why is it that my God sleeps with open, unseeing eyes.)

'It might not be very well crafted, but it's direct,' she says.

She admits she was a mess after her marriage broke up. 'Most of it was to do with the fact that I had failed at something. I don't like failure.' The divorce was not nasty, but it wasn't easy. It took years to heal.

When she worked on *Queen*, something shifted within her. Writing the lyrics for a song called 'Kinare', she wrote:

Kinaarey, kaisey hongey kam
Kinaarey hain jahaan hain hum
Kinaarey khud hi toh hai hum.

(I can never drown, I will never run out of shores. Wherever I stand will become the shore. I myself am the ground beneath my feet.)

For the first time, in a very long time, she could feel the sadness moving on. 'It was a song that said there is hope, that things are well. I was talking to myself.'

It turns out, she was talking to others too.

Two years after *Queen* released, Anvita was at a friend's home for lunch. There, she met a young woman who had stepped out of her house for the first time after her father's death. Speaking about her grief, she explained how the words of a Hindi song she happened to hear in a cab had given her hope. She had rushed home and bought the song on iTunes. Listening to it over and over comforted her. That song was *'Kinare'*, from *Queen*.

The young woman had no clue who had written the song. All she knew was it helped her face life again. 'There's no greater gift than if your writing can do that,' Anvita says. 'For that one reason, it's my favourite song.' When the lady found out that Anvita had written it, she gave her a heartfelt hug.

Not all of Anvita's songs are weighty and meaningful, nor does she takes herself too seriously. Her writing covers all genres, including comedy and fantasy. Sometimes her lyrics are appreciated, sometimes they're not.

In 2012, she wrote a song called *'Ishqwaala Love'* for the hit film, *Student of the Year*:

Surkh wala soze waala faiz waalaa love
Hota hai jo love se zyaada vaise wala love

Loosely translates to:

'Love with deep colour, with passion and with ardour,
which is more than just love
That kind of love . . .'

'It was ridiculous,' says Jatin Varma, founder of Golden Kela awards, which celebrate 'the best of the worst of Indian cinema'. Anvita won it for the Most Atrocious Lyrics of 2012.

Varma was totally unprepared for what followed. Taking the bull by the horns, Anvita flew down to Delhi to accept the award in person, wearing a broad smile and the most expensive sari she owned!

'One needs to have a certain sense of humour to accept it. And she did that. It was a lot of fun. She sat through the entire ceremony and she gave a victory speech. It just puts things in a very different perspective when you see someone saying, "Yeah, I get it, this isn't the best thing I've put out but I'm willing to take a joke,"' Varma says.

She is a good sport, self-deprecating and easy-going. The only time Anvita gets testy is if she's asked what it feels like to be a woman lyricist in Bollywood. 'How does gender matter?' she says. 'If you look at Gulzar's work, it is so beautiful and delicate. A poet wrote it. That's all that matters.'

She bristles when asked about gender discrimination behind the scenes in the Hindi film industry. 'Nobody hires me because I am a woman,' she says emphatically. 'Directors think about who is right for their film. A lot of money rides on it, so they are going to hire someone for the quality of their work, not because of their gender.'

'The only gender bias I face is when people ask me how it feels to be a female writer or a female lyricist. You know, that's discrimination. Because you don't say male writer, you don't ask a director, as a male director, what do you think? I am just a writer. I am just a lyricist. That's it.'

It's hard to overlook the sexual content of so many Bollywood songs—popular 'item numbers' that usually feature titillating dance moves set to provocative lyrics. That doesn't bother Anvita, and she points out that it's not new. It's been part of the fabric of our culture for generations. 'If you listen to our folk songs, they are very sexual. In gatherings around fireplaces, after the kids have been put to sleep, in a repressed society, people talk and flirt like that—through music, through dance.'

What bothers her is bad writing. 'You could be writing nonsense or a song about nothing in particular but the writing could be really good.'

Anvita is creative and driven, but her greatest strength is perseverance. According to her brother Mayank, 'Bollywood is not an easy place to make a mark in, but the fact that she has done it is a big accomplishment. Every time we see her name anywhere, be it in the media or in a film, it gives us goosebumps.' When their family watches one of her movies in a theatre, the high point is the credit roll. Anvita's parents hug each other every time their daughter's name appears on-screen.

For Anvita, a song is a story. 'It's a conversation with someone. I want that conversation to be as visual as it can be. It's like I am making you watch something, that I am painting a picture with my words.'

Words that tell you a tale, that tell you what happened, once upon a time.

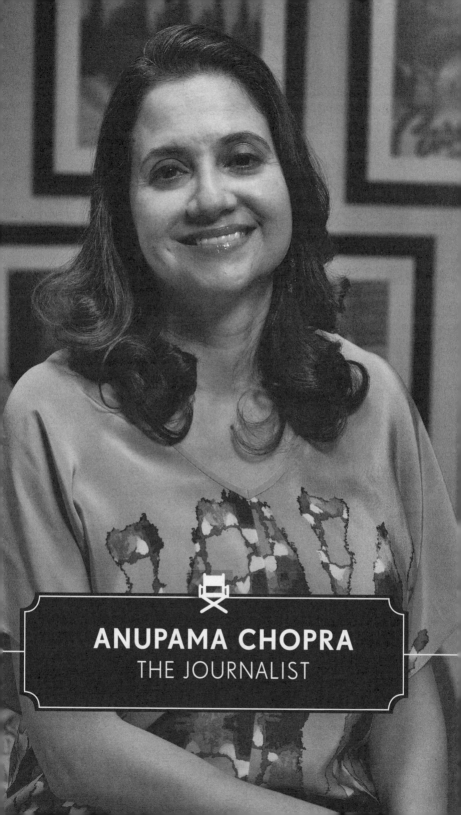

ANUPAMA CHOPRA
THE JOURNALIST

Over her twenty-five-year career covering Indian cinema, Anupama Chopra has faced all sorts of reactions. Some of them have been extreme. A top-notch director once saw her and fled. People she's known for years have ignored her socially. Her credibility has been questioned. She's been called a hack. Adored by some and reviled by others, it's hard to ignore India's pre-eminent film journalist and critic.

Anupama, or Anu as she's affectionately known, covers Indian cinema like no one else. From reporting on the underworld's financing of films—a story that launched her career in 1993—to dissecting the appeal of stars like Salman Khan and Madhuri Dixit, or chronicling the rise of independent cinema, Anu is a tour de force in film journalism.

She has reported from the front lines at the Oscars in Los Angeles, from prestigious international film festivals like Cannes and Toronto, and seen more movies than she can count. She has interviewed pretty much everyone in show business. Brad Pitt. Shah Rukh Khan. Angelina Jolie. Priyanka Chopra. Tom Hanks. Aamir Khan. Jake Gyllenhaal. You get the idea.

Anu's writing has appeared in innumerable publications, including *India Today, Los Angeles Times, New York Times, Variety, Vogue* and NDTV. She has written seven books. Her first book, *Sholay: The Making of a Classic* (2000), won the 2001 National Film Award for Best Book on Cinema. Two of her books are compilations of her articles and TV interviews.[1] She has been instrumental in reviving MAMI (Mumbai Academy of Moving Image), the annual Mumbai Film Festival, of which she is the director. Anupama Chopra breathes and lives Indian cinema.

In 2014, at age forty-seven, she turned entrepreneur, founding Film Companion, an online platform for entertainment journalism for which she files stories every week. Her content has been beamed on TV via the NewsX channel (she earlier ran a programme on NDTV). Her reach is further extended via her 1.4 million Twitter followers, and almost a million on Facebook.

Does a film journalist have the best job in the world? After all, what's not to love about watching movies and then sharing your opinion on them? Anu

---

[1] Anupama Chopra, *First Day, First Show*, New Delhi: Penguin Books, 2011; and *Freeze Frame*, Noida: Om Books International, 2014.

wouldn't disagree. 'Yes, there's glamour. You get to meet stars, attend film premieres and go to world-class movie festivals. It seems so . . . seductive.'

However, there is a flip side. A.O. Scott, *New York Times* film critic whom Anu admires, writes in his 2016 book, *Better Living Through Criticism*: 'People think of critics as failed artists, unloading long-simmering, envious resentments on those who had the luck, talent, or discipline to succeed. This assumption is so widespread as to amount to an article of public faith. Every working critic could easily assemble, from discarded letters and deleted emails, a suite of variations on the themes of "You're just jealous" and "I'd like to see you do better".'[2]

Anu is familiar with these jibes. On 6 August 2017, she tweeted the following about superstar Shah Rukh Khan's highly publicized film *Jab Harry Met Sejal* (JHMS): *I love Hindi cinema so much, I take it personally. When a film doesn't deliver it's a personal let-down. Sadness lingers for days. #JHMS'*

The reactions poured in thick and fast. Some said she was 'writing crap', others called her 'cynical'. Unfortunately, being at the receiving end is part of the job, especially when she dares to speak her mind about revered celebrities with huge fan followings.

'It's hard, yes, and there are people who just don't speak to you any more or get very upset,' says Anu, seated in her Film Companion office in Bandra, which is decorated with vintage film posters. 'I have massive affection for SRK but I did not like *When Harry Met Sejal*. I think he's hurt by the response the film got and by the critics' reviews, including mine. I can't be a film critic or reviewer if I am dishonest in any way.'

Bollywood trade analyst Komal Nahta, who has known Anu since she was a rookie reporter for *India Today*, describes her as a diligent journalist. 'She would not put down the phone till she got the information she wanted,' he says. 'I'll take five minutes, I'll take ten minutes, she would say. If it was a business story, she would say wait, wait, you have to go slow because I am not a Bollywood business person, so you'll have to explain it to me.' This is a trait that distinguished her from her peers.

---

[2] A.O. Scott, *Better Living Through Criticism: How to Think about Art, Pleasure, Beauty and Truth*, Gurgaon: Penguin Random House, 2016.

The veteran journalist Madhu Jain, who was once Anu's boss at *India Today*, says she has seldom come across anyone so passionate about movies. 'I left the entire coverage of Indian cinema to her,' Jain says. 'With her quick intelligence and lucid style of writing, Anupama could have written about anything while she was in *India Today*, but it was only cinema that interested her—despite the fact that cinema was sneered at as soft, "back of the book" stuff—and it certainly was not the shortest ladder to the top of the hierarchy. But Anu was not interested in clambering up that ladder.'

Anu's film analysis is sure-footed. She is at heart a reporter and has made a name for herself as a perceptive interviewer. 'My attempt when I go out to interview people is to find an insight that you don't have,' she explains. Before each interview, she prepares for a few hours, reading and poring over research notes that she and her team compile.

As a journalist and critic, Anu faces the conundrum of being a Bollywood insider who knows most of her subjects. Her husband is Vidhu Vinod Chopra, the Oscar-nominated award-winning film-maker, whose credits include hits like *3 Idiots*, the Munna Bhai series, *Parinda* and *1942: A Love Story*. (The last one happens to be written by Anu's mother, Kamna Chandra, whose own illustrious screenwriting career is the stuff of celluloid dreams. But more on that later.)

'The fact is, she has talent and she is making good use of the access she has,' Komal Nahta notes. 'She makes sense when she talks or writes. If you are a good journalist, nobody shies away from talking to you. It may give her a slight edge but to dismiss her because she is Vidhu Vinod Chopra's wife would be belittling her talent.'

Anu is gifted in her metier and has a way with words. Her style packs a punch but she isn't a sledgehammer. Sample these pronouncements on *Film Companion*:

'Like the barfi in the title, *Bareilly ki Barfi* is sweet, enjoyable and low on nutrition,'[3] she says about Ashwiny Iyer Tiwari's film *Bareilly ki Barfi* starring Ayushmann Khurrana, Kriti Sanon, Rajkummar Rao.

---

[3] Film Companion Reviews, 18 August 2017, https://www.youtube.com/watch?v=VAXvO4qIDYI

And of *Pari*, Prosit Roy's film starring Anushka Sharma:

> '*Pari* asks the big question—are human beings in fact the biggest
> monsters? I say the biggest horror is a lame script.'[4]

Anu's flair for writing and use of clever, distinct turns of phrase to capture
the essence of a movie or a person gives her a unique voice. Her 2007
biography of Shah Rukh Khan is a page-turner. She sheds insight into
the superstar. 'I'm just an employee of the Shah Rukh Khan myth,' says
the actor in the book. She also dexterously posits him against the larger
sociological transformations under way in India post-liberalization:

'In films like *Dilwale Dulhania Le Jayenge* (1995), *Dil To Pagal
Hai* (1997), *Kuch Kuch Hota Hai* (1998), *Kabhi Khushi Kabhie Gham*
(2001) and *Kal Ho Naa Ho* (2003), he told Indians that an Indian could
be a hybrid who easily enjoys the material comforts of the West and the
spiritual comforts of the East. You didn't have to choose between the
two; the twain could meet without friction or confusion . . . Shah Rukh
personified the new millennium Indian who combines a global perspective
with local values and is at home in the world.'[5]

In India, film journalism is as old as the industry itself. *Bijoli*, a weekly
Bengali film magazine was founded in 1920. *Mouj Majah,* the first magazine
devoted solely to cinema, started four years later in Mumbai. From the
1930s onwards, new magazines and periodicals on cinema proliferated. In
1951, *Indian Express* started *Screen*. And trade papers like *Trade Guide* took
shape in the early 1950s. But most of the coverage was superficial, dealing
with the personal lives of superstars rather than the films themselves. When
Anu was a child, Devyani Chaubal's saucy gossip columns in *Star and Style*
magazine had both punctured and boosted many star egos.

But it wasn't just all gossip. Serious film critics began looking at
India's movies through a critical lens. Bhawana Somaaya, who began her

---

4   Film Companion Reviews, 2 March 2018, http://www.filmcompanion.in/
    pari-movie-review-anupama-chopra-anushka-sharma/Published
5   Anupama Chopra, *King of Bollywood: Shah Rukh Khan and the Seductive
    World of Indian Cinema*, New York City: Warner Books, 2007, p. 14.

career in 1978, is a well-known film journalist who has written more than ten books on the industry. She received a Padma Shri in 2017 for her contribution to the field of literature and education.

For Anu, work is worship. She loves her job and is a self-confessed workaholic. At Cannes in May 2008, she was on the jury of the Un Certain Regard section, which showcases films with stories told in unconventional ways; simultaneously, she was reporting for *Picture This*, her TV show.[6] She was overworked and hadn't eaten much. As a result, she fainted. Paramedics were immediately called. But Anu had a deadline to meet and her TV crew could not wait around. She anchored the shot sitting in a wheelchair, and stared into the camera, starting with her usual introduction: 'This is Anupama Chopra.'

Her husband fumed from behind: 'Are you mad, you're going to die!'

'I am your quintessential type A,' she says with a grin. 'I need to work all the time. I have no idea what to do during downtime.' She approaches her job with a zeal that is refreshingly youthful. It seems like she's having the time of her life.

She traces this attitude to her parents, especially her eighty-eight-year-old father Navin Chandra, whom, she says, 'has no concept of retirement'. He goes to work every day, focusing his energy on non-profit causes like the environment and the education of economically backward girls.

When Anu started Film Companion four years ago, she didn't know how to run a digital platform and had no business plan. There were months when the company didn't break even. Today, Film Companion has grown and has a serious roster of reputed journalists and film enthusiasts. The team of fifteen includes National Award–winning critic Baradwaj Rangan. The company adheres to strict dos and don'ts, clearly separating the business and editorial side so that advertising doesn't influence reporting. In the media business, this is popularly known as the separation of church and state. At Film Companion, reviews and interviews cannot be bought. (Although she has heard the practice exists, Anu says she has never been propositioned for a paid review ever.) Film Companion does do branded

---

[6] *Picture This* was a half-hour TV show that was aired on NDTV from January 2007 till June 2011.

content and advertorials—editorials paid for by advertisers—but these are clearly labelled.

Anu laughs frequently, and has a ready smile that constantly illuminates her face. Now fifty-one, she looks much younger. At 5'2", she's petite but appears taller. There's something warm and enveloping about this entertainment chronicler who is now a celebrity in her own right.

As a critic, what distinguishes Anu from her compatriots is her intellectual prowess and ability to glean a larger narrative of the country through the films she reviews. Writing in *Open* magazine in March 2012,[7] she said, 'I know it's hard to feel sorry for people who watch movies for a living but spare a moment to ponder our lives. We see at least four to seven films a week. We love our job, but the truth is that the movies are often staggeringly mediocre and eventually, they fray our Olympian enthusiasm. Over years, lesser film critics become cynical and dismissive. But the best among us retain their passion, hone their skills, and, like the best wine, get better with age.'

Anyone who has seen Anu on screen knows that her programmes make for engaging viewing. She comes across as a journalist with a genuine interest in the artistes she is interviewing. Her manner is disarming, allowing her to build an instant rapport with her subject. Anu says she forgets that the cameras are rolling. She just has a conversation.

How did a girl who never watched Hindi films growing up come to adore an industry that she had once found infra dig?

Her journey began in 1989 when she joined *Movie* magazine as a reporter. She had just completed her bachelor's in English literature from St Xavier's College. 'I worked at *Movie* for eight or nine months and I was just hooked. I thought, "This is it, this is what I want to do."'

What was the draw? 'It certainly wasn't the cinema because in 1988–89, it was really bad,' she giggles. 'It was the film industry itself, which was a mad place then. It was the Wild West. We would go to Film City, and go from

---

7   Anupama Chopra, 'The League of Extraordinary Critics', *Open*, 3 March 2012, http://www.openthemagazine.com/article/voices/the-league-of-extraordinary-critics

one set to the other and do on-the-set reports! That's unthinkable now when there are thirty minders between you and the talent. Back in the day, you could just do it and the talent would be really nice; they'd say, "Hey, come on, let's chat."'

In the introduction to her book *First Day, First Show*, Anu writes:

> In those days, the journalist–star relationship was more casual and far less suspicious. There was very little professional distance between the subject and the reporter. There were only a handful of film journalists and everyone knew each other. Stars felt like our most attractive and powerful friends. I remember going to long sessions of tea and gossip at Dimple Kapadia's house in Juhu; studio rounds during which the *Movie* magazine staff went from one shoot to the next at Film City or Filmistan, most of us giggling madly and barely doing any work; and photo shoots during which we spent more time hanging out with each other than actually taking pictures. Admittedly, it didn't produce great journalism, but it was great fun.[8]

For a twenty-one-year-old, it was heady stuff. Her first assignment was to speak to Amitabh Bachchan's heroines about him. 'I would go on set and it would literally be me, the actress, her mom and the hairdresser. There would be 200 people and we'd be the only women. I don't remember seeing women without chaperones, and I don't remember seeing many women at all on sets. It was so male!'

Working at *Movie* made Anu realize that she didn't want to be a regular film journalist. *Stardust* was the pinnacle and everyone read 'Neeta's Natter', and *Cine Blitz* too. 'Look, I enjoy gossip as much as the next person, but that's not what I wanted to do with my life. I wanted to learn the craft of journalism.'

Language and writing come naturally to her. It could be the genes. Anu is the youngest daughter of Navin and Kamna Chandra, originally from Uttar Pradesh. Navin was an engineer who worked at Union

---

[8] Anupama Chopra, *First Day, First Show: Writing from the Bollywood Trenches*, New Delhi: Penguin Books, 2011, p. xxi.

Carbide. Kamna, a highly accomplished woman of letters, had an MA in Hindi literature and a BA in both Hindi and English from Allahabad University. They were married in 1963 when Kamna was twenty and Navin twenty-three. The Chandras were part of a new, post-Independence generation of Indians who valued education and hard work. They instilled those traits in their children. Anu's older brother is the celebrated author Vikram Chandra who wrote *Sacred Games*. Her sister, Tanuja, is a well-known film-maker and author. The Chandras' eldest child, Milan, died in a tragic accident when she was five, before Tanuja and Anu were born, a pain her parents carry to this day.

The Chandras moved every three years because of Navin's job. In 1978, they found themselves in Mumbai, where they lived in Paradise Apartments on Napean Sea Road. The sisters were enrolled at Villa Theresa High School. Vikram was away at Mayo College.

Kamna says that her youngest child was always peaceful and Navin remembers Anu as very studious. 'She was always the best student,' says Kamna with obvious pride. 'If she had an exam the next day and she hadn't finished her portion, she would have tears in her eyes.'

Less than a year after the family moved to Mumbai, Kamna, who had written for magazines, television and radio in Delhi, managed to meet Raj Kapoor, India's greatest showman. He treated her graciously and with respect. She pitched him a story—the result was *Prem Rog*, for which Kamna was nominated for best story by *Filmfare* in 1983 and for which Raj Kapoor won the best director award that same year. Subsequently, she wrote four more screenplays. They included the hits *Chandni* (1989) and *1942: A Love Story* (1994).

Prem Rog was Anu's first time on a film set. She was fourteen. 'Raj Kapoor was very affectionate, and I just kick myself for not paying more attention when he was directing. I was a kid and I thought my mom had written this story, like whatever!'

Perhaps it was that early encounter with a cinematic genius that makes Anu at ease around stars. She admits she has had some fan-girl moments though, like the time she interviewed Angelina Jolie. 'Mainly, you're just amazed at your own good luck, that you have these opportunities,' she says with a smile.

Soon after *Prem Rog*, the family moved again, this time to Hong Kong. Anu eventually finished school in Kodaikanal after which she returned to Mumbai and studied English literature at St Xavier's College. In college, one of her professors was the late Eunice de Souza, an inspirational and admired poet and novelist. Before Eunice passed away in July 2017, she spoke fondly of Anu. She remembered the beautiful essays Anu wrote.

'Eunice shaped the way I think,' says Anu. 'She opened our heads up; she wasn't just teaching us literature; she showed us great cinema. She showed us *King Lear* and the Russian greats and asked us to think beyond what was on the pages. She really inculcated in me a love for words. It was the first time I responded to the beauty of just how a sentence can string together.'

Anu topped her class in Xavier's and received a gold medal. When she got a job at *Movie* magazine after graduation, her mother was taken aback at her academically accomplished daughter pursuing film journalism. 'She thought it was really below my level,' Anu says. 'Even though she had worked in the industry, at that time people thought that it was a bit seedy, and film journalism was really the dregs.'

Her days at *Movie* convinced Anu that she wanted to pursue journalism and study the subject seriously. Anu and Tanuja both decided to go to the United States for further degrees. 'I'm from a middle-class family, so I had to get student loans, scholarships, I had to put all that together,' Anu says. In 1990, she was accepted at the prestigious Medill School of Journalism at Northwestern University in Chicago for a year-long master's programme.

For Anu, university was life-altering. She loved the rigour. She was surrounded by smart people and she was on her own. It was transformative.

'Everything I know as a journalist was taught to me there. This whole idea of a church-and-state separation between editorial and advertising, the idea of getting your facts right, the basic things of what you need to have as a journalist.' She never forgot these tenets.

She focused on the medium of magazines—it was 1990 and the Internet was a foetus. She found a great professor in Abe Peck, who headed the magazine department.

Peck remembers Anu as someone who was smart, friendly and a compassionate leader. 'In a programme whose alums are editorial directors at several magazine companies, she was awarded the Harrington Award in our sequence, symbolizing "academic excellence and promise for success in the field of magazine journalism",' he says.

Bill McDowell was editor-in-chief of a magazine prototype that Anu and her peers put together. He remembers her in flowing Indian skirts paired with an oversized, grey athletic sweatshirt. He also recalled that despite being whip-smart and well read, Anu was constantly carrying around a trashy paperback novel. In Bill's words, 'Anu could be refined and proper but was never afraid to insert a well-placed four-letter word to add some seasoning to the discussion.'

Here too, Anu topped her class. But this was 1991, and the US economy was in the doldrums. Jobs were hard to come by.

Always tenacious, she kept hounding the entertainment editor at *Harper's Bazaar*, the chic fashion magazine. Eventually, her persistence paid off and she was hired as his assistant. But New York City seemed intimidating and in the early 1990s, it wasn't the gentrified, family-friendly place it is today. Anu decided to move in with Tanuja who was studying film at Temple University in Philadelphia. She commuted every day, taking the train from Philadelphia to New York's Penn Station and back, two hours each way.

Though Anu's primary role at *Bazaar* consisted of photocopying and fact-checking, working at a high-fashion office had its perks. Where else can you run into Brooke Shields in the bathroom?

The daily commute took its toll. Anu got very ill, developing a condition called ITP, or idiopathic thrombocytopenic purpura, where the body's immune system mistakenly attacks platelets. She was rushed to an emergency room and remained in hospital for a week while the doctors tested her for leukaemia. Her parents had no idea.

By this time, Tanuja had finished her degree, so the sisters headed home to Mumbai. Anu was twenty-three. Her immune system was shot. She had to stay at home for six months till she was better. ITP is a chronic condition and she still gets regularly tested for it.

Back in Mumbai, she accepted a job at *Sunday* magazine in December 1992. The following month, Anu reported a big story—on how Mumbai's underworld had permeated the movie business. There had been whispers that unseemly characters were financing films to launder money. People tried to dissuade her from reporting such a controversial issue but she persisted. The piece ran in January 1993.

Two months later, twelve bombs exploded in Mumbai, killing 257 people and wounding many more. The underworld was in the news again. Suddenly, everything changed. The police made it a mission to neutralize the menace and the film world realized they could no longer hobnob with shady characters in order to access funds.

With that story, Anu's career sprang to life. She got a call from *India Today*, then the reigning news magazine and a must-read for India's intelligentsia. Anu met proprietor Aroon Purie and editor Shekhar Gupta, who later told Anu that all she did was giggle in the meeting. According to what Gupta told Anu, Purie wasn't impressed, but Gupta reassured him by saying, 'It's fine, she's just covering films, she doesn't want to cover Parliament!' Purie offered her a job.

Anu wanted the film beat to be taken more seriously. Her job at *India Today* gave her a platform to do just that. She began work in July 1993 and in September, she had her first cover story. Titled 'The Madhuri Magic', the piece explained the actress's appeal. Anu wrote: 'So what is the Madhuri phenomenon all about? It's about dancing, for one. No other actress can match her suggestive, come hither mobility. In the profusion of bare midriffs and wiggling hips, her sexuality stands apart, marked by an apparent innocence. Her expressive eyes retain a childlike look even as the breasts heave and the pelvis thrusts. Her slim body lends grace to the most blatant and suggestive choreography. She doesn't ooze sex, only suggests it. With no overt come-on, she is the ultimate Indian male fantasy—a desi, middle-class Madonna.'[9]

Hindi cinema rarely got that kind of attention from mainstream press. 'When I did the *India Today* cover story on Madhuri Dixit, I was told it was only the third cover with a film personality in years.'

Anu pounded the pavement as a shoe-leather reporter, covering Bollywood as a business. Her salary was Rs 20,000 a month—she eventually worked herself up to Rs 40,000. 'We didn't do telephone interviews. We met people, reported, got out there, which is what I try to tell young reporters now—to not Google this shit, it won't give you colour for your story,' she says.

---

[9]   Anupama Chopra, *First Day, First Show*. This excerpt is from an *India Today* article that appeared in September 1993.

Anu worked with *India Today* till 2002. Her articles were compiled into a book called *First Day, First Show: Writings from the Bollywood Trenches* for which Shah Rukh Khan wrote the foreword. In it he wrote,

> Anupama was a serious journalist, by which I mean that she wrote about Hindi films in a serious way. Her writing reflected research. She didn't gloss over facts and figures. Over the years, Anupama became more involved with Bollywood. She married a filmmaker—Vidhu Vinod Chopra. Like me, she was an outsider who became an insider. When you make a film, if you are an insider, you're usually the last person to know that your film is not right. But when you are an outsider, you have a little more objectivity.[10]

Anu married in 1996. It was Chopra's third marriage, the first two having ended in divorce. The couple's paths first crossed in 1989, when Anu called Chopra for a feature she was doing on 'directors of tomorrow'. But he was dumbfounded that the rookie reporter didn't know anything about his past—like the fact that he was nominated for an Oscar at twenty-three. 'I got a slight dressing-down,' Anu said in a television interview with Abu Jani and Sandeep Khosla.[11] She learnt her lesson, and was never unprepared again.

The couple has two children, a son, Agni, who is nineteen, and a daughter, Zuni, who is seventeen. Although her husband makes Hindi films, Anu is definitely more obsessed with Bollywood than he is. Hers is the *Sholay* generation and her tastes gravitate more towards pulp, commercial cinema compared to her spouse's, whose inclinations are more rarefied. They do not often like the same films. At home, Anu doesn't talk to him about her work because she prefers to keep their professional lives separate. Vidhu never speaks about his wife or her work in public, and certainly not with journalists. Anu, in turn, seldom turns to him for advice, but sometimes, when she's struggling with how many stars to give to a film, she errs on the side of generosity. That's Vidhu, the film-maker's

---

[10] Anupama Chopra, *First Day, First Show*, p. ix.
[11] NDTV, 22 January 2010.

influence. That's the part of work she finds most difficult—the star rating. She hates it but unfortunately that's what audience looks at.

With the advent of social media and 280-character headlines, does the public take film reviews seriously? Anu thinks it does.

'Now, with digital, there is space to create blogs but the audience also wants mashable content. You are in a battle for eyeballs and it has sort of set us back in terms of the level of the conversation. Film Companion is an attempt to create a platform where you can have engaging conversations about cinema that doesn't have to be only high-brow and esoteric. I don't ever want the conversation to be about the star rating.'

Her careening into film criticism from journalism sort of just evolved. But Anu doesn't consider herself a film critic. 'I'm a film reviewer,' she says modestly. 'A film critic is A.O. Scott or Anthony Lane,' naming two acclaimed American writers. 'They are people whose knowledge and reference is not just cinema, it's music, art, literature. You evaluate a piece of cinema against other art forms. I don't know enough!'

Every Friday, her team puts together a file of writings by critics she admires from around the world so that she can keep abreast. She watches interviews by *Hollywood Reporter*. She constantly consumes inspirational content so that she can better her journalism. 'I would love to go back to school and study a bit more and be worthy.'

There is no typical workday for Anu. Friday is dedicated to watching a film in the morning and then reviewing it. She's up at 6 a.m., working by 6.30 a.m., and makes her way to the office mid-morning. She says she tries to put her phone away by 7.30 p.m., but it often doesn't happen. The family always has dinner together.

Anu has also done much to transform MAMI, Mumbai's annual film festival, which was languishing till she and Kiran Rao came on board. Together, thanks to their efforts, and those of its creative director, Smriti Kiran, the festival has turned into a window for Indian and world cinema.

Anu's work chronicles Bollywood's evolution, which reflects the evolution of India itself. If the public's perception of Hindi movies has changed over the past quarter of a century, it is in no small measure thanks to her journalism. Today, pop culture is mainstream and people recognize the power cinema wields on society. Anu's writing and reportage plays a pivotal part in shaping India's broader cultural narrative.

SHANOO SHARMA
THE CASTING DIRECTOR

Trying to track down Shanoo Sharma is not easy. Dubbing her the 'Gatekeeper of Bollywood', the press often describes her as reclusive and enigmatic. Rarely seen behind her office desk, her whereabouts remain a bit of a mystery in Mumbai. Upon hearing such talk, Hindi cinema's leading casting director dismisses it with a roll of her large, heavily kajal-rimmed eyes. 'We are here,' she says, referring to the casting department at Yash Raj Films which she has headed since 2010. 'Anyone can walk in.'

The hype around her inaccessibility may be far-fetched, but is indicative of the power she wields. Shanoo has cast for over thirty Hindi films, including some of Bollywood's biggest blockbusters such as *My Name is Khan, Ra.One, Dhoom 3, Tiger Zinda Hai, Ae Dil Hai Mushkil* and *Sultan*. She is credited with discovering new talent. Introducing the wildly popular Gen Next star Ranveer Singh to the film world was a milestone in her own career. And he is just one of her finds. She has played a key role in launching the careers of several successful actors including Parineeti Chopra, Vaani Kapoor, Bhumi Pednekar and Arjun Kapoor, who says earnestly, 'Shanoo believed in me before I believed in myself.'

Forty-year-old Shanoo is changing the way actors are cast in Hindi films. Transparent about her casting calls and auditions, she is credited with professionalizing the process. She is a no-nonsense risk taker, intimidating but personable, confident but vulnerable, tough but soft-hearted.

Shanoo is a head turner with a distinct personal style. Dressed in jeans, a crisp white kurta, a stack of silver bangles, oversized rings, dangling earrings and a large silver nose ring, she can't be missed. Her jewellery, which she wears a lot of, tinkles when she moves. Unmistakably girly, she loves eye make-up and lipstick—sometimes mixing as many as four colours to get the perfect pink-brown shade. Her appearance matches her dramatic personality.

'Shanoo is a force of nature,' says director Karan Johar, who works with her to cast his films. 'She has a personality that is unique. I mean she has this kind of joie de vivre, she has a passion for what she says and does. She has a gifted sense of humour and a personality that is unique to her. From her look to her projection to the way she expresses herself— I've never met somebody like her.'

When asked about the labels the media has given her, of a gatekeeper or starmaker, Shanoo bristles. She insists she is neither.

'If I was a star maker, everyone I have cast would be Ranveer Singh. That's not happened. My kids are still aspiring. Some are still struggling. Some of them have gone back,' she says.

Not one for tags and titles, she prefers to be known as a 'casting director'. 'That's credible,' she says, adding she would rather be known as 'someone who does her job well and makes a difference in a person's life.'

Worldwide, casting directors are finally being recognized as specialists in their field. This is true of both Bollywood and Hollywood. Though there is no separate Oscar category for casting directors, American casting director Lynn Stalmaster became the first to receive an Honorary Academy Award for his pioneering casting work in 2016. Remember Christopher Reeves as Superman? Dustin Hoffman as Tootsie? Stalmaster cast them.

The Los Angeles–based Casting Society of America (CSA) is a professional body that casts actors in film, television, theatre and new media. It says its mission is to 'uphold and honor the highest standards of professionalism in the casting field'. Though a handful of casting directors from India are part of the CSA, the Hindi film industry is dominated by individual casting directors. Shanoo is a central figure here and according to industry talk, one of the most powerful. Though she comes from filmy pedigree—her maternal grandfather was the legendary singer, Mukesh, and her paternal grandfather, B.M. Sharma, was a film distributor— Shanoo grew up far away from the bright lights and studio sets of Mumbai.

Born in Mumbai on 25 June 1978, to Udesh and Rita Sharma, Shanoo is their younger child. Her brother, Sameer, a film-maker and director, is seven years older. The Sharmas place family above everything else. 'My parents are retired. All they do is love each other,' Shanoo says. The four of them live together while the head of the family, Shanoo's paternal grandmother, who is in her nineties, lives upstairs. That's where the family gathers to eat their meals. Home is a big part of Shanoo's life—both professionally and personally. For Shanoo, who keeps long hours, works late into the night and doesn't switch off on weekends, the lines between the two are blurry.

'Welcome to the Sharma studio,' her father jokes, feigning annoyance at Shanoo's work that has taken over their apartment. A bevy of assistants hovers around, filling the flat with their youthful energy. 'They are such kind children, they have left the bedroom for us,' he says, his soft eyes twinkling. Her mother, Rita, 'the most selfless person I know', Shanoo says, dishes out fruit and chocolates to the team. 'She's the feeder, the caretaker,' Shanoo says sincerely, her voice softening. 'She is a woman of great, great character. If there is any good in me, my mother is responsible for it.'

Though Mumbai is home now, Shanoo spent much of her childhood in Johannesburg, South Africa, where her father ran an Indian restaurant called the Maharaja. Udesh, who was in the hospitality business, decided to work overseas so that he could save money. Located by the water, with a breathtaking view of a valley dotted with houses whose lights twinkled in the evenings, Shanoo remembers the night the Maharaja opened its doors. It was 1991. 'Oh my God, we didn't know what hit us! There were so many people. There were queues. It was amazing!'

Shanoo became an integral part of the Maharaja's story. After her classes at Brescia House convent, a Catholic girls' school, she would walk up the road and spend the afternoon at the restaurant. She would study there and when she got tired, she would grab a few bolsters and curl up under a table to take a nap. It was her happy place.

Shanoo pitched in at the restaurant almost every evening. Father and daughter agree that she was an incredible waitress. 'When I wasn't at the Maharaja, their business would drop,' Shanoo says, laughing. 'I knew how to take orders for up to fourteen people without writing it down. When the food would come ten to fifteen minutes later, I would know exactly where each dish would go.'

Those early days at the Maharaja left a lasting imprint on Shanoo. 'Restaurants are my life,' she says. She loves the rhythm of a restaurant—the quiet hours before it opens, the waiters cleaning the glasses, the tables being set. 'It takes me back to a comfortable place. And if you are comfortable in your life, you will be better in whatever you do.' Today, a good place to look for Shanoo is at a cafe—she spend most of her day working out of one of Mumbai's coffee houses. 'That's home to me. I feel safe.'

Evenings at the Maharaja were lively—but Shanoo's teenage years in Johannesburg were fraught. 'I was not a good kid,' she says. Living abroad meant straddling two cultures and living in South Africa during the apartheid era wasn't easy. Shanoo says she was the only Indian girl in a school full of white people. With that, came the inevitable push and pull of two very different worlds.

Shanoo rebelled. 'I had my own issues that I dealt with as a kid. My parents had nothing to do with it. You hide from your parents. You do shit on your own. I was very troublesome. My parents were going crazy, trying to keep me as Indian as possible.'

Udesh was worried. He was strict, but 'not like Amrishji in *Dilwale Dulhania Le Jayenge*,' Shanoo says with a laugh, referring to the romantic blockbuster in which Amrish Puri plays a conservative Indian father raising his daughters in the United Kingdom with an iron fist. 'But my father is not like my best friend either. He's my father. In South Africa, there is crime. You don't want your daughter out at night,' Shanoo says. After a pause, she adds, 'I was a bad kid. And *I* am saying that.'

Soft-spoken and courteous, Udesh admits Shanoo went through a challenging phase. 'She was out of my hands.' Shanoo's teenage years were tough on the whole family. One day, when Udesh was at home in Johannesburg and Shanoo in India, he received a disturbing call. 'I get news that Shanoo had shaved her hair, completely. I remember thinking, I am still alive, why has she shaved her head?' Shanoo's explanation is more pedestrian. 'I guess I just wanted to be bald.' When probed, she exclaims, 'It's hair. It grows back!'

Going bald was done on an impulse. The teenage Shanoo loved to party. 'I loved dancing with my hair like this,' she says, covering her face with her shiny, long hair. After a night of revelry, she landed up at the Sun N Sand, a beachfront hotel in Mumbai's Juhu area, with a group of friends. They hung out till 4 a.m. The hotel's salon, run by leading hair stylist Anees Muss, would not open till 10 a.m. 'I said we have to wait till Anees comes.' When he arrived, she said, 'You have to shave my head.' Anees declined. 'So I took his buzzer and went bzzzzzzz.'

'I thought it was crazy, it was stupid,' her father says. When Shanoo returned to Johannesburg, she grew her hair back, but she started colouring it. 'One day it was red, then green, then yellow,' Udesh recalls. 'I said Shanoo, you will remove this. Shave this immediately, otherwise I will throw you out of the house!'

It never came to that. 'Let us put it this way,' he says gently, 'I was not happy about it. But I stood by her.'

They've supported her through all her ups and downs, her wild ways and calm days. Today, they look at her with deep adoration. 'She's a very focused person, she's intelligent and she's creative,' her father says. Overcome with emotion, he breaks down. Sitting across from him in their cosy living room, Shanoo tears up. 'One feels very proud of her,' Udesh says. 'Whatever she does, she excels. It's a miracle.'

After finishing high school, Shanoo began to spend more time in India. In 1998, Udesh and Rita decided to move to Mumbai for good—a decision driven by Rita who wanted to be closer to her extended family. Back then, they had no idea how transformational the move would be for their daughter.

Since Shanoo did not want to go to college, she tried her hand at a variety of jobs—bartending, hairstyling, public relations. Nothing was arresting enough to stick with for more than a few months. The driving force was to earn money. Through these various gigs, Shanoo built an extensive network of friends and associates. 'I used to be a party animal so I knew a lot of people.' When her brother, Sameer, who was an assistant film director, asked her to scout around for new faces who wanted to work in Bollywood, Shanoo agreed. 'My job would be to take a lump sum of money from talents for six months and make sure they got a one-on-one meeting with directors.' It was a natural fit.

Then came a request from Sameer that would prove to be a turning point. He was working as an associate director with acclaimed director Sudhir Mishra on *Khoya Khoya Chand*. He asked Mishra if Shanoo could cast a few characters. Mishra agreed. Shanoo became the casting director for the film—a decision Mishra is glad he took.

'She had an instinct,' he says. 'She took very brave choices.' He says Shanoo's ability to think unconventionally means she comes up with unusual casting choices that often make a character more interesting. 'She uses her imagination instead of plainly working on a brief.' According to him, Shanoo reads the script and thinks on a director's behalf. 'I am a particular kind of director, my films have a particular style and I need a certain kind of actor. All sorts of actors don't work for me. I am not working with people who are just interested in looking pretty.' He says Shanoo understands that because she understands cinema.

According to Johar, Shanoo thinks out of the box 'because that's what Shanoo is, she's out of the box. She is unique and therefore her choices are unique. So when you ask her for casting options, she will always choose an option that is away from the beaten path. Suddenly, she will find you a name that you had perhaps forgotten or just wasn't in your vista of thought.'

Like the time she suggested Zarina Wahab play the role of young Shah Rukh's mother in Johar's 2010 film, *My Name Is Khan*. Johar had been struggling to cast that role. 'Suddenly, Shanoo said, "Why not Zarina?" And I was like wow, I hadn't even thought of it. That was the first time I discovered that there was an inherent genius to Shanoo.'

Shanoo worked on her first big project, *Khoya Khoya Chand* in 2006, when casting was slowly coming into its own in Bollywood. Though there were others, including Amita Sehgal and Nandini Shrikent, doing it, most of the casting decisions were taken by directors and producers typically concerned with casting leads. Secondary roles were filled at the last minute, without much thought.

At the dawn of the century, things began to change. As studios, both domestic and international, set up shop in India, the business became more professional. That brought in much needed reforms in an industry that had long resisted change, writes Tejaswini Ganti, professor of anthropology at New York University. One area that began to get more attention, was casting.

> Until the advent of corporatization, the industry contained very few non-value-added people such as executives, lawyers, agents, professional managers—i.e., the 'suits,' who did not contribute to the actual film-making process. Also, for much of its history, the industry did not have intermediaries such as casting agents, talent scouts or agencies like ICA and William Morris. However, since the mid-to-late 2000s, such intermediaries have been on the rise in the industry as a consequence of new approaches to casting and the increased significance of film stars for consumer brand advertising.[1]

---

[1] Tejaswini Ganti, *Bollywood: A Guidebook to Popular Hindi Cinema*, London: Routledge, 2013.

Till the early 1990s, Hindi films did not give anyone credit for casting. It is widely reported that *Bandit Queen*, released in 1992, was the first Indian film to include a casting director in its closing credits. It acknowledged Tigmanshu Dhulia, a screenwriter, producer and casting director. Prior to that, the biggest Hindi blockbusters—be it *Guide* in the 1960s, *Sholay* in the '70s or *Mr India* in the '80s—did not credit casting directors.

The early noughties brought in a noticeable change: Indian directors began recognizing the work of casting directors. Amita Sehgal was cited for Sanjay Leela Bhansali's *Black* (2005) and Elaine Granger for Rakeysh Om Prakash Mehra's *Rang De Basanti* (2006). Loveleen Tandon was acclaimed for her casting work on Danny Boyle's Academy Award–winning *Slumdog Millionaire* (2008). And Yash Raj Films gave Shanoo credit for casting several of its hit films, including *Ishaqzaade* (which introduced Arjun Kapoor), *Befikre* (starring Vaani Kapoor), and *Dum Laga Ke Haisha* (Bhumi Pednekar's debut).

In Shanoo's eyes, anyone can have a shot at becoming an actor. 'But it's up to the audience to make you a star.' The days of needing industry connections to get your foot into the door are on the wane. She says being an actor's child may give you an initial break but if you don't perform at the box office, your pedigree doesn't matter.

What about the elephant in the room, the casting couch?

Since the downfall of powerful producer Harvey Weinstein rocked Hollywood, stories of sexual harassment have put a spotlight on the predatory culture surrounding movie industries across the world. Women in the US, UK, Spain, Italy, France and Australia have come forward with their stories of exploitation under the #MeToo movement. In Bollywood, a handful of actors have spoken up about facing the casting couch but the campaign has, at best, been tepid.

According to Amit Behl, Joint Secretary of CINTAA (Cine and TV Artists Association), sexual harassment is a growing problem in India. Nearly fifty formal complaints were registered with CINTAA between 2015 and 2017. Prior to that, between 2012 and 2015, only twelve cases of sexual harassment were registered. 'I don't know if the instances of sex exploitation have increased or decreased but instances of reporting have definitely increased. And that, I suppose, is everywhere,' he says.

'Apparently it does exist but it doesn't exist in my corner,' Shanoo says. 'It's too credible a space now. We are professional people. No one will cast someone because they have been through the casting couch.' Although she has heard stories about people making advances on vulnerable aspirers, promising to help a struggling actor in exchange for sexual favours, she doesn't believe that it works. 'Do you get a film as a result? I don't know.'

'I am sure the casting couch phenomenon may exist, not just in Bollywood but in every walk of life' Johar says. 'But the fact that there are prolific casting directors like Shanoo Sharma in the business completely takes away from the sadness of that situation. She brings credibility to the job of casting, she brings integrity and more than that, she gives access to so many people who may not have had a route to Yash Raj Studios without her.'

Sudhir Mishra rates Shanoo one of the top casting directors in the country, and says that she has brought respectability to the profession. 'Now there is a fair way of coming into the industry. It's becoming democratic. You can walk in and audition for a part. Otherwise minor roles would be cast through friends of heroes or via recommendations. Now anyone can walk in, you don't need connections.'

Shanoo says her main criterion for casting someone is talent. She insists she does not give out favours, not even to sons and daughters of famous people. 'Talent wins over bloodline, always. I have met almost every star child and if this industry was ruled by nepotism, I would have cast all of them.'

One star kid she helped cast for his first film is Arjun Kapoor. The son of the well-known producer Boney Kapoor, Arjun did not want to be launched by his famous father. So he found himself sitting before the most powerful woman in the casting industry, his future in her hands. According to Arjun, it was one of the worst meetings he has ever had. 'She told me, "You are not the best looking, you have to work harder, lose more weight. You have an attitude, you have a chip on your shoulder, you look like you are upset with the world. So you need to improve yourself."'

They were harsh words that Arjun remains grateful for. He took her advice. He exercised and worked on his attitude. It paid off. Shanoo landed him a leading role in *Ishaqzaade,* his debut film. Arjun was praised for his performance in the romantic drama and is now one of Bollywood's leading young men, with an impressive roster of hit films like *2 States*, *Finding Fanny* and *Mubarakan* to his name.

He remains a Shanoo loyalist. 'She has the ability to speak the truth and not mince her words. That is the best quality that Shanoo had, has and will always have. She is my truth serum. Today I can just pick up the phone and call her and she will just inject me with truth. She will tell me exactly what I need to hear. She is who she is, unapologetically, and that's what makes her so dynamic.'

'Shanoo has made a great contribution,' says Honey Trehan, a fellow casting director in Bollywood. He describes Shanoo as a change agent and goes as far as to say that Shanoo's casting choices are not just bringing in fresh faces to the industry, but changing the texture of Hindi films.

'I happen to be part of that revolution,' says Arjun. 'For a long period of time, mainstream actors were only known by the way they looked. If casting was not important then I would not have made it. I am defined by the roles I play, not by the way I look.'

'Shanoo doesn't just focus on the lead characters,' Honey points out. 'By casting carefully for supporting roles as well, she helps a director shape an entire ensemble, lending films a certain authenticity. Hindi films are no longer recycling the same faces for cliched roles.'

Professional as she may be, there are still some areas within the industry that are forbidden, even for the most powerful woman in casting. 'Obviously, I don't cast Mr Salman Khan,' Shanoo says dryly. The leading spots of big budget films or those by established directors are often filled by their favourite actors, without auditions. Asking any one of the Khan trinity (Shah Rukh, Salman, Aamir) to try out for a role is unheard of. In fact, it would be considered downright disrespectful.

This exclusive club aside, aspiring film stars clamour to meet Shanoo but the film world buzzes with tales of how it takes months to get an appointment with her. 'These are stories made up by the media,' she insists. 'My team and I *are* available to meet people. I work out of coffee shops, I walk on the road. I get followed by people saying "ma'am, one minute, one minute" when I go for an evening walk—that's when I draw the line. I take my headphones off and say this is my personal time. Otherwise, my team and I are around.'

There is a simpler route to get Shanoo's attention—she holds open auditions twice a week. On that day, anyone can walk in to Yash Raj

Studios. About a hundred budding actors do and she makes sure she sees every candidate. No one is turned away. People of all ages, sizes and shapes come in. Senior citizens are always given a place to sit and everyone is offered tea and coffee. 'That's a rule,' Shanoo says. 'We are a good office.'

There is always email too. She gets around 200 a day, which can go upto 700 when she puts out a casting call, and her team looks at each email that comes in. She makes sure of that. 'Because If I don't see that, that may be the one thing I am looking for.' So she warns her assistants, 'A friend's son could email me and then call me to say the email wasn't seen. And if I bust you doing that, then nobody gets salaries for a month.' Shanoo's bark is worse than her bite—she's never acted on that threat.

When she needs to cast someone for a film, her team posts the requirement on social media. One entry on the Yash Raj films (YRF) casting pages on social media and retweeted by the official YRF site looks like this:

CASTING CALL!!!
For the first time we are looking for actors with a very particular brief for a part in an upcoming feature film. Any photographs that do not fit the brief will not be considered. Below mentioned is the description:
HEIGHT: 5'9"
SHOULDER: 15–19"
BICEPS: 11–15"
AGE: 25–30 years old
COMPLEXION: WHEATISH TO FAIR
BODY TYPE: FAIRLY BUILT
All photographs concerned with the above description can be emailed to casting@yashrajfilms.com with SUBJECT AS S2017. Also, apart from the ones mentioned above, please also mention your Head to Waist, Waist to Toe, Hip, Chest, Thigh Round, Head Round and shoe size measurements in the mail.
THANK YOU
LOVE AND LIGHT,
SHANOO

With almost 200,000 followers on her personal Instagram page, another 122,000 following the official Yash Raj Films casting page, word that Shanoo is on the lookout for an actor spreads like wildfire. Once aspirants send their details in, her team handles the first round. This usually consists of a thirty-second video recording of the candidates introducing themselves. The shortlisted ones get sent to Shanoo. Anyone, anywhere in the world, can apply.

She watches each video like a hawk. 'I am particular about these things. After a while, the faces start to look the same and when they start to look the same, that's when I say STOP! My assistants say, "Ma'am, we have only forty more to go", and I say no, it's unfair. He could be the next one.' Every candidate deserves her undivided attention. So she takes a five-minute break, closes her eyes, does something else for a few moments and gets right back to work. She demands professionalism, but leads by example.

What she looks for in an audition is 'watchability'. She asks herself, 'Am I interested in going beyond twenty seconds?' If she likes something about a person, she works with them. In her trademark blunt style, she'll spell out what needs to be done—fix your teeth, sort out your make-up, lose some weight, change your hairstyle.

She has a meticulous system of filing every audition she has ever held. She confesses she is 'very, very organized'. Pictures of young female leads go in one folder, Bengalis are placed in another, middle-aged men go into a separate folder, there's a another for overweight people, and so on. If she needs to cast a sardar for a role, out comes that folder, where she expects to see every Sikh she has ever auditioned. Given Shanoo has seven million auditions stashed away, being organized is critical. When you are a casting director in Bollywood, you don't have much time. There's always one more struggling actor waiting to be seen.

None of the auditions are deleted. 'That's a rule. You can be good, you can be bad, you can be horrible but you are not going to be deleted. A person comes to us with hope. How can I delete hope?' If someone who has auditioned passes away, their videos and photographs go into a deceased folder. 'I don't like deleting,' Shanoo says. 'It's a memory. Deleting feels rude.'

Once in a while, she receives a portfolio that she finds distasteful. Like the time a young woman sent her pictures in a school dress and bra. 'That pisses me off. I used my driver's phone and I called her and said—you don't know who I am but you don't need to be doing this. She said "No, my photographer said this is how it works."' Shanoo heard her out and then repeated, 'In this industry, you don't need to be doing this.'

She doesn't sugarcoat her words when talking to anyone—be it an aspiring actor or her assistants. Her style has been compared to Miranda Priestly, the infamous fashion editor played by Meryl Streep in *The Devil Wears Prada*, who was feared by her underlings and contemporaries alike. Priestly lorded over her team. Shanoo does too. 'When I hire my assistants, I tell them that I am not going to be nice them for two years. After that, I will be your slave.'

Her reputation as a demanding diva doesn't bother her. 'In a way, I want people to be scared of me because intelligent people will go beyond that fear.' But if her assistants get something wrong, they are not spared a verbal lashing. 'It's very simple. They don't get shouted at for no reason. I am a perfectionist. If I want things done a certain way and if they are not done like that, I get irritable.'

She doesn't go into her office at Yash Raj Films that much—her team handles the operations there. She is constantly in touch with them, messaging, texting, exchanging photos and videos through a WhatsApp group appropriately called *Kamdham*. She used to insist that her assistants send her selfies when they got to work every morning so that she could see what time they came in. She doesn't do that any more but has installed CCTV cameras in the office which she views through her mobile phone. Yet, Shanoo denies being a control freak. She says she is just being practical. 'I need to know what's going on.'

'When I met her for the first time, I was very intimidated. She has a strong personality,' says Charmi Gondalia, a former assistant. For the three years Charmi worked for her, she did not have a life of her own. 'My life was hers.' And it had its moments. 'She yelled at me a *lot* of the time. After me, a lot of assistants have come, but I am still the one she's yelled at the most,' Charmi says, adding, 'but I also am still the one she loves the most.'

Despite being a tough boss, Shanoo has great affection for those who work for her. 'See, my team is my family,' she states like there is just no doubt about it. 'On the eve of my birthday, I am with my team. They become my family.'

It works both ways. 'Charmi gave me blood for three years,' Shanoo says. Now, it's her turn to reciprocate. Charmi is teaching dance and wants to become an actor. Shanoo promoted her dance classes on her Instagram page which got Charmi immediate visibility and a lot more students. 'Today we have a wonderful equation,' Charmi says. 'I know she's going to be there for me whenever I need her and I am there for her, no matter what.'

Shanoo exhibits the same unflinching loyalty towards her boss, the reclusive Aditya Chopra who heads Yash Raj Films. She appreciates the freedom and trust he gives her to run her department. But if Shanoo gets something wrong, he lets her know. 'I had my boss come up to me one day and for the first time in the history of casting, we had to delete a scene because he didn't like the actor. I turned around and said the director head chosen the actor. He said, "No, if you take responsibility for a Ranveer Singh, you have to take responsibility for everybody."' His words hit home. 'I realized that's where I had been messing up. I have to take responsibility for everyone I cast.'

She has a philosophical approach towards failure. 'I cast a whole bunch of kids but of course not all of them make it. But I don't call that failure, I call that life.'

Shanoo is whimsical, emotional and sensitive—that's reflected in her choice of tattoos. There is an Om with wings, a heart, shooting stars with musical notes and three Michael Jackson tattoos because she's a huge music buff. Each tattoo tells a story. There's one of a bottle on her left leg, inspired by a childhood dream. 'Since I was a kid, I would always fantasize about one of those bottles washing up on the shore with a message for me,' she says.

Her parents don't approve of the tattoos. 'My mother still thinks they are going to come off,' Shanoo laughs loudly. 'She thinks they are mehendi!'

The romantic in Shanoo often thinks about what lies ahead and is refreshingly honest about what she wants. She says she would like to continue working but when it happens, there is room for love and marriage. 'I think I can be amazingly independent and strong in a marriage too. I've waited forty years for this man, I would like to spend time with him. I'd like that. That is the dream,' Shanoo says softly.

As she chases her dreams, both professional and personal, her father offers her advice. 'I tell her to lie low,' says Udesh protectively. 'In the film industry, a lot of people love getting pictured, love getting talked about. I advise her, stay away from it. As far as possible, just do your work, have job satisfaction, have the feeling that you are doing well.'

India's most sought-after casting director refuses to acknowledge her success. 'I don't think I am at the top of my game,' she says. Shanoo insists she's not saying it to be humble. 'I don't want to feel like I am at the top. If I feel I am at the top of my game, my journey here is done.'

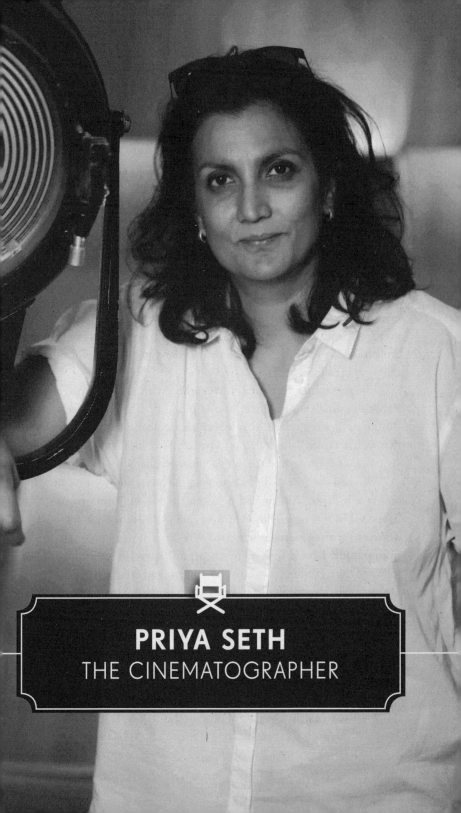

PRIYA SETH
THE CINEMATOGRAPHER

Ranjit Katyal, a rich Indian businessman based in Kuwait, bursts into his home to find the furniture in disarray, the decorations smashed and the place destroyed. Rushing from one room to another, he calls out to his wife, Amrita, and daughter, Simran. He gets no response. He screams their names again. His shrieks are met with silence. He collapses on the bed and cries copious tears. He takes a child's teddy bear and presses it against his face. He fears the worst. Ranjit is experiencing first-hand the immediate aftermath of Iraq's invasion of Kuwait in August 1990, which sparked the first Gulf War and eventually led to the world's largest civilian air evacuation in history.

Less than half an hour into the 2016 blockbuster *Airlift*, this gripping scene, hauntingly portrayed by lead actor Akshay Kumar, shows a desperate man searching for his family in his home, which has been wrecked by the invading Iraqi troops. The camera pans back and forth between him, the broken objects and the strewn clothes. It darts in and out of the various rooms in the house.

It makes for tense viewing. Just moments earlier, troops had stopped Ranjit's car and shot his driver in cold blood. Viewers could see and feel the horror of war up close. That we experience physically the terror of war, that we live through the drama in so personal a fashion, is testimony to the virtuosity of Priya Seth, the film's cinematographer.

'We had shot the soldiers destroying the house and then we froze the set,' recalls Priya. 'Akshay had not seen the set, he hadn't rehearsed, it happened in real time.' Priya chose to shoot this scene with a hand-held camera to give it a more authentic feel. 'Akshay came running on to the set from outside. I could hear his footsteps, so I knew he was coming. I just followed him. I didn't know what he was going to do. He came in, crying. He went into the bedroom, collapsed on to the bed, and snot was coming out of his nose. We got it all in one shot, and we knew we had something special. It was unbelievable.'

The movie, realistically shot and raw with emotion, is a gripping action film about a real war in a foreign land, and it made Priya a cinematographic star. 'It finally gave me credibility,' she says about her first big-ticket Bollywood feature. Till then, she had been shooting ad films and had a small cult classic movie under her belt, *Barah Aana* (2009).

Priya recalls wanting to throw up on her first day at the *Airlift* shoot because she was so nervous. 'But when I got on set, I was fine, since I've been doing this long enough. I work really hard, I do a lot of homework, and I know that those are the things that I can handle. It was a massive platform, this Akshay Kumar film.'

Thanks to *Airlift*, Priya is one of the most celebrated women cinematographers in the country today. She is widely featured in the media and is a poster child for the way Hindi cinema is changing. If there were any misgivings that women couldn't handle complicated, technical shoots, or carry bulky equipment, Priya's work in *Airlift* puts that to rest. It was her breakout film, one that demonstrated that women who work behind the camera are equal to their male counterparts. Priya's success was a victory for all women cinematographers in India.

Though she had worked behind the camera for several years, it took her a decade to land the job of director of photography (DoP) in a big Hindi film with a superstar. Raja Krishna Menon, who wrote and directed *Airlift*, pushed hard for Priya to get the job. They had a history of working together and he had complete faith in her ability. After some resistance from the producers, who were keen on picking their own crew, he finally had his way. 'Akshay asked me, "So who's the cameraman?"' Raja recalls. 'I said, "There's no cameraman." So Akshay says, "Who's doing the film?" I said it's a camerawoman, to which Akshay said, "*Achchha? superb yaar!*" That was his reaction. It never came up after that. He was very supportive of Priya, he loves her work.'

While the film was being shot in the UAE, the actor tweeted, '*Checking a shot filmed by #Airlift's female DOP Priya, unfortunately cn only see her arm, bt wat an arm she hs #WomenRule.*'[1] It was a clear public acknowledgement that gender doesn't matter when it comes to cinematography.

Unfortunately, that realization hasn't sunk in fast enough across the world. The year 2018 marks the first time a woman, Rachel Morrison, was nominated for an Oscar for Best Cinematography for her work on *Mudbound,* at the Ninetieth Academy Awards.

---

[1]   Akshay Kumar on Twitter @akshaykumar 3/11/15 18:35

Chef, the 2017 Saif Ali Khan–starrer, was Raja and Priya's third feature film together—evidence of the faith the director has in Priya. 'Technically, she is one of the top four or five DoPs in the country today, without a doubt,' he emphasizes. 'She's very diligent and puts a lot of thought and work into how she approaches something. In our industry, that's not normal. It's a "we will wing it" industry.'

In India, the number of women working as cinematographers has increased since Priya first started out. Meghna Ghai Puri, who heads the Mumbai-based film academy Whistling Woods International, says, 'Earlier, girls didn't want to do cinematography. Perhaps they felt cinematography was going to be a job where you have to carry lights, you have to carry a camera and bulky equipment. But I'm quite happy that it's one of our more popular choices and that there are girls who want to become cinematographers.'

As a technical field, cinematography requires strength and stamina. Film schedules can be gruelling. For *Airlift*, the unit shot for forty-nine days, sometimes moving between two to three locations a day. Priya is a tall, strong woman. That's just as well, given that she works with an Arriflex Alexa, an expensive 18-kg camera that costs about $250,000. She finds it most suited to big-budget cinema work. It also captures low light well.

Despite the number of women cinematographers increasing, the battle for recognition continues. Priya is no exception. Even after *Airlift*'s success, her phone didn't exactly ring non-stop.

As a cinematographer, Priya has done more than 200 ad films, umpteen music videos and three features. She has also earned her stripes as the first woman in India to film underwater for Kiran Rao's 2010 film, *Dhobi Ghat*. She credits ad guru Prahlad Kakkar for pushing her to learn diving more than a decade earlier because he felt underwater cinematography was a nascent field with a lot of potential. Today she's one of India's best underwater DoPs. Priya loves underwater shoots, even though they can be gruelling.

For Priya, cinematography is an art form. 'It is painting. It's just that it's painting in 3D,' she says. Cinematography has been described by journalist and film historian Pamela Hutchinson in the following terms, 'The cinematographer or director of photography (DP) is the director's right hand on set. It's a demanding job, combining artistry, advanced technical knowledge and team management, as the DP selects the camera, lens and lighting for each shot, and commands a crew of electricians and camera operators. A good cinematographer works closely with the director to achieve the desired visual effect in each scene. A great one imparts their own unique vision to the film. Evocatively, cinematographer John Alton described the trade in the title of his 1949 book, as "painting with light".[2]

Priya distinguishes herself through her passion for cinematography. Vishnu Rao, Priya's former husband and a fellow cinematographer, says, 'More than technical know-how, which everybody on a certain level of cinematography will have, it's the interest that Priya has. She fully dives in, she researches, she cares about all aspects and wants to be creative because it helps the narrative. She's damn hard-working, she's got tenacity, grit and spirit. At the same time, she's all heart, soft, wonderful. That combination is what makes her so special.'

With sharp features, shoulder-length hair and a winning smile, Priya comes across as approachable, but not one to tolerate any nonsense. Her cosy apartment in Mumbai's Bandra suburb is neat and tidy. The first thing that catches one's attention when you enter it is a bookshelf. Priya is a voracious reader. There's nothing overly *filmi* about the home or its inhabitant.

For someone who had never watched a Hindi film till she was twenty-one, it has been quite a journey. As a child, Priya watched a lot of Hollywood movies with her siblings, either at the cinema or at home on a VCR. She was typical of the anglicized Indians of that era. It was not unusual for a certain subset of Indian society—the English-speaking, urban educated set—to eschew Hindi movies for Western ones. In the decades after Independence, the attitude towards local cinema among the country's elite tended to be snobbish. 'Bollywood movies were despised as the movies necessary to keep the illiterate masses amused and hopefully out of trouble,' writes Mihir Bose in his definitive history of Hindi cinema.[3]

[2]   https://www.theguardian.com/film/2018/jan/25/woman-cameraman-snubbed-mudbound-rachel-morrison-nominated-oscar, 25 January 2018.
[3]   Mihir Bose, *Bollywood: A History*, New Delhi: Roli Books, p. 33.

Reputed cinemas in the neighbourhoods Priya grew up in never showed Indian films.

'I feel embarrassed sometimes because my Hindi film history is zero. But growing up, there was no exposure to Hindi films or Hindi music,' Priya admits.

Born on 14 July 1975, Priya is the fourth and youngest child of Pimmi and the late Dharam Paul (D.P.) Seth. She comes from a large Punjabi business family. Pimmi, who was raised in Mumbai, has five sisters and two brothers, and D.P., who hailed from Amritsar, had five brothers and a sister. D.P.'s family had businesses across India. The Seths were living in Amritsar when Pimmi found out she was pregnant, at thirty-four, with her fourth child. She was nervous. She already had two boys and a girl and had just started to study again. Pimmi's friend, who lived across the road, reassured her, saying that the new baby would be the most intelligent. The logic: an older woman's maturity would permeate the baby. The friend's words turned out to be prophetic.

According to her mother, Priya was a happy, bouncy baby, adored by her parents and older siblings. Vikram is twelve years older, Vivek eleven years older, and there is a six-year gap between Devika and Priya. She was bossed around and as the youngest, learnt the art of keeping everyone happy. In Amritsar, the family lived in a sprawling house. The kids climbed trees and played outside in their spare time, with the girls participating in the same rough-and-tumble games as their brothers.

In 1981, when Priya was five, the family enterprise in Amritsar was struggling. The Seths moved to Mumbai so that D.P. could work with his brother. They lived in fashionable Maker Tower in Cuffe Parade and Priya joined the elite Cathedral & John Connon School. For a while, things went swimmingly well. Then Priya's uncle persuaded the family to move into his home in Walkeshwar. Priya says she could not put a finger on it, but she did not like living there.

On Vivek's twenty-first birthday, Priya and her family stepped out for dinner. When they returned, they found themselves locked out of the shared house. They had nowhere to go and no money. Another family member took them in. It was a difficult period as the family moved homes every two years. The Seths coped through humour.

'For my thirteenth birthday, we couldn't afford to go out,' Priya remembers. That didn't come in the way of the Seths celebrating this milestone. 'My mum decided we would cross-dress. She got my brothers, who were twenty years old, to dress as girls and us girls to dress as boys. My dad wore a skirt and my mum wore pants and we had a party in the house, just us. We would do this kind of stuff because all we had was each other. It never felt like it was makeshift because it wasn't an expensive experience. It was just about being together and laughing. Black humour is a tool I have held on to. Growing up like that makes you resilient, and nothing can faze my siblings and family. When you've had enough kicks through childhood, you can face anything.'

Her family shaped Priya's personality, especially her mother. Priya calls her mother a 'firebrand'. Pimmi was keen on studying, and after completing her bachelor's from Sophia College, wanted to pursue chartered accountancy. Her family objected, saying she would never find a Punjabi man to marry if she was 'too educated'. Pimmi looks back at that time and says that in Punjabi business families, girls were not allowed to be brighter than the boys.

While Pimmi resented this, she was dutiful and fell in line. But her dreams of studying further never left her. When her children were born, she vowed to give her daughters the same opportunities as their brothers. 'I was very sure I would let the girls do what they wanted,' Pimmi says. 'My husband was wonderfully liberal and encouraging.'

'My mom was always driven and ahead of her times,' Priya says. 'She focused on her two girls. We didn't grow up with "girls dress like this" or "you must look like that". We played sports our whole lives. She allowed us to thrive.' That attitude led Devika and Priya to believe they could do anything.

In grade 7, Priya went to Welham Girls' School in Dehradun, a reputed boarding school founded in 1957. Her parents did not want to send her, but Priya was determined to follow her sister there. She loved Welham. She felt like she belonged. 'Welham was a wish-box of everything I wanted to do. You know how in school, in every class, there are ten to fifteen kids who are good at everything? I was one of those kids. I did well academically, I debated, I played every sport. In basketball, we made it to the nationals.

I even threw javelin! I was the school captain. When I left school, I thought I owned the world because everything I had touched was great.'

'Priya has always been a natural leader,' says Shimona Shahi Rana, Priya's best friend and classmate. 'Priya can be the serious, intellectual thinker, who reads numerous non-fiction books, ranging from the history of salt to *Sapiens*, but she is also the funniest person I know. She has always been very sure of herself, confident in her ability to get things done, and has a calm and mature disposition, which was unique for a teenager.'

Shimona calls Priya her go-to girl. When Shimona had her second child, she turned to Priya for support. 'I knew she would be the only person who would fit the role of mother, friend, hand-holder, spokesperson, everything. I knew she would shake the hospital down if anything went wrong. She is the most reliable person I know.'

After Welham, it was back to Mumbai, where Priya studied economics at St Xavier's College. ('I wanted to be practical and have an option to fall back on in case nothing else worked out,' she says.) It was during this time that she got her first exposure to the film business. Her parents knew UTV's Ronnie Screwvala. In 1994, Priya began interning there during the summer, doing all sorts of odd jobs. 'It was donkey work, I was a gofer,' Priya says with a laugh. Indeed, running errands for the crew was far from glamorous. But she did realize that she liked this world and wanted to be a part of it. Being on set was electric and she felt herself drawn to the technical side of the business. 'There was this great attraction to the camera and the lighting. It's image-making, at the end of the day. It's the cameraperson who has control over the imagery.'

As a child, Priya was drawn to art history, and photography in particular. 'I think at one level, if I could have, I would have become a fine artist. I can't draw to save my life, not even a stick figure, but in my head I can, and it was a way to express that.'

In 1996, with an economics degree under her belt, Priya wanted to explore cinema courses. Studying cinematography in India in those days required an educational background in science, which she lacked. At this point, her sister Devika, who was living and working in New York, gave her a generous gift to enrol for a short diploma course at New York University's (NYU) School of Continuing Education.

Pimmi remembers asking Priya what she was studying. Her daughter replied, 'Cinematography.' 'I couldn't even pronounce it correctly,' Pimmi says. 'I asked her to explain what she meant and she said she wanted to shoot films and ads. Later, Priya's *nani* asked me what Priya was studying. When I told her, she said, "*Camera ka shooting matlab kya? Camera saath jayegi shadiyon mein photo lene?*" My mother was not impressed at all.'

At that time, Priya was dating Vishnu, whom she married in 2003 (and later divorced). He wasn't all that surprised by her choice. 'I thought it was damn cool and she was a cool gal,' he says. 'It felt normal for her to want to do this because she has that adventure in her. It's a testament to her personality. She always had a creative streak, and didn't want to do anything conventional,' he says.

Priya loved her time at NYU. She embraced cinematography completely. 'I would pull the camera apart, look at the nuts and bolts, and enjoy that it was a combination of science and art.' When she finished her diploma, her professor pointed out that the field was heavily male-oriented all over the world. He wanted Priya to be aware that it was going to be an uphill slog to work in such an environment. But Priya took his warning lightly, too naive to think that her gender would impact her ability to get assignments. 'I was a javelin thrower in school and used to win national events. I did plenty of things boys did, so I just didn't think it was important. Later on, when work was erratic, I recalled his comment and thought, "Yeah, someone did warn me!"'

The history of female DoPs in India is not particularly long. B.R. Vijayalakshmi was the pioneer, becoming the first Asian woman to helm a camera in 1984. Since then, more women have joined the field. Priya's contemporaries include Neha Parti Matiyani (*Waiting*, *Badrinath Ki Dulhania*), Savita Singh (*Hawaizaada*), and Fowzia Fathima (*Mitr: My Friend*), among others. In 2010, Anjuli Shukla became the first Indian woman to win a National Award for cinematography for the Malayalam film *Kutty Srank*.

Priya is a founding member of the Indian Women Cinematographers' Collective (IWCC), which began in 2017. She describes it as a platform for women working in the field to come together to inspire each other. She estimates that there are about seventy women now working in the field across the nation, including assistants, those immediately out of film school, cinematographers, and basically anyone who works with a camera. This figure doesn't include those who work in television.

After returning from New York, Priya landed an unpaid job with Gopal Shah, one of the top cinematographers of that era, who got some of the best assignments. Working for him meant Priya could gain significant experience.

Wary of the profession, her parents wanted to meet Gopal. He put them at ease, but admits he thought Priya wouldn't last very long. He assumed she was another south Mumbai kid whiling away her time. Plus, he was sceptical since there were so few women cinematographers working in films at that time.

'She came in to meet me, and I saw her and thought, "She is so pretty, how will she handle the camera?"' recalls Gopal. 'I said to her, "Why are you interested in this tough job? Just marry a rich guy, you're so good-looking." She said, "No, no, I am really serious." I couldn't say no to her.'

She spent the next six years under Gopal's tutelage. Cinematography is like a guild system where one joins as an unpaid apprentice, climbs the ranks and learns the craft on the job. Years later, Gopal happily accepts that Priya proved him wrong. 'I am so proud of her,' he says.

The respect is mutual. 'Gopal is a lovely person, and my experience as a woman in cinematography was completely based upon the safe environment in which he operated. We had late night shoots in places far from where I lived, in Ghatkopar and Goregaon. My mom would call me every day and ask me how I was coming home, and I would lie because I was coming home on someone's bike and she would never have approved of that! I can't believe the stuff I did then, but I was young and being foolhardy was part of it.'

'Cinematography is the toughest department of a film,' Gopal says. It requires solid technical and personal skills, since a DoP has to have a great rapport with the director and with various crew members. It is physically and mentally demanding. Just a few days into the job, Gopal was surprised to find Priya picking up heavy lights and moving things around. 'She worked like a man,' Gopal says, still sounding surprised. Priya would bombard Gopal with tons of questions—complicated, technical ones, as well as questions on the emotional aspect of a shot. 'I used to tell her, I don't mind giving you tuitions, but please don't ask me on set, it's too difficult! Within one year, she was more qualified than anyone else I had worked with in that amount of time.'

She eventually moved from being an unpaid apprentice to a paid first assistant. Gopal says she was one of the best assistants he ever worked with. 'We reached a stage where Priya was a tigress on set. The way she could handle the manpower—three to four hundred men—and she was the only girl. She handled herself so well. She would never even blink on set, she was so focused.'

Priya quickly learnt how to deflect attention from her gender. She intentionally wore baggy, shapeless clothes. That continues to be her uniform. She is usually in pants and a loose T-shirt, and wears comfortable shoes when she is working.

In the early days, she worked on Deepa Mehta's *1947 Earth* as a third camera assistant and on *Holy Smoke*, a Hollywood film starring Kate Winslet and Harvey Keitel. Eventually, the time came for Priya to strike out on her own. She was reluctant to leave Gopal, but he encouraged her to become an independent cinematographer. In 2004, Priya took the plunge.

That's when she realized how difficult it was to get assignments. 'When I became independent, everything came crashing down. It took me many years to get work, and I didn't know how to deal with it. I wasn't used to not succeeding.'

For about six years, she didn't get many assignments. This was an unsettling and difficult phase in her life when she constantly questioned her abilities. She coped by finding solace in reading. One of V.S. Naipaul's essays in *A Bend in the River*, in which he writes about how insecure he was as a writer, gave her comfort.

'I remember reading that and I held on to it, because I thought here's someone telling me that this is normal. As a freelancer, you never know where you stand because you're only as good as your last job, and you don't know where your next job is coming from. This is a unique profession because I am not sitting in an office where I have other people to draw upon. It is isolating. In hindsight, I can say that I was depressed. When you're in a creative job, you can't separate yourself, your whole person is defined by it and if you're not successful, it shakes you to the core.'

Priya's absolute devotion to her craft kept her going. She is nothing if not determined and tenacious, which she credits to her upbringing. Priya has a message for all aspiring cinematographers, men and women, but especially women—to persevere and be prepared for a slog. Her advice— develop a 'thick skin'.

At this point, a Pimmi had a brainwave. Priya's parents had a defunct textile mill, Ellora Silk Mills, located on Mumbai's Western Express Highway, which had shut down in the 1980s. Her father had been approached to rent out a portion of the space to erect a temporary studio for shoots of television shows. Pimmi suggested that Priya accompany her father and help out at this studio. Priya, who felt she was being 'fobbed off' with something to occupy her time, went along, though reluctantly. At that time, the 4.5 acre property didn't even have a bathroom for her to use. 'It was a dump, so after staring at my father's face for a few weeks, I thought, "OK, let's at least clean it up!" The first thing I built was a bathroom.' She worked day in and day out to make the place presentable, putting in everything from dustbins to drainage pipes.

'Slowly, over the years, we built a studio, and then another one.' Today, the family-owned Ellora Studios has nine sets, and is one of the foremost locations to shoot at in Mumbai. It is a large, verdant space with state-of-the-art sets that are booked year-round for television and film shoots. Priya runs it with her Delhi-based brother, Vikram. With her artistic flair, Priya has designed all the sets herself. There is a hospital, a village house, a large garden, a police station with a jail, a contemporary office, a restaurant, a large villa and plenty of room to build more ready-made sets.

In the early days, Priya was embarrassed about being associated with Ellora Studios because she was desperate to be recognized as a cinematographer. She didn't want people to think of her as anything else—certainly not as a studio owner. 'Cinematography was my first and only love, so I rejected any other label. Now that I have proven my worth with a big movie, I don't care any more.'

Airlift's success was bitter-sweet, because Priya's father passed away before the film was completed. The unit was in Jaisalmer when Priya was urgently called back to Mumbai. D.P. Seth died on 26 October 2015. Priya stayed for the cremation and was back on set two days later. Her siblings and mother encouraged her to resume work, saying her father wouldn't have wanted it any other way.

When Priya returned to the location, no one knew how to react, so she did what she does best—diffuse the situation with some humour. '"Can we get back to work? No one died here!" That is what I said—I cracked a joke, like I always do,' she recalls. '*Airlift* was a seminal period in my life because I realized I could deal with anything. Nothing worse could have been thrown at me than my father's death. I thought I could survive anything [after that].' It was only after the movie was released that she felt the grief, finally letting her emotions sweep through her. For six months after *Airlift*, she couldn't bring herself to go on a set.

Raja Menon had worked hard for Priya to get the *Airlift* gig. The two had met in 2006, when Priya was commissioned to do an ad for Ford in Ahmedabad. Raja was the director. They got off to a tricky start. The first shot was of a guy walking across a monument. Raja thought they got the shot, but Priya wanted to do it again. Raja isn't one to take extra shots, so he declined. But Priya insisted on a retake. The director was puzzled. That's when Priya admitted she had put in a filter and hadn't prepared for it. She had made a mistake, but owned up to it. 'She was honest about it, and that says something about her,' he notes.

Since then, the two have worked on fifty ad films, and every feature film directed by Raja, starting with *Barah Aana*, which starred Naseeruddin Shah. They have a strong working relationship and friendship.

Raja says, 'When you think of cinematography, you imagine it's about lighting—you come in and light a shot or set this fantastic frame. But actually, that is the least important part of cinematography. What you want is to understand the subject and understand why that particular sequence or shot is to be presented, lit or shot in a certain way. That process can take up a lot of time. Directors have a particular vision they wish to convey, and that requires contextualizing and understanding. The cinematographer has to get into a director's head to understand what they are trying to convey and to make it better than that.' Priya, Raja says, has the technical ability and finesse to shoot his vision.

Looking back, Priya realizes that being a woman was a disadvantage, although at the time she attributed it to her lack of ability. 'This is a creative profession and as a newly independent cinematographer, you are insecure about your ability. I think it's taken me ten years too long to get my first film, when I see 100 other people getting films easily, good or bad. I think, how did they get opportunities before I did? I do good work, so what took me so long? Was it a lack of motivation or drive? Not at all! I work as hard as most people. It definitely is gender, and at a certain age, you have the security and self-confidence to admit it. I know guys can't sit with me and slap me on the back on set and we can't exactly go and have a few drinks after work.'

Given her own struggles, Priya always tries to meet aspiring female cinematographers who call her seeking career advice. While she doesn't have much space on her crew because they work in small teams, 'if I can help her out, have a chat, tell her I have struggled too and encourage her, I try to do so,' she says.

Sajid Sanwari has worked with Priya closely for about five years and is her chief assistant on many assignments. 'Priya is like an encyclopaedia—she's aware of what's happening in the world of cinematography, and is also very well read and knows a lot. She's the best mentor because she's approachable—you can ask her anything and she will answer all your questions. She teaches you, and she also trusts you and gives you opportunities.'

Priya takes care of her crew, who can sometimes number up to seventy to eighty people and comprises mostly men. She makes sure they get their breaks on time and are well fed. For them and for any aspiring cameraman or woman, she repeats a mantra she herself swears by: 'Know your craft, study everything, because cinematography is not intuitive.'

It is a profession that requires talent, of course, but also significant hard work and courage. 'Moviemaking is not easy, but I felt I could work on it instinctively,' Priya says. 'The first time I was on set, I felt like I came home.'

ROHINI IYER
THE REPUTATION MANAGER

On a balmy night in August 2017, a corner of Mumbai's Bandra neighbourhood was buzzing. The paparazzi was in overdrive. Flashbulbs popped, dozens at a time, as one fancy car after another pulled up, announcing the arrival of yet another movie star. After striking a pose for the cameras, the celebrities disappeared behind heavily guarded doors. The who's who of the Hindi film industry was out in full force to celebrate Rohini Iyer's birthday.

Inside, Bollywood's favourite celebrity brand manager, wearing a sparkling red dress, beamed as she mingled with her guests. Within hours, pictures from her party began appearing on multiple social media and entertainment blogs. Shilpa Shetty, a friend and a client, posted this on her Instagram feed: *Happy birthday my darling bestie @rohiniyer, to many more successes, unconditional love and unending friendship.* ☺ ☺*#friendsforever #brat #love #gratitude*[1]

One of India's most popular celebrities, Priyanka Chopra, who was not in town, tweeted to her 22.5 million followers: *Happy birthday @rohiniyer stay the amazing girl you are and have a wonderful year! Adore u!* ♥ ♥[2]

There were more posts, each one equally effusive—proof of the immense sway Rohini has over Bollywood and the affection her clients have for her.

The petite powerhouse has a high wattage roster of clients which includes Priyanka Chopra, Katrina Kaif, Kareena Kapoor Khan, Sonam Kapoor and Anil Kapoor. She also manages high-profile directors Sanjay Leela Bhansali and Farah Khan, producer Ekta Kapoor, and Masaba Gupta, the fashion designer.

Rohini is co-founder and director of Raindrop Media, a one-stop shop for celebrity management. 'What I do is called business reputation management—we look after the reputation and the image of people.'

By doing that, Rohini has developed a formidable one of her own: as a no-nonsense straight shooter who is at the same time, all heart.

'I call her a Habanero,' Priyanka Chopra says, referring to the chilli pepper. 'She is in a small packet, a really spicy spice.'

---

[1] Instagram entry by @theshilpashetty on 9 August 2017.
[2] Twitter entry by @priyankachopra on 10 August 2017.

Rohini is known for shaping the careers of many leading celebrities but when asked about the role she plays in their success, she demurs, 'I feel that stars are born. But superstars are created. There is an X-factor that an actor is born with. The talent is ingrained. What we do is take that to another level. Perhaps we take them from point A to B.'

A regular on power lists in India, Rohini was awarded the 'Woman of the Decade in Celebrity Media' at 2017's Women's Economic Forum in London, weeks after being named one of India's Outstanding Women by *Outlook Business.* 'I am obsessed with awards and titles. I love them. It's a validation. It's like getting a report card,' she says candidly.

What role does Rohini play in a star's meteoric rise? Take Priyanka Chopra for example. Rohini has represented her since 2012. 'I love PC,' Rohini says, using the nickname the popular press has for the superstar. The two women, who share a strong professional relationship, are also close friends.

Over the past six years, the Bollywood actor's career has soared. One of the few Indian stars to bridge the gap between Hollywood and Bollywood, Priyanka now divides her time between the US and India. She has an impressive international fan base following her role in the American TV series *Quantico* and the film *Baywatch*.

'It would be unfair to say that I had a major part to play in building Priyanka Chopra,' Rohini insists. 'I've known her since we both began our careers and I've never seen anyone so determined, so hard-working and so ambitious. But we are extremely happy to be a significant part of her journey and I'm extremely proud of what Priyanka has achieved.'

When rumours surfaced in 2012 of Priyanka Chopra being involved with a married superstar, local media credited Rohini with turning things around for her. An article in Scroll.in, a leading Indian news website reported:[3]

Shortly after, Chopra made an appearance at a high profile party. All smiles and dressed in a gold number, she walked towards the

---

[3]   Chandrima Pal, 'Image Building', Scroll.in, 6 March 2017.

flashbulbs clutching Iyer's hand—a powerful statement about the trust she had placed in her crisis manager.

Rohini rubbishes that. 'None of this is true,' she says, making it clear the subject is a non-starter. Rohini says Priyanka and she would hang out at events even when they were not working together. 'So there was no public moment of her holding my hand or any of that.'

Discretion is an integral part of Rohini's personality. She will never break a client's trust, never utter a word that could tarnish a client's image.

There are many publicists working in Bollywood, but the top talent picks Rohini because, as Priyanka says, 'She is not someone who can be pulled down. She can go toe to toe with anyone in the industry and that's the kind of person you need as a publicist.'

For Rohini, the stars she manages aren't clients. 'They are friends,' she says.

This approach, which forms the DNA of Raindrop, sets it apart from competitors. Stars express their affection for her on social media but the greatest validation comes in the form of loyalty. Most of her star clients have stayed with her for years. Rohini represented Akshay Kumar for ten years. Vidya Balan was a client for just as long. Ask Balan about Raindrop Media and she answers, 'They are one of the best in the business.'

Rohini speaks fast but chooses her words carefully, which is hardly surprising given the business she is in. The thirty-six-year-old has a friendly face, framed by a trademark mane of highlighted curls. She is warm, easy to chat with and has the reliable air of a 3 a.m. friend. To many of the actors she manages, she is exactly that.

'She is my all am–pm friend,' says Sushant Singh Rajput. He met Rohini at a common friend's birthday party and the pair hit it off instantly. They have been close friends since and have also worked together. 'She is a happy insomniac like me and we are accessible almost all the time to each other. She is absolutely honest, giving, and her love for you is non-negotiable,' he says. 'She is a rockstar in the truest sense.'

Rohini is on call for her clients 24x7. She's always switched on. 'I never have to call her for anything or chase her and say we need to do this and do that. She's always on top of it,' Katrina Kaif says. 'She gets things done and she gets things done quickly. There is never a delay and that's important.'

Rohini admits she has no work–life balance but it doesn't bother her. She works long hours and free time is limited. 'Until I have a personal life, which I don't, I don't need to have work–life balance. I give time to my mother, I give time to my company. Apart from that, I have nothing else to do. When I do, I will think about it.'

She's devoted to her career and the pay-off is evident. Ask anyone who has signed on with her.

'I think she's very trustworthy,' says Katrina, who has known Rohini for twelve years. Katrina was working on the film *Humko Deewana Kar Gaye* when Rohini came to the set to meet the male lead of the film. Something about the diminutive publicist caught Katrina's attention. 'We chatted a bit, bumped into each other at a few places and I remember that she just seemed very caring,' Katrina recalls. 'There are lots of options for good publicists, but what I really look for in the people who work on my team is that they care on a personal level.' Katrina believes Rohini cares deeply.

'A lot of people do reputation management but their work is superficial,' Rohini says. 'I work on "inner engineering". Once I know the person, I find out what is holding them back from achieving something. In every relationship, you need someone to tell you that you can do it. It would not have happened if I had a cut-and-dry relationship with my clients. A lot of people say it's a negative point to be emotionally invested in my clients but that's the only way I work. How can I know them or see things in them if I am not close to them?'

Building that sort of intimate relationship takes time. Rohini earned Katrina's trust over the years. 'When she does advise me on something she tends to be right,' the actor says. 'I know that. Although at times I may still choose something else, I know her sense is right and she's always giving you correct advice, having analysed the situation and seen what is best for you so you always come out as a professional. I always trust what she is saying.'

The business of reputation management is a nascent one in the Hindi film industry, not more than a decade old. Till the early noughties, stars' lives were run by secretaries who sometimes were as well known as the stars themselves. Rekha was rarely seen without her secretary, Farzana. Rikku Rakesh Nath served as Madhuri Dixit's secretary for almost three decades. They managed stars' lives—they organized their schedules, granted interviews to journalists, issued statements on their behalf, kept track of their accounts, advised them on which brands to endorse, set up meetings for them and decided which promotional events they should attend.

'There was no method to this madness,' Rohini says, remembering the days before professional celebrity managers shook things up. 'If an actor went to three malls to promote a film and the movie was a success, every actor wanted to add a mall visit to his list of promotions. It was all trial and error. If one actor appeared on the cover of a particular magazine, it created a frenetic race amongst the others to get the same level of publicity. There was herd mentality.'

Media interviews were done on an ad hoc basis. Journalists who used to be taken along on outdoor shoots would just hang out with the actors. 'They used to talk about what song was being shot, what food was being served on the set. It was crazy!'

Instinctively, Rohini knew what the industry needed. She also knew she would be the one to fix it.

Raindrop. It's an unusual name for a media company but there's a good story behind it.

'*Raindrops keep falling on my head . . . they keep falling.*' B.J. Thomas' classic from *Butch Cassidy and the Sundance Kid* played softly on the car radio as Rohini drove to her friend and co-partner, Rahila Mirza's home in Bandstand. She had a lot on her mind. The two young women had been offered the opportunity of a lifetime—a chance to manage the publicity for a mega Bollywood film that had just been announced. The pair had done freelance publicity for smaller projects before. But a big Bollywood entertainer? That was an entirely different story.

Before they had time to digest the news, they needed to register their fledgling business as a company. 'We were kids, we were nineteen, we didn't want to look like we did not know what we are doing,' Rohini laughs. But first, they needed a name for their business.

'Raindrop?' suggested Rohini when she reached Rahila's home. 'It's one of my favourite words,' Rohini recalls years later, over a glass of wine at a stylish bar in Bandra where the waiter brings her 'her usual'—a glass of house Bellini. Rahila liked the name too and that's how Raindrop Media Pvt. Ltd was born.

The two girls, one five feet ten inches tall, the other, around five feet, often called 'the long and short of things', formed Raindrop to bring some order into Bollywood's public relations. 'We were two amateurs, realizing that we needed to bring about change. We were like, this has got to be more structured,' Rahila says. So they hired two more girls, who admittedly knew very little about cinema, and set up a small operation. 'We didn't think we were a mom and pop shop, by the way. We thought we were cool! There was a very delusional factor about us. But it was amazing,' Rahila says.

The film they had been approached to work on was *Main Hoon Na*— the much anticipated directorial debut of choreographer-turned-director and producer Farah Khan. Starring mega stars Shah Rukh Khan, Sushmita Sen and Sunil Shetty, the film had created a sensation the moment it was announced. Farah, who knew Rahila personally, hired the two girls. They would be responsible for the film's overall marketing strategy and take a 360 degree approach to promoting the movie. Entrusting two relatively inexperienced girls with the movie was a risk but Farah took the chance.

That single decision changed Rohini's life. 'Farah looked at me. Initially, she had her reservations on whether a kid like me would be able to manage the film. I'm so happy that she put her faith in me,' Rohini says. The film was a huge hit and Raindrop Media proved its mettle, making an instant name for itself in the cut-throat business of public relations. Farah and Rohini became firm friends and Farah continues to be Raindrop's client.

Working in public relations can be difficult—it is certainly not for everyone. 'Handling PR is one of the worst jobs,' says Farah. 'When all is good, it is thankless and when all is bad, you are blamed for everything that goes wrong.'

Dealing with celebrities means there are often ego clashes and histrionics involved. A good celebrity manager must be unflappable—and honest. 'What I like about Rohini is she is not fake,' says Farah. 'She calls a spade a spade. She will fight with people and she will tell people "what you are doing is wrong". They may not like it at that time but after a point, it's a quality people appreciate. When you think about it, you say to yourself, "Shit! Rohini had told me, don't do this movie."'

Is Rohini feared as much as she is loved? 'Yes,' Farah smiles. 'That's a great quality to have in this industry.'

Though her principal job is to handle reputations, Rohini often advises clients on professional choices. 'Deciding which films a star should or should not work on or which brands they should endorse does not fall into the purview of a reputation management agency,' she explains. That's usually handled by an actor's management company. 'But because we have been working with our artists and brands for so long, they are like family and they consult Raindrop on films and brands they want to sign.' Rohini, part friend, part reputation manager, part brand consultant never says no when someone seeks her advice.

In the age of Instagram and Twitter, most stars communicate with their fans directly via social media. Rohini encourages this, explaining, 'I would always advise superstars to speak to fans directly because the public needs to know the stars. They need to have an emotional connection with an actor to go buy a ticket of their film.' Rohini can't create that. She says her job is to manage perception. 'Any actor can walk into this place right now. If you don't know him, you may think "Oh, maybe he's rude or whatever". That's a perception. My job is to manage that and say this is not who you think he is, but this is the real person.'

Rohini is known to be fiercely protective of her clients. Having been part of the Hindi film world for fifteen years, she knows how challenging it is to make it in this field. 'I hate it when people say actors have it easy. They don't. They have the most difficult lives ever.'

'They can't have a bad mood day, a bad hair day, or just a bad day. The show must go on. If something goes wrong, they have to work. If someone dies, they have to report for a shoot because forty-five people are answerable to them, and they are also answerable to their production houses and their staff. It's a very, very tough life. Of course they earn whatever they earn but if they have chosen to be in that line, they deserve to earn it. They make a *lot* of sacrifices.'

Rohini, an only child, was born in Mumbai on 9 August 1982. Her father, Krishnan S. Iyer, was the head of a pharmaceutical company and her mother, Geeta, a consultant at a builder's firm. Her parents divorced when she was in the grade 4. 'I was too young to remember it,' Rohini says. 'I was so attached to my mom, I never felt the lack of another parent. I was pretty much brought up by my mom only. I owe a lot to her for making me the way I am.'

She did not grow up in a conservative environment but she says, 'Like all south Indian families, there was a heavy emphasis on academics.' She attended Canossa Convent High School, Mahim, and St Mary's High School. She describes herself as a serious student. 'I was always that crazy kid who used to wait for my report card and I wanted to be ranked first or second in class. If I wasn't, I would cry for days. I was very, very competitive. I used to hate anyone else winning. I am still like that.'

She started reading at an early age. It was the pre-Internet era. Kids could play outdoors or curl up with a book and read. Rohini read. 'We had a library at home and would collect books. Discussing history, culture, politics and philosophy was something that was ingrained in me since childhood and has shaped me as an individual.'

Books would influence her but films define her. As a child, she was mad about movies. 'I was the only Tam-Brahm filmy Hindi-speaking child who used to bunk classes and watch films,' she chuckles. 'When I was really little, I used to be obsessed with Amitabh Bachchan. Of course, the whole country was, but I was too.' She loved *Sholay*. Guru Dutt's *Pyaasa* was another favourite. 'For me, it's one of his best works and it taught me the most amazing truth about life—*Yeh duniya agar mil bhi jaaye toh kya hai?*'

She watched Rajinikanth, Kamal Haasan and Mani Ratnam films and those that starred Shashi Kapoor, Shammi Kapoor and Raj Kapoor. *Mera Naam Joker* and *Prem Rog* top her list. 'These films were made before my time but I used to love nostalgia, I still do,' Rohini says. 'Then there's *Andaaz* and *Aag*. I've watched Dilip Saab's *Devdas* several times and Sanjay Bhansali's *Devdas* and *Khamoshi* twenty-two times. And I cannot forget to mention *Mughal-E-Azam* and *Mother India*.'

She didn't limit herself to Hindi films. Rohini devoured French movies, old Hollywood classics, Tamil, Malayalam, and even Iranian cinema—anything she chanced upon. Sometimes she would catch a film on TV, at times she would go to the theatre, or tune into Turner Classic Movies. She would watch movies on VHS tapes and LPs. She gets animated remembering the movies she watched as a young girl. 'I loved Quentin Tarantino films like *Reservoir Dogs* and *Pulp Fiction*. *True Romance* written by him is among my favourites. Akira Kurosawa, Charlie Chaplin, Elia Kazan's work, Marlon Brando and Paul Newman's early work,' she carries on breathlessly, adding that she was heavily influenced by James Dean, Sophia Loren, Elizabeth Taylor, Katherine Hepburn, Audrey Hepburn and Bette Davis. 'I loved *All About Eve*. I was deeply influenced by Frank Capra's work. Godard's *Breathless* is one of my favourites. Belmondo is my favourite French actor.' Her list is long. The girl who was serious about cinema watched a mixed bag of films, often two a day!

Rohini viewed the movies with a critical eye. She would pay attention to the way a particular shot was framed or how an actor delivered lines in a specific scene. She was fascinated by the overall business of moviemaking. 'Since I was a child I always wanted to do something related to the movies. Because that was my fantasy world, my escape from reality.'

She describes 'reality' as boring. 'I hated routine and fixed schedules and that is what I associated reality with. Movies helped me escape routine. I cannot be tied to a watch and cannot be bound by reality and schedules. I don't subscribe to the theory of waking up in the morning and then going to work or eating at a particular time.'

When her mother, who remains a guiding force in Rohini's life, realized movies were more than just a form of entertainment for her daughter, she sat Rohini down for a chat. 'She understood that I wasn't in it for the glamour,' Rohini says. 'Once she spoke to me, she realized I was there for the craft.' At the age of sixteen, Rohini knew the movie bug was real.

By the time she started college at St Xaviers in Mumbai, nothing else mattered. She was studying arts but did not enjoy it. 'I used to sit in on lectures and think, "Why am I learning this? How is it going to help me in my real life?" I can safely say that experience comes from learning on the job. I believe life is the best teacher.'

The film enthusiast picks a scene from a movie to describe how she felt while she was a college student. 'I was like that girl from Woody Allen's film, *Purple Rose of Cairo*.' In the film, a girl in the audience imagines herself entering the screen and living the life being depicted on it. 'I was always daydreaming. I was always fantasizing about an alternative reality while I was in the classroom.'

So the studious girl did the unthinkable. She dropped out of college.

It was the summer of 1990. Legendary film journalist Bhawana Somaaya had just launched a new film magazine called *G*. Word got around that the magazine was hiring writers.

One day, Somaaya's telephone operator called her to say a young girl was standing outside her office, requesting to meet her. 'My door opened to a smiling face,' Somaaya recalls. In walked a teenage girl, blazing with confidence. She looked around at the walls of the office adorned with magazine covers and said, 'I think I have the making of a terrific journalist.' Somaaya was intrigued. In her twenty-year career, she had never heard that line from someone looking for work. She decided to give Rohini a chance.

Somaaya asked the rookie reporter to write an article on the portrayal of dacoits in Indian cinema. She gave her a week to do it. Rohini returned the next day and submitted the piece. Somaaya hired Rohini on the spot.

'She was young, vivacious and raring to go. She was reverential and yet unstoppable. I knew when I set my eyes on her that she was going to be someone special and soon,' Somaaya says.

Somaaya's hunch—and Rohini's promise—came through. Rohini did a terrific job at *G* and later at the film magazine *Stardust*. But her true calling lay somewhere else.

'I am not a deadline person,' Rohini says bluntly. 'I love journalism and I have a lot of respect for it. It's a great field.' It just wasn't for her. She became a film journalist to get a foot into the movie industry. Once she was part of that world, she knew she belonged in it—but not as a reporter.

The timing was fortuitous. As Rohini began making inroads into the Hindi film industry, international studios started setting up shop in India and introduced a more systematic way of working. Stars began giving the responsibility of their calendars, career choices and image management to professionals. The days of the ubiquitous secretaries started waning. Sensing an opportunity here, many entrepreneurs, including Rohini and Rahila, jumped into this space.

Rohini doesn't like being called an entrepreneur. 'It has the sound of money to it with which I have a problem,' she says. 'Money is great. I love it but that doesn't drive me.' Her love for cinema does.

The person who says greed is not a dirty word says that for her, greed is not monetary. 'If you are good at your job, money will come. There's this quote of Rumi that I stand by,' Rohini says, '"If all you want is money, you'll be bought and sold all your life." I don't want to be bought or sold because I'm not for sale.'

A few years after establishing Raindrop and enjoying early success with hits like *Main Hoon Na* and *Yuva*, Rahila decided to exit the company to pursue a career in production. 'But for Rohini, *this* was her passion,' Rahila says. She handed over the reins to Rohini, who decided to have a go at it alone, against the advice of many friends. People called and said, 'Are you sure?' She didn't have much money in her account but whatever little she had, she had earned herself. 'I don't take money from my dad or mom. I've never done that,' Rohini says emphatically. She had been earning since she was a teenage film journalist and had some savings. She used that as capital for her business.

Rahila and Rohini remain friends and meet whenever Rahila, now based in Dubai, returns to Mumbai. 'I had no idea she would bring Raindrop to this extent,' Rahila says, with obvious pride and a little surprise. 'Kudos to that girl, kudos.'

Today, Raindrop consists of a team of fifty people who manage six verticals that serve regional cinema, rising stars, fashion and lifestyle brands, digital services, and public relations—plus a division through which it acts as a media director to films. Raindrop currently has offices in Delhi and Mumbai but plans to expand the business across India.

Rahila says Raindrop is where it is because of Rohini's business acumen—but the real driver is the integrity of Rohini's friendships. 'If I had to pick one thing that works for her, and this is being as candid as I can be, she has always maintained her relationships with people. Even if you have not signed with her as a client, if you need her to manage a situation for you, she will step up and help you. If I pick up the phone and call her and say, "Iyer, I need this done," she will not hesitate even 1 per cent. She will say, "Ya ya, I will sort this for you." And I know that it is done.'

The willingness to help is genuine, not driven by the need to please others. With Rohini, there is no sugar-coating involved. 'No, none at all,' Rohini says. 'I feel if I don't tell my clients the truth, they will lose respect for me. They may be angry about a particular point and walk out on me. I have had actors who have had fights with me, they've not spoken to me for a month, six months, one year. Whenever they have come back to me, the only thing they've said is, "I am just so glad you told me." So I stick to that.'

Sometimes the process gets unpleasant, but fallouts are part and parcel of the film world. 'I don't have a thick skin. I get hurt all the time,' Rohini admits, suddenly appearing a lot younger than her age. She copes by remaining focused on her job. 'I will still show up. It's autopilot. But personally, it hurts. My actor friends call me and say you've been there for so long, how can this affect you? I say, it *is* affecting me, I have to deal with it. I drink coffee, play gangsta music, and I move on.'

Rohini is emotional and sensitive, qualities that help and hurt her. Farah, says, 'I always tell her, just detach and do your work. Why are you getting so upset that he is doing the wrong thing or he is signing the wrong movie? She gets very personally involved but then I think that could also be a strength because she goes all out to make sure the best things happen for all her clients.'

The reputation manager lives by a mantra—never let success go to your head, never let failure get to your heart. Fate is fickle. Rohini has witnessed several cases of actors rising rapidly to achieve superstardom, only to see their careers fall flat soon after. In the fickle world of movies, it's a roller-coaster ride. 'I just feel when they are on a high, they lose perspective because you are surrounded by people who only tell you how amazing you are. When you fail, nobody wants to be around. It's sad but I guess that's the case.'

In her inimitable style, Rohini has blazed her way through a male-dominated industry. She is aware of the gender dynamic within Bollywood and admits men get intimidated by strong women. 'Yes. True. They do. They do,' she says with emphasis. 'When you are starting out as a woman, they are encouraging and supportive. It's more like, "let's see what she can do". But when you reach a particular place or start to threaten them in some way, there is a thin line that gets drawn. Then they are wary of you.'

Though there are so many women working both on and off the screen today, they are not paid at par. The gender pay gap is a very real problem. 'Of course it exists,' Rohini says. 'It's been there for the longest. Actresses do get paid a lot less than actors or mainstream heroes. But slowly, I can see that changing.

Vidya Balan says the Hindi film industry has a peculiar attitude towards successful women. Assertive women are often perceived as domineering or ambitious—which is not meant as a compliment. 'They would say that Rohini is very aggressive because she is a woman who is demanding the pound of flesh due to her artist, and that was not OK. But today with all the success she has seen, they don't call her aggressive any more. Now, they call her a go-getter. That is an interesting shift that has happened.'

This go-getter is shy about her private life but her eyes light up when she speaks of her mother, who has been a deep influence. 'I have seen her manage work, manage me, manage her life,' Rohini says. 'She never complained but made sure I was happy. I have always been inspired by her because she did that with limited resources. I never had to ask for anything because it was provided for. Besides, she did all this as a single mother.'

Geeta still fusses over her daughter. She packs a case of water bottles in Rohini's car so that her daughter, who is always on the move, stays hydrated. 'I don't drink water, I forget to!' Rohini laughs. 'At the end of the day, before my mother and I say hello to each other, she will ask, "Have you had water today?"'

Rohini has a lot on her mind these days—mainly, more movies and more work. She's thinking about an international division and experimenting with app-based communication tools. There's no blueprint for it yet. 'I'll figure it out as I go along. I never plan ahead. It comes to me. If it works, it works. Luckily it has worked so far.'

Don't mistake that for complacency. 'I suffer from chronic dissatisfaction,' Rohini says, laughing. She says she wakes up feeling the same way every morning—that she must get out of bed and make the most of the day. 'It's a realization that I have so much more to achieve and so much more to do.' Bollywood's most coveted publicist says she hasn't even got started.

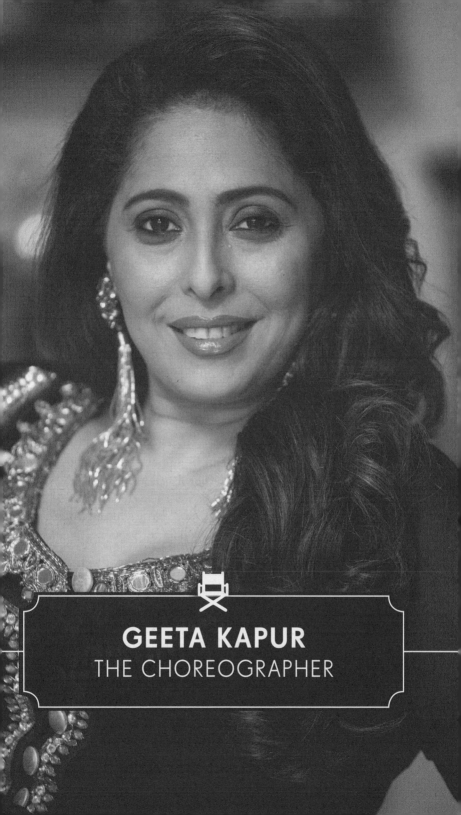

GEETA KAPUR
THE CHOREOGRAPHER

S tupendofantabulouslyfantasmagoricallymagical

That's the tongue-twister choreographer Geeta Kapur coined to compliment a particularly impressive dance contestant on season one of *Dance India Dance*, the popular dance competition TV show that premiered on Zee TV in 2008.

It's a mouthful, but it has become Geeta's trademark. She uses it frequently, on social media and in public appearances—to praise and encourage people, and to wax lyrical about life. The phrase captures Geeta's personality. Exuberant and cheerful, Geeta cracks jokes, is seldom serious and makes lots of self-deprecating comments. She pokes fun at her size and her front teeth. Yet when it comes to dance, she's passionate and focused. Geeta is one of India's most lauded choreographers.

Thanks to television, 'Geeta Maa' beams into our homes most nights of the week as one of the three judges on *Super Dancer*, a dance reality show on Sony TV, alongside Shilpa Shetty Kundra and Sajid Khan. Coined when Geeta wasn't even forty, the honorific has stuck. Young and old alike, across the country, call the forty-five-year old Geeta Maa. So does the press. A guru, teacher, judge—given her maternal instincts, the term suits her.

Moving with grace and agility, Geeta has taught many Bollywood stars how to bust a move. Remember Katrina Kaif in the chart-topping item number '*Sheila ki Jawani*'? Geeta co-choreographed the song with mentor and guru Farah Khan, who in turn received *Filmfare*'s best choreography award in 2011 for it. Actor Shahid Kapoor publicly thanked Geeta for teaching him his first dance step as a child for the Pepsi *Yeh Dil Maange More* ad.

'Geeta is fabulous at her job and she's a fabulous dancer,' says film-maker and ace choreographer Farah Khan, who has known Geeta since she was fifteen. Geeta has danced, assisted and choreographed with Farah for years.

'I used to do dance shows and Geeta was my dancer and you would see her move, and compared to her, the heroine looked like shit,' Farah says. 'She could demonstrate steps exceptionally. She's a trained classical dancer in Kathak and Bharatanatyam and she was a great help to me because I have no training in Indian classical dance at all.'

Vidya Balan is full of praise for Geeta—not just because of the way she moves. 'I was petrified of dancing and I remember her being extremely encouraging and nurturing,' says the actor. 'She makes you feel comfortable. For someone who is not a natural dancer like me, that is very precious. That's the personality you see on TV. People love her, from TV audiences to people who have worked with her. Geeta has just got a lovely vibe.'

Shilpa Shetty Kundra, a fellow judge on *Super Dancer*, says that Geeta has a grasp on her craft. 'She is a graceful dancer. Being a choreographer she's handled actors and actors, are nothing short of children. She knows how to pamper them.'

Director Tarun Mansukhani and Geeta go back a long way. 'I've known her since 1997–98 when we were all assistants on *Kuch Kuch Hota Hai* and we formed a bond,' he says. He describes her as an amazing dancer.

From Indian cinema's earliest days, music and dance have been an integral part of the storyline. Classical Indian dance forms, like Bharatanatyam, Kathak, Odissi and Kathakali, were fused with folk techniques like Lavani to produce a unique Bollywood hybrid style. The world over, 'screwing the light bulb', and shaking the hips are seen as quintessential Hindi film moves. But of course, movie dance moves are far more intricate. Effort, sweat, inspiration and emotion go into making sequences that make a film come alive. Bollywood dance moves are so rigorous that cities across the world, from New York to London to even Moscow and Seoul, offer exercise classes inspired by them.

Facial expressions are as significant as body manoeuvres in Indian dance. The rise of an eyebrow, the hint of a smile, the expansiveness of the eyes, all convey feeling. Geeta's face is a dancer's asset—expressive and attractive.

'Geeta's like a storm when she's dancing,' says Rick Roy, a close friend and designer who worked with Geeta on the 2012 film *Joker*.

Geeta has worked on some of the biggest films in recent decades. She enjoys training, whether it's a famous star or an unknown actor. When it comes to performing herself, however, this super dancer still gets nervous before going on stage. Her hands and feet go cold. She trembles. She knows that this will be her true test, this is when her craft comes into motion. Despite momentary anxiety, she loves the do-or-die thrill of a live performance.

How does someone with no *filmi* connection become a top-notch choreographer in the industry? Lady Luck and wonderful mentors play a part, but it also requires talent, grit and determination. In a Hindi film, Geeta's life would be attributed to destiny. Perhaps it is so. Her mother, Rani Kapur, has said that Geeta loved to perform as a child and often danced on the bed. Although her mother didn't know it then, she was wise to enrol little Geeta in dance classes.

Geeta Kapur was born on a rainy, thundering day on 5 July 1973, at Northcote Nursing Home in south Mumbai's Colaba. Were the skies dancing as the gods showered the baby into this world? Geeta's mother certainly thinks so.

The family lived near the iconic Leopold Café in Colaba. Geeta's father worked for numerous airlines, he travelled frequently. Rani and Geeta lived with Rani's parents. Geeta's maternal grandfather, a chef on the cruise liner *Queen Mary*, was away for chunks of time. That left three generations of women together in a small room. While Geeta's grandmother and mother doted on her, times were tough. It was a 'hand-to-mouth existence,' Geeta says.

Thankfully, St Anne's High School in Fort was a happy place. 'I loved school, it was one of the best times of my life and I didn't realize it till I went into the real world,' Geeta says with a laugh.

The school day would end by 3:30 p.m. After a quick lunch, Rani would take her daughter to various after-school classes. There was swimming but mostly there was dance. Geeta studied Bharatanatyam with Hema Malini Chari in Cuffe Parade. 'Geeta was a regular student and very good,' recalls the teacher. 'I choreographed a popular song *Ek Radha Ek Meera* and Geeta danced beautifully to it. I am so proud of her success.'

Geeta also learned folk dance. Dancing took up at least six hours a week. Geeta often wonders what life would have been like if her mother hadn't enrolled her in those dance classes. To her, dancing was innate, a way to express her creativity and channel her energies.

Hindi movies were a source of great pleasure for the Kapurs. Unfortunately, Geeta could only watch them on videotape because local cinemas near her house played mostly English movies. She admired dancers like Helen, Rekha and Madhuri Dixit, whom she still holds in awe. When Govinda burst on the scene in the 1980s, Geeta was mesmerized by his fluid dance style. As a thirteen-year-old, she first saw him in the 1986 release *Ilzaam* and loved his moves in the song '*Main Aaya Tere Liye*'. She had never seen any actor dance like that. She dreamed of dancing with him.

Are some things fated? From Geeta's experience, it would seem so. Even though she didn't know it then, Geeta met her future in 1989, when she was in grade 10. She saw a group of young performers doing a Western-style dance on stage. One of the female dancers, about seven years older than Geeta, danced with remarkable grace and agility. Geeta immediately bought the videotape of the performance and played it at home. Her father remarked on how wonderful the same female dancer was. 'My father complimented that girl and it pissed me off,' Geeta recalls. 'I thought, I can do this! I watched that tape so many times. Rewind. Pause. Play. Repeat. I learned that dance.'

Later, when Geeta went to meet her choreographer friend Padmini Haldankar, she was told that the much admired dancer had fallen ill. Geeta showed Padmini the same dance moves—the ones she had learned by watching the videotape on repeat. The choreographer immediately asked her to fill in as a replacement.

When Geeta and the dancer met again, the latter thanked Geeta for filling in. That dancer was Farah Khan.

'All the dancers idolized Farah. She and her dance partner could do lifts and we were just in awe.' The two have a special, unshakeable bond. Geeta's devotion to Farah is absolute. She refers to Farah has her 'mom' and is grateful to her for teaching her and providing her with opportunities for professional growth. In a cut-throat industry where many actresses have male mentors, a woman championing another woman is rare and deserves to be celebrated.

After finishing grade 10, Geeta began performing with dancers across the city. Javed Jaffrey was a star performer at that time and Geeta quickly progressed from being a back-up dancer on his shows to dancing in the front with him. Jaffrey used to tell her that she was too heavy and didn't have control over her body. 'Trust me, I am heavy today—back then I had a waist of twenty-four and that was heavy for him,' Geeta jokes, rolling her eyes. She loved working with Jaffrey and enjoyed the intimate group rehearsals at his house, where dancers ate, practised and hung out together.

By then, Farah had begun choreographing dance performances and Geeta joined her troupe. At sixteen, she was the youngest. She went on to do numerous shows and music videos which were extremely popular in that era.

In 1994, Geeta met director Ken Ghosh, who was India's top music video creator. Amongst the iconic videos Ghosh made were Baba Sehgal's *Dil Dhadke* (1992), Alisha Chinai's *Made in India* (1995) and Nusrat Fateh Ali Khan's *Afreen Afreen* (1996). By 1997, Ken Ghosh had made about one-third of India's 150-odd music videos, according to journalist Anupama Chopra. In a magazine article, she wrote that his work was 'happy, peppy-stuff'.[1]

When Geeta ended up dancing in one of Ken's music videos, she caught his eye. 'Geeta was the dancer who remembered all the moves and helped other dancers,' Ghosh says.

Clearly impressed with her, Ken asked Geeta to choreograph some of his videos. She was flabbergasted. She had never given choreography any thought. She immediately called Farah. 'She told me not to think twice, that this is the way forward,' Geeta says.

Her first gig was choreographing Suchitra Krishnamoorthy's *Dole Dole* in 1995. Looking at it now, the video is typical of the 1990s—a young, urban, college love song. It features a curly, long-haired girl in silhouette, dancing vigorously in the dark. This was Geeta. Ken kept telling her to smile while she danced. When she saw the video later, Geeta realized her face couldn't be seen. She hadn't realized lighting mattered!

Ghosh set up Shadow Films, a production house, and Geeta worked there with him. She handled every role, from assistant to choreographer to dancer to actor to writing production reports. She was even the stenographer because her mother had made sure Geeta took typing and shorthand classes in school!

---

[1] Anupama Chopra, *India Today*, 4 August 1997.

At Shadow Films, Geeta received a salary of Rs 15,000 a month. Her salary helped support not just her immediate family but also extended relatives who were hard up. The renumeration didn't go far. Geeta realized she needed something more lucrative. Once again, she turned to 'mom' Farah, who was blunt: Geeta couldn't dance in shows because audiences wanted slim girls and Geeta didn't fit the stereotype. Instead, Farah suggested Geeta assist her. It was painful leaving Ghosh, but it was time to move on.

Farah had started choreographing films. *Duplicate*, starring Shah Rukh Khan and Juhi Chawla, was Geeta's first film as Farah's assistant. She never looked back. Geeta enjoyed being on set, teaching steps. She also loved working for Farah. 'Farah is one hell of a secure boss. She gives you so many opportunities. If she's not taking on a job, she hands it over to someone she trusts. She has no insecurities.'

In 1999, Geeta got a choreography gig for *Pyar Mein Kabhi Kabhi*. Songs like '*Woh Pehli Baar*' and '*Dil Se Mere Dur Na Jaana*' show young lovers singing and frolicking through jungles and other scenic locales in a manner typical of Hindi cinema in the 1990s.

Two years later, Geeta helped Farah on Karan Johar's *Kabhi Khushi Kabhie Gham*. They shot frenetically, day and night, for the hit song '*Banno ki Saheli*'. The film was replete with all the elements of a KJo film—lavish sets, wedding scenes, high drama; and so it was with the songs and dances. Tons of backup dancers doing intricate steps were involved.

That same year, Farah and her team were brought on board to choreograph songs for *Asoka*, starring Shah Rukh Khan and Kareena Kapoor. Director Santosh Sivan called Geeta up one night and asked her to work on the song '*Roshni Se*'. They were to shoot the next day. As a reference, Sivan showed her a photo of a mirrored table. Geeta was flummoxed. What could she do with this opaque idea? But then she had a eureka moment. The two actors—Shah Rukh Khan and Kareena—would appear entwined like tree branches and mirror each other.

Geeta considers that song one of her finest works. 'I have never done a dance like that in my life. It can't be repeated. A lot of people come to you and say, "Can you do it again?" But I say no, because you get stuck in a rut. It's better to move forward and innovate.'

Ask her about item songs, and she bristles. Bollywood has received considerable flak for suggestive dance numbers whose sole aim appears to be to titillate. 'We are in the business of entertainment,' Geeta says matter-of-factly. 'Why aren't people asked to change their thought processes? Put a guy in an item song! Shah Rukh Khan has a six-pack, Salman Khan shows his body. Aren't we objectifying them?

'Once upon a time, Helen-ji was thought to be risque but today we look upon her as iconic,' she says, referring to Helen Richardson Khan, the Indian actress known for introducing sensuous cabaret dance to Hindi cinema. 'I don't understand why we are such hypocrites.' Instead, she urges parents to raise their children to respect women.

What bothers her is that musicals, so central to movies in India are losing their importance. As Farah said in a recent interview, 'I think the whole song-and-dance thing is dwindling unless you are making a dance film. I don't think it is there. The song culture is going away. Songs are played in the background.'[2]

Geeta couldn't agree more. Opportunities to innovate in film for dance are waning. Today's stories are more realistic. From the 1970s onward, films made for pure entertainment had an element of wild fantasy. 'Nowadays everyone wants reality, so song and dance have become a background score. When people call me to say they want to film an emotional song but it's in the background, I think, "Do they really need me?" It's the director's vision then, you don't need a choreographer.'

Typically, a production company approaches a choreographer on behalf of a director. The first step involves understanding the storylines for the songs. Next comes the music. When the choreographer hears the melody, he or she provides input on steps, emotion and sequencing. For Geeta, this creativity happens on the spot. She just starts dancing and instinctively knows the next move. Some steps work, others don't, in which case she and her dancers go back and start again. It is a feeling from within that spurs the movement. Her dance moves have soul.

---

[2] 'Farah Khan: Song and dance culture in Bollywood is fading away', *Indian Express,* 11 September 2017.

In India, film music budgets can be huge. In the past, music comprised a significant chunk of a movie's overall budget. These days, it can be significantly less. Some producers are known to spend up to one crore on a song-and-dance sequence, involving hundreds of backup artistes, multiple costumes changes and elaborate sets.

Geeta's most enjoyable experiences were filming for *Kuch Kuch Hota Hai* (1998) and *Main Hoon Na* (2004). The latter, Farah's directorial debut, is especially meaningful for Geeta because she was bestowed the honour of giving the mahurat clap. In Indian cinema, the person who gives the clap is supposed to bring good luck to the film.

Farah says she never thought Geeta would last with her as long as she did because she was so young when she entered the profession. 'She became so inherently responsible that even though I am anal, she is worse,' Farah jokes. 'For *Bombay Dreams* I had her in charge of the dance crew and she had it down to a T, she was so meticulous and detailed,' she says, referring to the 2002 musical that debuted in London and later travelled to Broadway. 'I would sometimes fight with her and say she had become an *angrez*.'

Geeta takes her job seriously and works hard. It upsets her that showbiz dancing is not taken as seriously in India as in other parts of the world. She realized the difference when she rehearsed for *Bombay Dreams* in the UK. 'The first thing you experience is discipline, which desperately needs to be taught in India. If rehearsal was at 10 a.m., dancers would come in at 8 a.m. because they didn't want to be late. I realized things can be done calmly, properly, and not in some kind of crazy, organized chaos which is how it happens here.'

On both a film and TV sets, Geeta doesn't dominate. On the reality shows she judges, she is effervescent but not overwhelming. Her go-with-the flow personality ensures that. She's a mentor and an inspiration to many dancers and aspiring choreographers. It's her way of paying it forward.

As friend Rick Roy says, 'When she performs it's one thing, but when she's training people, she's so patient. She can make anything dance.'

Choreographer and dancer Ruel Dausan Varidani, who's from the Philippines, met Geeta while filming the song '*Just Chill*', choreographed by Farah for the Salman Khan—Katrina Kaif film *Maine Pyaar Kyun Kiya* in 2004. Over 100 dancers had auditioned and Varidani had been selected as Geeta and Farah's assistant. Geeta helped train him. 'It's only because of Geeta that I am where I am, she pushed me,' he says. 'She is very particular when it comes to work, and after work, she takes care of you. If she says something bad, she will apologize if she feels she has hurt you. With any big film, Geeta always messages to congratulate me. She never forgets.'

Faisal Khan also considers Geeta a mentor. Khan first met Geeta as a contestant in 2011 in the third season of *Dance India Dance* and later on *Li'l Masters* in 2012. He remembers telling Geeta how nervous he was before a performance. Her reply soothed him. 'She said ultimately it's your spontaneity and energy on stage, just do it, *jaan lagao*. She taught me not to over-express, that expressions have to be perfect.' More than that though, Khan marvels at Geeta Maa's humility and at how grounded she is. 'Sometimes in front of a celebrity you get nervous but when I first met and talked to her, I felt she was someone I have known for a long time. And yes, she's very motherly.'

In an industry known for its pretence and lack of authentic friendships, Geeta's generosity of spirit is echoed by anyone who knows her well. Rick Roy says, 'She's one of the nicest, warmest people in the business. She is genuine. People are drawn to her.' Ken Ghosh agrees. 'There are a lot of talented people. But it's your personality, warmth and genuineness that sets you apart and that's what Geeta has.'

Unfortunately, dancing comes at a physical cost. Geeta has suffered umpteen injuries, including three slipped discs. She comes from a generation where safety was not paramount, where pads and special flooring were unheard of. Falling on the floor was par for the course. Luckily, she has a huge threshold for pain, she says.

Today she rarely choreographs for films. She enjoys judging dance shows on television instead. In 2008, she was approached to judge *Dance India Dance*. Television changed her life. She's now a known public figure, her talent no longer hidden. It also pays well. Geeta recently moved into a spacious new home along with her mother.

Eighteen years ago, she co-founded Work Station with her associate Binny Johny. Work Station handles all her work including bookings since Geeta doesn't have an outside agency managing her. It has five 'work family members,' as she refers to them, including a sound engineer. Eventually, Geeta hopes to utilize Work Station to bring aspiring talent under her wing.

Over the years, she has had the opportunity to work alongside people she once idolized as a child. As a teenager, she was a huge fan of Govinda's and in the early 1990s, when she did a small cameo with him at the Filmfare awards, she was ecstatic. Govinda had twirled her! Geeta remembers thinking that she didn't want to have a bath for the next four days. In 2015, she and Govinda were co-judges for *Dance India Dance Super Moms*. 'Who could have thought that this was possible?' Geeta says.

In 2015, Geeta moved to another reality show, *Super Dancer*. Judging dance shows has been great fun. It's much less physically laborious and she loves meeting new talent—especially children. It is tricky though to not hurt another person's ego. 'You try to make sure the kid who is dancing in front of you is told to go nicely, without punching him or her in the stomach.' Shilpa Shetty says Geeta is a diligent worker and wonderful at what she does. 'She's got those skills of treating children with kid gloves which is what we need on the show. She's great fun. I see that she's come up the hard way and I have a lot of respect for people who have come up on their own.'

In December 2017, Geeta had another fan-girl moment when the legendary Rekha made a guest appearance on *Super Dancer*. 'She came on set and as I went towards her, she cried "Geetu" and hugged me,' Geeta marvels. 'I didn't know what hit me!'

Given the proliferation of dance talent shows on television, choreographers are more abundant today than a decade ago. Geeta jokes about how reality TV shows, including the ones she judges, have ruined it for everyone. 'But seriously, I am very happy that people think of choreography as a profession, that there are job opportunities, because in my time, there were not. Today every dancer thinks he or she is a choreographer, but that's a problem too!'

As for the future, Geeta would love to do a big musical production for theatre along the lines of *Bombay Dreams* but bemoans the lack of budgets. Even when she's hired to perform at live shows, it's a tough slog because everyone wants out-of-the-box ideas at minimal cost. 'No one wants to invest. We have sold you the Oscars but end up doing the annual day function,' she says with a laugh.

Geeta wants to choreograph songs where the viewer can linger over the visual, feel the emotion the music conveys, feel the breeze or the rain being portrayed on screen. But till that happens, Geeta Maa continues to beam into our homes, bright smile in place, encouraging India's future super dancers—how Stupendofantabulouslyfantasmagoricallymagical.

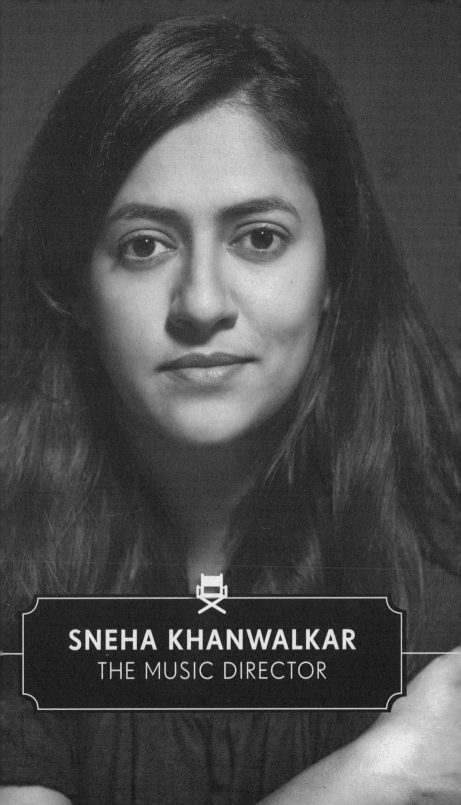

SNEHA KHANWALKAR
THE MUSIC DIRECTOR

Before daybreak, when the sky over the central Indian city of Indore was still ink blue, young Sneha Khanwalkar stirred in bed. As she rubbed the sleep from her eyes, her maternal grand-aunt, a petite lady wearing a 'bum divider'—Sneha's term for the way a traditional Maharashtrian sari is draped between the legs—pottered around in the kitchen, preparing tea for her husband. It was 3 a.m. The patriarch of the house, respected musician Pandit Vamanrao Rajurkar, would rise an hour later and immediately turn to his tanpura. The humming, pulsating drone of the stringed instrument would fill room after room, morning after morning.

It was the late 1980s and Sneha wasn't even ten years old. She would join her cousins for sleepovers at the old family home which Sneha likens to a '*train ka dabba*'—it had a long corridor with several rooms off it. The children knew the drill. They would wake up early to 'Baba' playing his tanpura. The pure, raw sound nourished the little girl huddled under a blanket. That sensation is burnt into her mind. 'I wish I could go back to that time. It was amazing,' Sneha says.

Sneha, now thirty-four, is a prominent music director in the Hindi film industry. As a woman, she stands apart in a field dominated by men. She sees herself as a storyteller. 'Music allows you to feel an emotion by time-travelling into your own library of events and memories. I feel that composing for films allows you to make a song for a specific emotion that underlines the story.'

Sneha's musical style defies categorization. It is unique: she fuses funky, contemporary beats with traditional Indian sounds. Her work on *Oye Lucky! Lucky Oye!* and the *Gangs of Wasseypur* series introduced India to a fresh musical aesthetic. Unconventional and alternative, the soundtracks for both these films were instant hits.

Her professional breakthrough occurred when she wasn't even thirty. Suddenly, the press, both domestic and international, could not get enough of this young composer. As part of its retrospective on a century of Indian cinema, the *Guardian* newspaper published a piece on the 'Top 10 Indian Cinema Soundtracks'.[1] Sneha's *Gangs of Wasseypur* made the list.

---

[1] 'Top 10 Indian Cinema Soundtracks', *Guardian*, 25 July 2013.

The newspaper wrote: 'This small-town gangster epic set in northeast India has a soundtrack like no other: bawdy Bhojpuri ditties and women's folk songs covering lusty liaisons and good-for-nothing-men, complement the film's blood-and-guts earthiness. Meanwhile the Indo-patois of I'm a Hunter (chorus: "She wants to see my gun") and the nursery-rhyme dancehall of Tain To To are refreshing and utterly bonkers. Take a bow, Sneha Khanwalkar. She has just turned 30 and is among a handful of female musical directors in Indian cinema.'

'Her tastes are dramatically different from Bollywood,' says Dibakar Banerjee who directed *Love, Sex Aur Dhokha* and *Oye Lucky! Lucky Oye!* Sneha composed the music for both these films. A music buff himself, Dibakar wanted a fresh, experimental sound for *Oye Lucky!* So he picked a composer whose sensibility matched his. 'Sneha and I share a healthy antipathy towards sentimental music,' he says, a reference to the soft, lilting melodies that have historically defined much of Bollywood's music. 'I think sentimental music happens when an urban middle-class person wants to weep over a glass of whisky and get into a never never land of nostalgia.'

Sneha rebels against that kind of sentimentality. It doesn't inspire her. 'There are so many people who do it quite well—I don't feel the need to aspire to get ahead in that race,' she says. 'I like those songs but I don't know if I am motivated enough to make one of them.' Light, sweet candyfloss music could give Sneha more typical hits but she's not chasing that. Her compositions are bold, hard and edgy and capture the imagination of a young, restless India.

'Sneha is basically a lone ranger,' Dibakar says. 'In an era where it's getting harder for music to reach an audience without it being attached to a film, Sneha is one of those independent voices who is part of Bollywood but is still carving out an individualistic course for herself. She looks for films that are a vehicle for her sound rather than the other way around.'

Sneha finds music in almost everything, including noise, and she approaches her work with that mindset. 'I feel everything can be included given good timing. It can all come together and communicate.' She finds the rhythmic pulse of machines in her father's factory in Indore soothing. 'I sometimes like noise. Pink noise, white noise on TV, sounds in a factory, my dad snoring—my mother hates it but I love it. And each time I find a boyfriend who snores, I feel bountiful. I am serious!'

Sneha prefers to leave the flaws in, which makes her music authentic. 'I don't like to alienate raw sounds or voices. I find it very odd to clean everything and put it in a shiny, dewdrop kind of presentation when in reality you heard something else,' she explains.

To make her music honest, Sneha does not delete mistakes that may have occurred during the recording process. 'I love human error,' she says emphatically. While composing a score for *Gangs of Wasseypur,* she invited a banjo player to a studio in Patna for a recording. On his way from Bhuj, the musician had a few drinks to warm himself up on a cold winter day. 'By the time he came to the studio, he was really drunk,' Sneha says, laughing. 'The studio guys were furious with him. They thought I would object.' She didn't. An excited Sneha welcomed him because she knew she was going to get 'a kick-ass recording'. The uninhibited music of a drunk banjo player became '*Tunya*', the film's popular background score.

There are other imperfections in the soundtrack. In one song, a dog can be heard barking in the background. 'I mean, there are dogs in Wasseypur,' Sneha laughs, 'so we kept that.'

'Her music in *Gangs of Wasseypur* was path-breaking,' says movie trade analyst and television show host Komal Nahta. 'The sound was so different, the voices were different and yet it became mainstream. Sometimes, the directors give different music but it stays in the realm of different music. That's all. The general public doesn't really pick it up and make it popular, they don't hum those songs. But with *Gangs of Wasseypur* she managed to break the routine and yet make popular music.'

'The fact that she travelled to the places where *Gangs of Wasseypur* was based and she did the same for *Oye Lucky! Lucky Oye!*—she sought out untrained singers, got local flavours and mixed it with electronic music. It was pretty radical,' says Amit Gurbaxani, a journalist who has been covering Indian music for two decades.

Her pursuit of authentic music formed the bedrock of an MTV India show called *Sound Trippin,* which became a runaway success in 2012. It was a bold and ambitious programme following Sneha as she travelled to various corners of India—backpack and recorder in hand, oversized headphones around her neck—to discover raw sounds and bring the country's vastly ignored local music into urban living rooms, to the MTV-watching generation. 'The goal was to have all sorts of cool people hang out together, whether they are from the village or big city. I thought it was a nice equalizing opportunity.'

For Sneha, that music could come from anywhere, even from a tractor. Many people find that sound harsh. But when Sneha heard a tractor engine running in the middle of the night in Ludhiana, she heard a rhythm. She recorded it, and the result is a delightfully original and catchy song called 'Tung Tung'. It became a massive hit and remains one of the show's most popular songs.

'When you are doing something for TV programming, the experience is different,' Sneha says. 'There was a time and budget crunch, which removed some of the intimacy. I felt it was a bit intimidating for the people. Half of my time was invested in trying to protect them from the flashiness of a Bombay TV crew.' Despite the difficulties that came with a TV crew shooting in rural India, the show gave her an incredible opportunity to make music. 'The younger generation was really happy that music like this was coming out on the MTV platform. There were no boundaries.'

Looking back, is she glad she did the show? 'Fucking, yeah.'

Sneha's music reflects her personality. She is distinctly modern, wildly independent, a touch irreverent, and she laughs easily. She isn't much of a planner and works on instinct. Take, for example, her casual approach to dressing for a TED Talk India recording in December 2017. While most presenters would have carefully considered what to wear on stage, Sneha did not plan her look in advance. She threw on whatever she could find at the last minute: an oversized T-shirt and track pants stuffed into chic knee-high leather boots. She carried it off with disarming confidence and cut a stylish figure.

At her presentation, Shah Rukh Khan introduced her as 'our country's young musical icon'. Sneha took to the stage to talk about her creative process. 'Wherever I go, whatever I hear, I find sounds that inspire me so much, I go into a different zone,' she told a packed audience. 'Now, this zone is inside my head. It's right here. With the help of technology, I have transformed this zone in my head to a physical zone outside.' Thanks to a synthesizer and a computer, Sneha can translate the orchestra playing inside her head into music we can hear.

Attractive, with a youthful face, she is a girly girl who loves clothes and make-up but isn't easily influenced by people or trends. Neither by the trappings of success. Film-maker and fellow music composer Vishal Bhardwaj says, 'She doesn't care about success markers like you should have a car, and you should have a big name and you should become one of the top leading composers. She cares about creating something. To her, that is the most important. That's what makes her feel different and crazy.'

Ruchi Bakshi Sharma, a multimedia artist, shared a home with Sneha when they were both young professionals starting their careers in Mumbai. Ruchi was directing a commercial and Sneha was composing a track for it. They remain close friends. 'We don't really talk about mundane things— she's not that friend,' Ruchi says.

Sneha occupies a different space in her life. The two women reach out to one another when either has a burning desire to discuss a creative idea that usually can't wait another minute—even if one of them is in the bathroom! 'It's like a mind map-making session on the phone, which happens out of the blue. It's a very joyful, childlike exchange of ideas,' Ruchi says. 'It's a creative, no-holds-barred conversation. You can't have that with everyone. Sneha's excitability has a very childlike quality—of course she wants to come across as an adult, but her innocence and her brilliance are what work for me.'

Born to Subhash and Shobha Khanwalkar on 28 April 1983, Sneha grew up in Indore, Madhya Pradesh. Her father, a mechanical engineer, owned a factory that makes spring washers. 'It's extremely noisy, very greasy and supercool,' Sneha says. Her mother Shobha is a homemaker whose side of the family is deeply involved in the celebrated Gwalior gharana of Hindustani classical music. Some of Sneha's relatives teach music, some play an instrument, others sing.

Music has a central place in the family and they have a deep, almost spiritual respect for it. 'These Maharashtrians are stuck up about music and culture,' says Sneha with a laugh. 'According to them, everybody else is a bania!'

The boys in her family were trained to play the tabla. The girls learned to play the harmonium. When the cousins met, they would sing together, and Sneha, the youngest, would watch. She would join in occasionally but says she was considered the least musical in the family. 'These cousins were kickass singers. They all still wonder how I am the one meeting Shah Rukh Khan!'

Sneha wasn't expected to be the breakout star. She was different, a little mischievous, often lost in her own world. Her brother Sanket, who is seven years her junior, was academically more conventional. 'He is an ideal son who did his master's degree in the US and is now an IT engineer working in California. He is the good boy of the family,' Sneha chuckles.

Sneha's father puts it more gently. 'In her school days, she was a little naughty. She was always talking in class; so one day, a teacher told her to clean the classroom floor as a punishment. Sneha said okay, I would love to do so. And she did it. She cleaned the floor without having any inferiority issues. At that point I realized that her biggest strength is her honesty,' Subhash says. 'Whatever she does, she gives it her all.'

This dedication distinguishes her. For *Oye Lucky! Lucky Oye!* Dibakar wanted the soundtrack to consist of fresh voices and an earthy undertone. The movie was set in north India, so that was Sneha's sound laboratory. She convinced a friend to travel with her. They went to the interior belt of Punjab and Haryana, microphone and recorder in hand, to see what they could find. In Haryana, she attended the Ragini music competition—a popular and dynamic festival that lasts through the night and is attended mostly by men. Sneha loved it. She zeroed in on some village voices that stood out—they are the ones you can hear in the Haryanvi-influenced soundtrack of *Oye Lucky! Lucky Oye!*

The startlingly fresh music caught the attention of Anurag Kashyap, considered one of India's most cutting-edge directors. He asked Sneha to work on the soundtrack for his upcoming film—a testosterone-fuelled two-part crime series centred around the coal mafia. His brief was simple: get me nice, raw sounds like you did for *Oye Lucky! Lucky Oye!*

Sneha did not want to repeat the same music. 'I felt like this film had to be different and gritty and really close to the simple folk and yet evocative, so that's the challenge I gave to myself.' The film was set in Bihar. Sneha packed her bags and set off—this time, for Patna. She roamed through the villages of Bihar, doing what she loves most: recording whatever caught her ear.

One winter morning when the sun was high in the sky, she found herself in a Musahar village, surrounded by happy, smiling children. They were desperately poor. The Musahars, who are illiterate and unemployed, are one of India's most marginalized communities. Unable to find work, they go from village to village to kill rats that destroy farms. India's rat catchers are so destitute, they even resort to eating the vermin when food is scarce.

No one visits the community. When Sneha did, it created a stir. Curious village children gathered around her. Some recited poems for her, others laughed and joked around. They wanted to perform. Sneha was ready. She thrust a microphone in front a child who had mucus running down his nose. He sang a song. Another child came forward, then another. 'We had a blast,' Sneha says. She recorded their performances and while they spent a blissful day lost in music, something unpredictable happened simultaneously. 'Our sound palette formed on the side.'

Gangs of Wasseypur's '*Bahut Khoob*' song, which includes the chatter and giggles of children's voices, is the result of the time Sneha spent in the Musahar village. 'These are the experiences I really thrive on.'

After the success of *Oye Lucky! Lucky Oye!* and *Gangs of Wasseypur*, the offers started coming in quickly. A romantic Bollywood film, *Khoobsurat*, starring heart-throbs Fawad Khan and Sonam Kapoor landed in her lap. Sneha was applauded for her remix of the old Rajasthani folk classic, '*Engine Ki Seeti*'. But she prefers to talk about a song called '*Preet*' from the film. Haunting and melancholic, there is a dreamy quality to it.

The producers of the movie commissioned Sneha to make two songs for *Khoobsurat*. First, a happy one, then a sad one. She could not crack the upbeat one. 'I was very sad those days, very sad. I know this is unprofessional but I just couldn't handle it,' she admits. She had just come out of a relationship and felt disoriented. 'My foundations were shaken about love and relationships and friendships and myself. It was a terrible time. To other people, I had just had so much good stuff going for myself that they never felt I could be sulking.'

She decided to compose the sad song first. 'I booked the studio, got the singer and recorded a few lines and then I called Rhea (Kapoor), the producer. It was quite a risk to do that because I had already recorded some stuff without the producer approving it.' Fortunately, Rhea loved it. 'She was sold in the first two lines,' Sneha says. Working on this song was therapeutic. It gave Sneha a chance to heal and find peace.

Sneha never formally learned to play an instrument but she is a gifted singer. At every family gathering, puja or birthday, a pushy aunt or uncle would prod her to sing. It was irritating but Sneha would oblige—sometimes by picking a Marathi song, sometimes, a semi-classical piece. After A.R. Rahman burst on to the Hindi film scene in the 1990s, she would choose one of his compositions. In 1994, Rahman's massive hit 'Roop Suhana Lagta Hai' released as part of the Hindi film, *Gentleman*. Like the rest of India, Sneha fell in love with that song. Her face lights up at the memory. In a flash, she's singing the chorus and clicking her fingers to the beat. She has a deep, distinctive voice.

'If I did not sing well, I would see the family's reactions. So, I was like if I am going to sing, I better be good. That's how I started paying attention to it.' Hungry to improve, she would listen to a song over and over again on a cassette player. 'I would have at least three copies of each because I would listen to them so often the tapes would wear out.' She would also write down the lyrics so she did not mess up the words. 'It wasn't a shallow audience,' she says of her family. 'There was always one aunt or the other trying to correct my pronunciation and they were all from Gwalior or Bhopal so their Hindi wasn't bad,' she chuckles.

Rahman quickly became a favourite. In 1995, he composed the soundtrack for the Hindi film, *Bombay*. Desperate to get their hands on it, Sneha's cousins found a way to buy it at midnight, hours before it hit the stores. They drove around for hours, listening to the cassette in the car's music player, on repeat. Sneha, the youngest, was tired but couldn't doze off. The sound coming from the car stereo was haunting. 'I couldn't sleep for many days after that because there was something about that music. The bassline could be heard loud and clear. The harmonies. The language. I could understand it.'

Music was an integral part of Sneha's childhood. She would sing at school performances and win trophies at inter-school competitions. Her proud father bought her a synthesizer. Sneha would tinker with it, she enjoyed it, but she never saw a future in music.

A gifted visual artist, she spent much of her spare time sketching. 'I used to doodle a lot and my hand had become really strong. I could draw a perfect circle.' That piqued an interest in animation which led her to learn the software it required. The principles are similar to working on a DAW, a digital audio workstation. That's when Sneha developed an interest in altering sound digitally.

Her tastefully decorated apartment in Mumbai's Bandra neighbourhood is testimony to her love for art. It has beautiful paintings, a plum-coloured wall, a retro-glass lamp and an inviting black-leather couch. Behind it is a constantly evolving blackboard wall. One day, there's a calendar on it. On another, there is a business plan drawn up by a friend. Sometimes, there is a to-do list. 'It's amazing for conversations, notes, explaining and just plain scribbling,' Sneha says. Inside is her personal space: she's converted one of the bedrooms into a den and soundproof studio.

After Sneha completed grade 10 in Indore, the Khanwalkars moved to Mumbai so that she could attend college in the big city. She enrolled at SNDT, a university for women, to study Hindustani classical music. Her parents felt it was 'the right thing for her'. But Sneha didn't enjoy it at all. 'I felt like I was wasting my time sticking to a syllabus and giving exams for a bunch of not so motivated teachers.' A year later, she quietly changed her subject to English and sociology. She didn't tell her parents. Do they know now? Sneha grins.

The kind of music Indian masses were listening to at that time—which typically featured female singers with high-pitched, thin voices—did not attract her. But, something about music had her hooked. 'I did not know where to put the finger. It was just bizarre that composing never struck me.' That is, until she went to meet a music director in Mumbai. He told her, 'You can be a singer, you have a good voice, but because you don't have the experience, maybe you can assist me. And you know, nobody minds a PYT in a studio.'

'I had to ask him what it meant,' Sneha says, laughing at the memory of her seventeen-year-old self who didn't know that PYT stood for 'Pretty Young Thing' or that she could be considered one. 'I was so driven by ambition that I was not aware of the fact that the world was looking at a grown, fuckable girl.' In her mind, she was just a young girl who loved music.

Would she react differently if a male music director called her a PYT today? 'I don't find PYT that threatening.' She's aware that some people may find it offensive. But to her, PYT will always remind her of a time in her youth when she had no idea what it meant.

On her way home after the PYT incident, something clicked. And it had nothing to do with sexuality. 'I was like, I am going to be a music director! Unknowingly, he had sorted something out for me, know what I mean?' she asks rhetorically. 'I felt, I love music, I want to do something with music, so why not make music?'

In the movie business, composing music remains a man's domain. Though there are more women working in other aspects of film-making in India—directing, producing, writing—there are very few women music composers. It's the same story in the West. In Hollywood, women comprised 3 per cent of the composers working on the top 250 grossing films of 2017.[2] According to the Center for the Study of Women in Television and Film, this figure is the lowest of all the behind-the-scene crafts of film-making.

Sneha isn't the first woman music composer in India. Jaddanbai in the 1930s and Saraswati Devi in the 1950s were accomplished composers. They were followed by Usha Khanna (of *Dil Deke Dekho* fame) who had a prolific career composing music from 1959 through the early 2000s. Sneha is only the second woman, after Usha, to receive a Filmfare nomination for best music director in 2012 for her work on the *Gangs of Wasseypur* series.

Sneha is surprised more women are not drawn to this profession. 'I used to think about that a lot.' But she still doesn't have an answer. After a long pause, she says, 'It's a multi-departmental job. You need to

---

[2]   Martha M. Lauzen, Center for the Study of Women in Television and Film, 2018, https://bit.ly/2zDTXw0

be interested in lyrics as much as in the script and in what the director is saying. Then you have to see it through execution and production and get the singer that you want. It's almost like being a director, hence the term music director. I don't know why there are female directors but not too many female music directors.'

'The work is ambiguous,' she adds. Few people know the specifics of what the job entails. She says it took her extended family a while to figure out what she does. 'They were like you didn't play the guitar, you didn't play the harmonium. What the fuck do you do?'

Dibakar, who shares a close professional relationship with Sneha, admits the industry wasn't always kind to her because she is a woman. 'Sneha has had to fight her way through the absolutely stifling patriarchy of the Bollywood music world,' Dibakar says. 'You have to see it to believe it. It's all about sitting with an old experienced programmer and telling that person, don't do it like this. And he says no, it does not happen like that and you have to say, it can and this is how it is done. Then, the guy does it. By that time we have lost about thirty minutes.'

The decks were stacked against a woman trying to break into the cinematic music world. But that didn't stop Sneha from trying. She told herself, 'Directors *ko* trust *karna padega*. If I liked the film, I would like to know how they think, I would like to work with them.' Her parents were apprehensive. 'We were really scared about Bollywood. What would the crowd be like? What would the picture be?' Subhash says. 'But Sneha is very particular about our family values and overall culture. She is a professional.'

Although reams have been written about her being a path-breaking female music director, it's a tag Sneha isn't entirely comfortable with. 'It's not very exciting beyond a point,' she bristles. 'Initially it was fine. People got attracted to it but eventually they had to listen to the music. There are usually a lot of magazines that keep coming up with women's day features and I find that a bit regressive. It's women's day, *phataphat list nikalo*.'

'But,' she adds, 'if this inspires chicks to come out of their homes and attempt music, that will be cool.'

That will be very cool.

AMRITA PANDEY
THE STUDIO EXECUTIVE

It was Oscars night on Sunday, 4 March 2018, and among the 3,400 guests packed into the glittering Dolby Theater in Los Angeles was Amrita Pandey, one of the senior-most executives at Disney South Asia. Wearing a fitted blue Gaurav Gupta sari gown, her long hair cascading down one shoulder, she looked every inch a member of the global film fraternity. She was beside herself with excitement when she spotted award-winning actor Meryl Streep walking down the red carpet. 'It was my fan-girl moment; my hands were shaking,' she recalled afterwards. 'It felt like a fairy tale. I have been watching the Oscars since I was a kid. You never think you are going to be there yourself. What incredible talent, energy and aura in one place!'

It was a huge opportunity to be at one of cinema's most important awards ceremony. Scoring a ticket is exceptionally hard and she was one of the chosen few from Disney to attend from India. That's not surprising, given Amrita's professional track record. As one of just a handful of women studio executives in Bollywood, it was a fitting testament to a fifteen-year career.

Since her first job in 2003 at what was then a small television production house called UTV, Amrita has spent the past decade and a half mastering the ins and outs of the film business. Her official title at one of the world's largest and most powerful media companies, the Walt Disney Company, is regional head, Media Distribution and OTT (Over the Top) for South Asia, which includes India, Singapore, Indonesia, the Philippines, Thailand, Malaysia and Vietnam. Prior to this, she was vice-president, Studios, at Disney. She is one of the top business heads in this region and is part of a ten-member core business management team across seven countries.

Not yet forty, Amrita looks a decade younger. Her youthful manner does not scream 'corporate executive'. She has a cherubic face that exudes friendliness. Her long hair, seldom tied, falls down her back and makes her look like the girl next door. In keeping with Bollywood's relaxed style, she's more comfortable dressing down than up. You're likelier to find her in jeans or trousers and shirts, than in saris or power suits. For work, she likes to wear pieces by Tory Burch, Michael Kors, Banana Republic, Massimo Dutti and Anita Dongre.

Setting aside her youthful demeanour, however, there's no mistaking that the 5' 6" tall powerhouse is widely recognized as a major player in the Hindi movie industry. Amrita radiates confidence and drive, and not for nothing has she built up a reputation for marrying her business acumen with solid creative instincts.

Moviemaking is less science and more art, which makes it hard to predict what will work and what won't at the box office. When *Jagga Jasoos*, the much anticipated but much delayed film starring Ranbir Kapoor and Katrina Kaif, released in 2017 to a tepid box-office response, Amrita felt like someone had kicked her in the gut. Disney had produced the film. Naturally, Amrita was anxious. The musical adventure, originally meant to release in 2014, was delayed for various reasons. Given that it was officially Disney India's last production (the studio has an indefinite moratorium on all new film projects in India), there was a lot riding on its success. It offered up the type of family-friendly fare on which the studio had built its storied worldwide reputation.

'It was like an arrow straight to the heart, and of course it's subjective, but I thought it was a special film,' Amrita says, thinking back to that opening weekend, always a litmus test for any Hindi movie's success.

Hits and misses are a way of life in the film business. Amrita understands that. But when a film bombs, it hurts.

Jagga Jasoos eventually went on to recover its costs through various other distribution deals, and while its lead actor won plaudits for his acting skill, some loved the film and others didn't.

Within the industry, Amrita is well respected. She is known for both her technical and interpersonal skills, which include the tricky business of managing talent. Over the past few years, she has won accolades. In 2016, she was on *Fortune*'s '40 under 40' list of the most influential young people in business, the *Economic Times*' Women Ahead List as one of corporate India's fastest-rising women leaders, and in 2015, *Business Today* named her as one of its Hottest Young Executives.

'Amrita has a very strong business orientation, which is why we entrusted her with heading syndication and distribution across India and six other countries in South-East Asia,' says her boss Mahesh Samat, managing director and senior vice-president at Walt Disney International,

South Asia. Samat describes Amrita as extremely driven, efficient, and as someone who always has a solution to a problem. 'She's able to handle stress, stands her ground, and while she doesn't talk much, when she does, she does so in a very articulate manner and always has good points.'

Her former boss, Ronnie Screwvala, the founder of UTV and an early mentor, concurs. 'She is very focused, consistent and has a no-nonsense approach which can appear stern, but eventually works in her favour. She understands what it takes to build relationships and gain respect.' Amrita, in turn, says Ronnie taught her: 'Your job as a studio is to nurture talent and to foster collaboration, not to show tough love and have an ego.'

Aamir Khan has worked on multiple movies with Amrita. He says she is hard-working, committed to her work and a team player in a business that is all about teamwork. 'She is someone who really enjoys the whole process of film-making and she is very dependable.'

Karan Johar dealt with Amrita when she was at UTV Disney. He calls the studio executive rock-solid. 'She talks shop in such a way that you feel she knows exactly what she is talking about,' he says. 'She has a corporate demeanour but she has a heart full of passion for the work she does. She understands the business but also loves the art of it. That balance of commerce and art really strengthens and distinguishes her.'

That a young woman, from outside the closed network of Hindi cinema, could rise to prominence so quickly in an industry that had once been the exclusive purview of men is impressive, but also illustrative of how rapidly the business of Hindi cinema has changed in the past two decades. Where the old boys' club had run the show, a new crop of women executives has emerged, many of them from UTV's stables, who now hold important decision-making positions at studios. Among them are Rucha Pathak at Fox, Sneha Rajani at Sony Pictures and Priti Shahani at Junglee Pictures. Amrita's blend of business aptitude, interpersonal skills and creative instincts have made for a unique career trajectory.

When Amrita joined UTV, it focused on the business-to-business segment, creating content for broadcasters. Despite being shy, from the beginning Amrita took pains to step out of her comfort zone and assert herself professionally. 'I wanted to be taken seriously and prove myself really quickly. Work is a major anchor in my life, no matter how casual I may appear. I am an anxious person. I felt I had to deliver, deliver, deliver, and I was very hard on myself.'

Her inner confidence comes from having strong female role models at home—her mother and sister. It also stems from a difficult childhood and knowing she would have to stand on her own feet in the absence of fallback options.

Although she has worked on more than 150 films since she started out, Amrita says the thrill of going to work hasn't subsided. She loves her job. After mastering international distribution and marketing, conquering the digital market is the next frontier. Some of Disney's movies are on Netflix and the studio has its own section on Hotstar, Fox's online streaming site. There are plans to distribute directly to the consumer.

Industry players speak highly of her. Rajkumar Hirani, one of India's most successful film-makers, with whom Amrita worked on distributing *PK*, the second highest grossing Hindi film ever, says of her, 'She's always smiling, and had a huge amount of willingness to accept out-of-the-box ideas. A lot of people come with an attitude, but what I saw in Amrita was a genuine desire to understand what the film was all about and brainstorm on ideas. She was absolutely open to creative thoughts on marketing.'

Vishal Bhardwaj has known Amrita since her early days at UTV and respects her aesthetic instincts as well as her marketing prowess. He has worked closely with Amrita on four films, including, most recently, *Haider* (2014). Bhardwaj recalls that the UTV/Disney commercial team was nervous about *Haider*'s publicity posters, which displayed the principal character holding a skull. 'I remember Amrita saying that we have to prepare the audience for what the film is and not show something else in the poster and draw them in and disappoint them. She believed that marketing should represent the film. That's her the sharp marketing mind.'

Siddharth Roy Kapur, Amrita's former boss, believes Amrita has great instincts. She is self-aware and constantly analyses her actions, is quick to accept responsibility and is resilient about failure. In this business, you tend to get swayed by a lot of things, but I have noticed she has a very solid creative instinct.'

Farah Khan thinks that Amrita's greatest asset is being able to communicate problems in an affable way. At the same time, Farah describes her as 'steelier than most men in the business'.

Vishal Bhardwaj has a similar opinion. 'In a meeting, she's very pleasant. She never lets you feel she is the head of a studio. Sometimes, people tell me you don't know how bossy Amrita is, so I told her one day that I have to see that side of you!' He still hasn't. Even when she has a gruelling schedule, the smile remains intact. Bhardwaj remembers that for *Haider*, the studio had to hammer out the final agreement with his office. The only day the Disney legal team could meet their counterparts was on Dussehra, a public holiday. 'We worked for twelve hours, and Amrita had to be present in case something came up during the negotiations, but she wasn't the least bit annoyed. She sat through it pleasantly.'

In 2003, when Amrita was interviewing for the UTV job, it was a newbie company. The offices were located in Worli's Nahar Industrial Estate, an unassuming compound without much character. Amrita had a forty-five-minute interview, where she was grilled by Ronnie and six other people. She nailed it and landed the job. Her starting salary was Rs 2.5 lakh a year, about Rs 20,000 a month. She could have got a higher paying corporate job elsewhere, but she was excited to join a growing media company where everyone was passionate about the movies.

UTV was an 'indie' production house founded by the visionary Ronnie, his wife Zarina and Deven Khote in 1990. Ronnie was an outsider in the notoriously insular and clubby world of Hindi cinema. Within a decade, he had expanded UTV's footprint into Singapore and Malaysia, acquired a Tamil language channel, Vijay TV, partnered with STAR to broadcast across the four south Indian languages, started a children's TV channel, Hungama, a youth channel called Bindass, three movie channels and eventually expanded into movie production.[1]

UTV was hoping to recreate the studio tradition that had once held sway in Hindi cinema during its earliest days. According to Mihir Bose's riveting historical account of Bollywood, cinema had arrived in India seven months after the world's first film was shown in Paris—incredibly, at a venue called Salon Indien that had been decorated to appear Indian.[2]

[1]   Ronnie Screwvala, *Dream With Your Eyes Open*, p. xii.
[2]   Mihir Bose, *Bollywood: A History*, New Delhi: Roli Books, 2007, p. 38.

On 7 July 1896, at Mumbai's Watson Hotel, on the same day that it was shown to the Tsar of Russia in St Petersburg, six short films were viewed by an audience of British residents (the hotel didn't allow Indians).

In the early twentieth century, Bollywood, like Hollywood, was built on the studio system, which lasted till the 1940s.[3] Dadasaheb Phalke's Hindustan Film Company was one such studio, as were the Pune-based Prabhat, Kolkata's New Theatres Ltd and the celebrated Bombay Talkies. But, unlike in Hollywood, where some of the earliest studios are around even today, these Indian pioneers eventually became defunct. Over time, movie stars became the real power centres, a trend that continues to this day.

With UTV, what Ronnie was trying to build was audacious—a movie business by outsiders with no connections or networks within the fraternity. In an industry that thrived on personal relationships, this took a lot of chutzpah. 'We adopted a director-based approach rather than a star-based approach, more out of default than design since we didn't have access to the star,' says Roy Kapur, who joined UTV in 2005 from STAR TV in Hong Kong. 'We thought, let's make the director the star. We started going after people who had great subjects and great scripts and got our foot in the door through that route, rather than the usual way of our grandfathers having known someone else's grandfather. The other thing was making marketing and distribution our strong suit. That was one way to convince talent that we were the best game in town when it came to releasing a movie.'

As the company grew, it began recruiting aggressively. Roy Kapur eventually became Amrita's boss. 'I remember this smart, wisecracking person in the international distribution team who clearly knew what she was doing, and knew that she knew what she was doing. From the beginning, Amrita made sure her voice was heard. She was quite sassy and had a lot of spunk. She had an irreverence and didn't really care about hierarchy but more about a person's ability, which I found refreshing.'

Years later, Amrita recalls a party her colleagues hosted to mark her ten years at UTV. Ronnie made a speech. He said, 'When Amrita walked

---

[3]   Ibid., p. 87. Bose cites historian Brian Shoesmith.

into the UTV office, she did so with two pigtails and an attitude. The pigtails have gone, but the attitude hasn't.'

Although Amrita never imagined that she would end up working at a fancy movie studio, looking back on her childhood, it seems almost inevitable. Born on 10 June 1979 in Ahmedabad, Gujarat, to Rita and Pradeep Kumar Pandey, Amrita arrived five years after her sister Alka. Ahmedabad was a textile hub, and Pradeep, originally from Delhi, had moved there to work as an executive in a textile company. Rita, a schoolteacher, was from Lucknow, where as a young girl, she and her cousins would watch two to three movies a day in theatres if they could. Movies were Rita's passion.

Alka and Amrita studied at Mount Carmel, one of the oldest and most respected convent schools in Gujarat and one that was known for its high-calibre women teachers. Amrita was a good student, although she would wait till the last minute to cram for exams. She always aced her subjects, especially Hindi.

In India in the 1980s, the mantra of 'save and invest for a rainy day' still reigned supreme. Frugality was valued, unnecessary expenditure frowned upon. The Pandeys led a typical middle-class existence in Ahmedabad. The family didn't own a television. 'My parents felt it would be a distraction,' Amrita says. So every Sunday, Alka and Amrita would go to their neighbour's house to watch *Spiderman*, *Vikram aur Baital*, *Chitrahaar* and the Sunday evening movie that most of India would tune into before cable television.

Movie watching was a family pastime. In addition to watching them on television, they also went to the cinema religiously. 'Both my parents are huge movie buffs,' Amrita says. 'Even today, my mum will watch every film that is released, irrespective of how good or bad it is, and she's very forgiving of most movies. So, if she tells me that a film is bad, we know it's really bad!'

The family would drive to Sunset Cinema, a popular drive-in built in 1973 that boasts of Asia's largest screen, which can accommodate 665 cars. 'I have the fondest memories of this cinema because Ahmedabad used to get really cold between October and February, and so we would go to the movies in our car,' Amrita says with a giggle. 'There was a shrill audio system, but it was great fun and you could carry your beach chairs and chill there and watch a film.' She recalls watching films starring Govinda, Mithun Chakravarty and Madhuri Dixit.

Although the drive-in cinema only played Hindi films, Amrita did watch a re-release of the 1969 Gregory Peck–Omar Sharif starrer *Mackenna's Gold*, a film about a group of bandits. Seeing that film turned out to be somewhat ominous. Amrita's family, while on holiday, had their own encounter with India's then-infamous dacoits.

The Pandeys loved to travel. In the 1980s and '90s, air travel in India was expensive and not widely prevalent, so like most Indians, they used trains and their trusted Fiat. They would head to Lucknow each summer to visit Amrita's maternal grandparents. They also saw much of central, south and west India by car. On one such road trip, in the late 1980s, Amrita had an experience that could have been straight out of the movies. Her father was driving the family through Madhya Pradesh's Chambal region when dacoits suddenly surrounded them.

'I was very young, but I remember there were many people on horseback who suddenly emerged behind the car,' Amrita recalls with a shudder. 'They threw a stone at the car to stop it, which hit the frame. My dad pushed the pedal and just revved up and sped away. It was really scary.' Despite this unnerving incident, the travel bug stayed with her. So did the movie bug.

In 1993, the Pandeys moved to Mumbai, when Amrita was in the grade 9. They found a place to live in the western suburb of Khar. It was a life-altering time for her. Ahmedabad was a small, safe, familiar city in contrast to Bombay (as it was known then), which was overwhelmingly crowded, frenetic and alien.

'I had a lot of friends in Ahmedabad and was sad to leave. I was traumatized and felt uprooted. It was not as though we were army children who had moved every few years. We had stayed in one place for a long time, and friends had always been important to me since I was a child. I always feel like they are family.'

She enrolled in St Joseph's Convent in Bandra, but felt 'everyone was so snobbish. No one wanted to talk to a girl from Ahmedabad. And I'm anyway shy, I wasn't gregarious and outgoing, so I felt like a complete outsider. Eventually, I befriended someone who had also shifted from another school and we were two little outcastes.' The two years she spent finishing up her grades 9 and 10 were tough.

It was also a time when things weren't going well at home. Her parents separated and that, coupled with being in an unfamiliar city, was difficult on the teenager. One easy escape was the movies. She saw *Rangeela* and *Dilwale Dulhania Le Jayenge*, both huge hits in 1995, six times each at Bandra's Gaiety Galaxy cinema (now the G7 multiplex). 'I would bunk and go and watch these two movies again and again. Little did I know while watching a movie like *Rangeela* that I would go on to work with Aamir in nine movies! I remember many things in my life that are associated with the experience of watching a film. I remember whom I watched it with. Otherwise, I have a terrible memory.'

After two years of studying science at Bandra's National College, Amrita was confused about what to study further. Always a good student, she had floundered academically due to the stress at home. She had always admired her father, a hard-working professional who ran a production unit in a company that manufactured textile screens. She wasn't keen on the usual paths of medicine and engineering. She thought of architecture and pharmacy, but eventually opted for microbiology at Jai Hind College in Churchgate—a subject 'nobody wanted to study'. It helped that her best friend Dipika Rang was also studying there. Alongside, she enrolled in a three-year computer programming course at NIIT, explaining rather drily, 'I was lost. Clearly, I didn't know what I wanted to do.'

Their parents had always encouraged Alka and Amrita to be independent and to make their own way, and so they did. In 1999, done with college, Amrita was smitten by the dotcom boom sweeping through India. She quickly got a job with egurukool.com, a company filled with young, smart people. 'My first day at work involved a white-water rafting trip in Rishikesh and I thought, "From here, everything has to be fun, it can't be boring."'

Her role was to convince blue-chip schools like Bombay Scottish and Bombay International to use egurukool products. She relied on a combination of charm and persistence. It was then that it dawned on Amrita that she enjoyed meeting people, marketing and distributing, and putting deals together. 'I realized that the more people listen to you, the more you realize you have the power of influence, and a compelling way of building relationships. It's not rocket science, you realize hey, I can do this, I can do more!'

Wanting formal business training, she quit her job and enrolled at the Sydenham Institute of Management, where she undertook a summer internship at the *Times of India*. The very suave Bhaskar Das was president, and Amrita was given an assortment of tasks, one of which included soliciting support from advertising agencies for a magazine called *Strategic Marketing*. The media industry appealed to her.

'I quite enjoyed my stint at the *Times*. There were so many young interns running up and down the corridors back then,' she says with a laugh. 'No one ever wanted to join the media, and the only media placements at that time were at Zee and Star.'

UTV, at that time a TV production house that did ads, animation shows and in-flight entertainment, came to the campus that year and Ronnie, gave a placement talk. Amrita hadn't thought to attend it, and was whiling away her time in Bandra. A close friend called and told her that if she didn't attend the talk, she wouldn't be allowed to interview. 'I went rushing from Bandra and just about made it; thank God I did. I was supremely impressed, because Ronnie is an amazing speaker and quite fantastic. I knew I had to land an interview.'

She got one and clearly made an impression. 'It was her first interview, fresh out of her MBA. We were interviewing a large group of graduates, a first for the media at that time,' recalls Ronnie. 'Her self-confidence and communication skills stood out and got her the job.'

The soft-spoken girl gave work her all and loved nothing more than a challenge. Her initial days at UTV were spent researching and pitching new ideas to broadcast networks, in particular to STAR, to whom the production house was supplying content. She spent time watching tele-novellas, game shows, soaps and analysing television ratings. Ronnie's wife Zarina was keen to start a children's channel in India. Amrita, as part of her rotation through divisions, was to research kiddie content from around the world. With an investment of Rs 100 crore, Hungama began operations in September 2004, airing Japanese anime like *Shin Chan* and *Doraemon* that became wildly popular with kids around the country. Soon after, Amrita moved into the motion pictures team, which then comprised three people focusing mainly on operations.

'I worked on everything, because when you join a company that was as small as we were, there are very few divisions and you end up doing so much more than in a larger firm where roles are more clearly defined,' Amrita says.

In the early 2000s, Bollywood was in a state of flux. The Indian government officially recognized film-making as an industry in 1998. Only at the turn of the twenty-first century were film-makers able to access bank financing and other legitimate funding sources. As a result, shadow financing from questionable sources, especially the underworld, began to wane. Increased legitimacy and proper channels of credit led to the practice of written contracts, once an afterthought in an industry where deals were settled with a handshake. Studios like UTV became instrumental in making the movie business more transparent.

In 2004, UTV was working on *Swades*, starring Shah Rukh Khan and Gayatri Joshi. Directed by Ashutosh Gowariker, fresh off the success of *Lagaan*, UTV wanted to release *Swades* not just in India but also overseas, to cater to the Indian diaspora market. The film was to release on 17 December 2004. Ronnie wanted to tie up on international distribution, something the company didn't know much about, but from his trip to the Cannes film festival that May, he had some leads.

Amrita, now a manager in UTV's international distribution division, was tasked with researching overseas markets like Indonesia, the UK, the USA and the Gulf. 'We just jumped into the ocean, pretty much the same way as we did with TV,' says Amrita, shaking her head in wonder. 'I was hungry to learn and it was a lot of fun.'

Her colleagues and she spent a few months following up on Ronnie's leads, researching price points, analysing how other Shah Rukh Khan films had fared in different countries, investigating which theatre chains ought to be approached in the various markets and what type of marketing to invest in.

Swades released in over twenty countries, grossing close to $2.8 million in the overseas market, compared to $2.4 million in India. The movie won critical acclaim, with Shah Rukh's performance considered a highlight of his career till that point.

Next up was *Rang De Basanti,* an Aamir Khan–starrer, about a group of young men who try to avenge their pilot friend's death, caused by corruption. Amrita was UTV's point person on the film's various sets, from Amritsar to Delhi and Jaipur to Mumbai's Film City. Responsible for maintaining budgets, reviewing cost reports, paying people, signing contracts, negotiating rates and general troubleshooting, as well as marketing, distribution, and later the awards process, she did everything. She was twenty-five years old.

'There's a story I love to tell about *Rang De Basanti*,' Amrita says. 'There is a scene where Aamir is talking to a buffalo, telling him they will loot this train, and he's rehearsing his dialogue. A buffalo man was duly brought to Film City and I had to negotiate the rates. That's why I always tell my friends that my job is not glamorous!'

After viewing the film's first cut, Aamir had a round-table meeting to solicit everyone's thoughts. Amrita was petrified because she hadn't liked what she had seen, but didn't feel like she was established enough to say so. They had gone around the room and everyone had offered polite opinions. She was the last to be asked. Though she wanted to hide under the table, Amrita also knew she couldn't lie. She plucked up the courage to say that the film didn't work for her and that it was jerky. Aamir took notes the entire time. 'I later realized that it was a rough cut, and that watching a rough cut is an art. They did rework it and it was then that I learnt that things change at every stage of the process. *Rang De Basanti* turned out to be the most beautiful film.'

The movie was a blockbuster hit, resonating with a nation fed up with the shady nexus between business and politics. It went on to receive a national award and a BAFTA nomination.

Amrita did nine more films with Aamir. She is an unabashed fan of the actor's, valuing his professionalism, work ethic, dedication to his craft and desire to make high-impact content which attempts to transform society. *Rang De Basanti* was a great film, one that solidified UTV's pioneering marketing skills. The film's actors were taken on roadshows around the country as the film released, to interact with audiences. Coca-Cola bottles were branded with the images of the cast. 'We used the content of the film to stir people's passions and to create a movement,' says Roy Kapur. 'The candle march in the film became symbolic of protest. Real life protesters got visual imagery that they enacted in the real world.'

UTV quickly established its credentials as a reputable movie studio. It had a string of cult hits. Using innovative plot lines that catapulted hitherto unknown directors to fame, the studio emerged at the forefront of a new kind of cinema, one that was aimed at an increasingly urban audience, hungry for quality Hindi movies. With swanky multiplexes taking over from the old-fashioned theatres of yore, watching Hindi movies became cool. Films like *Khosla Ka Ghosla*, released in the same year as *Rang De Basanti*, cemented UTV's reputation as the new kid on the block. Production successes included *Life in A Metro*, *A Wednesday*, *Fashion*, *Dev.D*, *Oye Lucky! Lucky Oye!*, *Delhi-6*, *Kaminey* and *I Hate Luv Storys*, while the roster of distribution successes included *Peepli [Live]*, *Delhi Belly*, *Barfi!*, *Rowdy Rathore*, *Chennai Express*, *Jodha Akbar*, *PK* and *Kaminey*, among others.

UTV's journey paralleled Amrita's own. Content distribution in India and overseas and marketing became her areas of expertise. She grew with the company, and wasn't afraid to admit to mistakes. 'I remember reading the *Dev.D* script and I didn't connect with it. It was one of those really polarizing films which you either loved or hated, and that film taught me how to think about reading a script in the beginning and understanding where it could go in terms of storytelling.'

Almost a century after Hollywood set up shop in India via Universal Studios, The Walt Disney Company acquired UTV for $454 million. Disney had held a 50.4 per cent non-controlling stake in the Indian studio, but completed its takeover in 2012. Ronnie stepped down a year later and Roy Kapur took over. Today, Disney South Asia is headed by Mahesh Samat.

There have been considerable successes and some failures. In 2014, *PK*, the Rajkumar Hirani–directed Aamir Khan–starrer, distributed by UTV, became a massive rage in China, where it released across 4,600 screens. The film grossed $120 million worldwide, the highest grossing Hindi movie at that time, helped in part by its distribution in the Chinese market, which Amrita was instrumental in figuring out. Hirani was so impressed with Amrita that he kept in touch with her. 'Even if we are not working together, I still can pick up the phone and ask her to advise me on something that is marketing or distribution-related,' he says.

Vishal Bhardwaj says he misses working with her. 'Most producers are interested in budgets and making sure things are on track. You feel they are financiers and you are being financed. Amrita is beyond that. She takes chances and participates in creativity.' Bhardwaj recalls the example of *Haider*'s promotions, which neither his team nor the studio liked. The promos were to release the next day, but the promo company refused to share the film's logo without considerable compensation. All this unfolded at 10 p.m. the previous night. Bhardwaj suggested that his own team work overnight to create a new logo and Amrita took a chance. 'She said, let's do it. And later, when there were protests against *Haider*, it was Amrita who was on the phone with the DCP and ACP in those cities. She was very active. With Amrita, you have this feeling that you have a partner in crime.'

When *Dangal* went on the floors, Disney and AKP Films knew that the plot, which centred on an ageing wrestler coaching his daughters despite a social backlash, would resonate with a Chinese audience that faced similar gender issues. In the end, the movie broke all box-office records, making it the first Hindi film to make over $300 million, with China contributing more than double its earnings. Till date, *Dangal* is one of the top twenty films by revenue in China. 'I feel so proud that an Indian film did so well in China. Why should only English films dominate that market?' says Amrita.

The Jungle Book (2016) was another feather in Disney's cap. Marketing it as a Bollywood film despite being made in Hollywood was a stroke of genius. Although there were internal arguments, Amrita was against the idea of inserting the song '*Chaddi Pehen ke Phool Khila Hai*', fearing a backlash, but listened to her team, which was eventually proven right. The song helped buoy the film at the box office. 'We fight and argue and that's part of the fun,' she says about working in a team filled with passionate, smart people. 'My first reaction to that song in *The Jungle Book* was, "Will this work?" I am glad I listened to my team.' She trusts their judgement and takes their opinions into consideration.

Her leadership style is best described as inclusive. Disney colleagues give her full marks for being firm without being aggressive. Echoing Disney boss Samat, Sujata Chanda, who handles communications and PR at Disney India, says, 'Amrita is shy, but when she's in a meeting with other producers or film-makers or talent, she gets her point across, though not in a dominating way.'

Besides the movies, Amrita is known to be a connoisseur of good food. Both Vishal Bhardwaj and Raju Hirani commented on how Amrita always knew where to eat and which dishes to order in any restaurant in any part of the world. From China to Italy, she knows exactly where to dine based on extensive research and tips. On a five-day trip to Rome to promote *Haider*, Bhardwaj said that even with complicated dietary restrictions—for example, Shahid Kapoor, his lead actor, is a Radha Soami follower and a strict vegetarian—Amrita had called restaurants in advance to ensure that everyone's needs were met. 'My assistant and I used to sing the *Omkara* song and change the line to "*sabse bada khavaiya re*—Amrita Pandey",' he says with a smile, citing a line from the title song of his 2006 film. 'Sometimes I call her from abroad to ask her for recommendations!'

How tough is it to be a woman executive in Bollywood? Because she's single, Amrita is used to being asked inappropriate questions like 'why aren't you married?' or 'are you ever going to settle down?' or 'will you have a child and quit?'. But those were more pointed in the early years. She also says that no one has ever behaved inappropriately with her.

Starting out at UTV was a blessing. Amrita maintains that she was fortunate to have walked into a firm where there was no gender divide and where she was surrounded by strong female personalities. 'We had Zarina as a co-founder, and the culture was phenomenal. I had more women in my team than men, except maybe on set. It's only when you go out there, outside the company, and then no one would take you seriously because you are told you look young, and you're female, so you must be an assistant type, you couldn't possibly be anyone else. If you're male and huge and tall, you have presence, you are taken seriously. I think the issue of gender mixed with age is a deadlier bias. My age has been a bigger problem.'

She adds, 'But yes, women should be projecting much more because men don't hold back. Why are women always called tactical thinkers and men strategic? What does this mean? I gave Sheryl Sandberg's book *Lean In* to my co-workers because the way men and women ask for a raise is so different. But I also think you shouldn't chase money. Chase excellence, and the money will come.'

Amrita hopes to encourage more young people to join the business. 'I never even knew that working in a studio was an option,' she says. 'I stumbled upon it. This is such a satisfying job. How many people get to work on things that impact millions? Films can change the way people think. Isn't that incredible?'

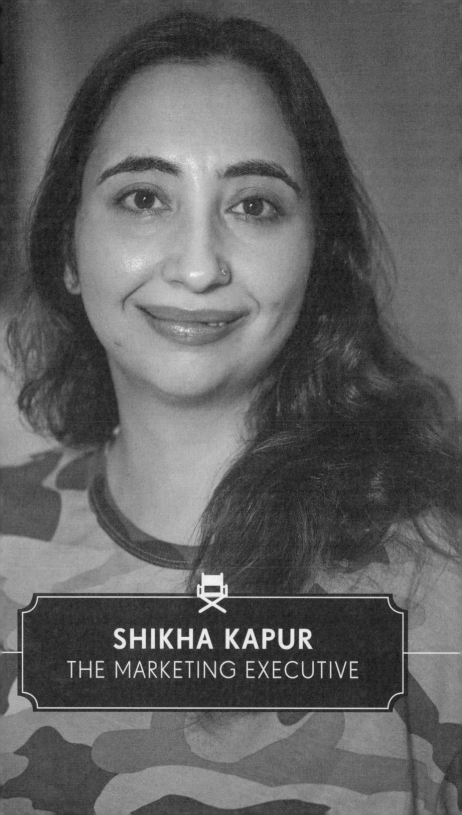

SHIKHA KAPUR
THE MARKETING EXECUTIVE

Shikha Kapur loves a stupid idea. At the heart of it, she says, usually lurks the germ of a wildly creative one. India's film-marketing genius, known for her out-of-the-box, innovative concepts, thrives on disruption. Seated at the dining table in her airy Mumbai apartment, she's having a late lunch. It's almost 5 p.m. In between spoonfuls of upma, she says, 'I want to be known for doing something that has not been done before.'

Shikha is the driving force behind some of the most innovative movie marketing campaigns to come out of Bollywood. She has scored plenty of marketing firsts—from distributing condoms to promote the romantic black comedy *Dev. D*, hanging cash on a Mumbai hoarding for the promotion of *Paan Singh Tomar*, a movie about an athlete turned dacoit, to launching a special edition of Coca-Cola bottles for *Rang De Basanti,* a film that targets India's youth. Bold and brave, they are a small sample of the unconventional tactics she has deployed to grab the audience's attention.

In a fifteen-year career spent in marketing, Shikha has promoted over a hundred films, won several awards, and is credited with creating unique campaigns to publicize blockbusters including *Chennai Express, Barfi!, Rang De Basanti* and *Neerja*.

Siddharth Roy Kapur, her former boss and one of her early mentors, calls her an 'ideas person'. She worked under him at UTV, now Disney India, before taking on her current role as the chief marketing officer at Fox Star India. 'The things we did on the marketing front at UTV while she was there were really quite something,' Kapur says. 'They were special, different, innovative and clutter breaking.'

In an era when movies compete with various other entertainment options, a good marketing campaign is key to a film's success. It is what gets people to purchase a ticket. Generally, the audience has a short attention span, so films have a limited window within which to make an impact—typically, the first three days following its release. Conventional wisdom suggests that films that do well during this period usually have a healthy run at the box office and deliver a good return on investment.

At Fox, Shikha is responsible for marketing the entire portfolio across Hollywood, Bollywood and Tamil films. Do people know about a film before it is released? Are they excited about it? Has it created a buzz?

Shikha's job is to give the target audience a reason to believe in a film months before it opens. Her boss, Vijay Singh, CEO, Fox Star Studios in India, says Shikha does just that. Here's how. 'It starts with a very deep understanding of the film business and it starts with her being in that space almost her entire career. It starts with her passion for the industry.'

In the past, film marketing was considered an afterthought, something the marketing department handled after a film was complete. In today's highly competitive film world where audiences are spoiled for choice at theatres and have a library of films readily available through streaming services, marketing has become integral to a film's journey.

Shikha gets involved with a film as soon as it gets the green light. Sometimes even earlier, during the scriptwriting stage. This allows her to be invested in it from the beginning, which in turn gives her a sense of ownership. With that, she says, comes accountability. 'I don't want to be told at the end of the campaign, "Oh this is shit, it didn't work," and I don't want to say, "Well, I just promoted this film, I have nothing to do with it."' Any film she's involved with belongs as much to Shikha as it does to its director, producer or actor. 'I must feel this is *my* film. That it's my blood and sweat.'

Once she absorbs the ethos of the film, Shikha starts teasing the audience with nuggets of information about it, relying on multiple platforms such as print, television, radio, star engagements, reality shows, the Internet, mobile phones and social media to get the message across. 'If I don't give them a compelling reason to watch it, it's going to fail.'

But first, she needs to be convinced of the film herself. Usually, she starts by posing one simple question to the director. 'I ask: Why do you want to make the film? Sometimes I get the answer right there. But if a director does not know it, the reason is flawed.'

Many of the groundbreaking ideas Shikha's department generates come from weekly brainstorming sessions. 'That's the one meeting no one is allowed to miss, at any cost,' says Pashan Jal, who was part of Shikha's team at UTV before he followed her to Fox.

Pashan is now pursuing a career in content production at a different company but remembers these meetings well. 'The team was allowed to suggest the most ridiculous, absurd, obnoxious, often unexecutable ideas,' he recalls, adding that Shikha always welcomed them. No one was ever ridiculed and no idea was shot down for not being good enough. 'That is not something marketing teams at other studios do. Those meetings were very Shikha-driven.'

Shikha is fiercely protective of those who work with her. They reciprocate by being loyal. 'I'm proud of the fact that anyone who is in my team will not want to leave me until I ask them to. And that's one of my key skill sets. For a person who finds it tough to be sociable, to be able to handle a team that is so consistent is a strength,' she says.

Pashan says team management is Shikha's fortitude. 'She's amazing with people.' During the seven years he worked with Shikha, no one left her team. In an industry where the churn is high, this is unusual. 'It's because Shikha always stands by you. I never had any fear of getting into an awkward spot with stars because I knew my boss would back me up. And she always did, without exception.'

Shikha's ability to call a spade a spade makes her stand out in an industry packed with fragile egos and an inflated sense of self, even if it doesn't always make her the most popular person in the room. 'Shikha's not the easiest person to work with,' Singh says. He means that as a compliment. 'She has the ability to take tough calls and speaks her mind which I think is a good characteristic.'

This honesty is the foundation on which she has built a strong relationship with leading Bollywood actors and developed a formidable reputation. 'If that means I have to take one for the team, or I have to play the devil, or that you may hate me, I am okay with that. Marketing does not cater to people's insecurities. It has to cater to the film.'

In the male-dominated world of Hindi films, it can be tricky for a woman to be in a position of power. 'I have felt uncomfortable at times, but I would not say there is bias. I have met a few people who just do not have respect for women. There *are* people like that in the industry.' But Shikha does not let that distract her. She keeps a steadfast focus on one simple mantra: The film always comes first.

The marketing wiz is a delightful study in contrasts. Shikha wants your attention but is an introvert. She has a business-oriented mind but operates on instinct. She follows the rules but is a risk taker. With a mane of glossy dark hair and a youthful face, Shikha, dressed casually in a T-shirt and comfy pants on an afternoon off from work, looks younger than she is. Her voice and body language ooze confidence and when she speaks, she commands the room.

How did she become a maverick, innovative, creative thinker? She looks to her childhood.

Born in Delhi on 27 September 1977, she was raised in Moradabad, an industrial city in Uttar Pradesh, where her father, Ram Kumar Khanna, ran a sugar factory and a moneylending business, and her mother, Savita, ran a children's clothing shop called Chinky Mod. Chinky is Savita's nickname for Shikha.

The Khannas loved movies and they indulged their passion by frequenting Chaddha Palace, a movie theatre across the road from their home. 'It was the kind of place where my dad would call up and say, "Don't start the movie yet, we are just coming!"' Shikha laughs. 'They would start the show when we got there.' The girl who 'loved love stories' watched the Aamir Khan–starrers *Dil Hai Ki Manta Nahin* twenty times and *Dil* at least fifty times.

Moradabad was a socially conservative and religiously sensitive city. Rocked by communal riots in 1980, the tension lingered for several years. Not keen to raise their daughter in this contentious, fragile environment, her parents enrolled her at the Convent of Jesus and Mary, a boarding school in Mussoorie. It was more than 200 kilometres away from their home. Shikha was in the grade 3 at the time.

At this school in the mountains, eight-year-old Shikha was miserable. Each time she returned to school after breaks, she would be overcome with dread. 'There was a really steep slope going up to my school, so my dad used to carry me on his shoulders on that stretch. He knew that was my cue to start crying, so he would just hold me tight and walk up that hill.' The little girl was desperately homesick.

Year after year, it only got worse. Shikha longed to go home. One day, her parents received a phone call from their distraught daughter. Shikha, now twelve years old, sobbed into the receiver, 'I am so sick, I don't know what to do. I have tuberculosis and I just want to get out of here.'

Alarmed, her parents rushed to Mussoorie and brought her home. It turned out that she wasn't sick at all. The frantic call faking an illness was a cheeky ploy to get out of boarding school. It worked. Her parents decided that she would stay at home with them and study in Moradabad. 'I was really happy about that,' Shikha giggles.

Her mother, Savita, laughs at the memory. 'She certainly knows how to get someone's attention,' she says, beaming with maternal pride as she talks about her daughter. 'She won't relent till she gets what she wants. Marketing is just the right career for her.'

The family is a close-knit one. When Shikha was going through a rough patch in her personal life, her parents moved to Mumbai to be closer to her. 'I only had to say, "Mamma, please come."' Her parents, who had moved from Moradabad to Delhi, sold their home in the capital and rented a flat in Mumbai. Today, they live with Shikha and her teenage son, Trish. Shikha's brother and sister-in-law live on another floor in the same building. They are constantly in and out of each other's apartments. Shikha shares a particularly close bond with her mother and says, 'I can't live without her, that goes without saying.' Savita, sitting beside her daughter, smiles.

Shikha's rise in the marketing world runs parallel to a paradigm shift within the Hindi film industry. More studios have entered the fray, content is changing, directors are experimenting with new themes and audiences are more discerning. Bollywood, the world's most prolific movie industry, produced 225 films in 2016, providing consumers with a dizzying array of choices each Friday. Which film does one watch? Among other factors, it is inevitably the film that has been marketed the best.

Though film marketing is as old as cinema in India, contemporary marketing strategies have come a long way from the days producers relied on posters to publicize their films. India's first full-length feature film, *Raja Harishchandra*, released in 1913, relied on printed literature—newspaper advertisements, handbills and publicity booklets—to spread the word. But when the film opened, the response was lukewarm. So director–producer Dadasaheb Phalke introduced novel marketing techniques. Madhavankutty Pillai, writing in *Open* magazine, explains, 'He came out with funny descriptions of the film, announcing in crowded marketplaces that it is a mile long strip of 58,000 little pictures put together. He offered prizes to ticket buyers. The audience started coming in and the movie went on to make money.'[1]

In the 1920s, hand-painted posters became a popular marketing tool. Artists would use bright colours and bold strokes to paint eye-catching images on billboards and hoardings. Celebrated artist Maqbool Fida Husain began his career thus. In fact, billboard and poster painting became an important source of income for many artists. Over the next few decades, Indian cinema gradually introduced new methods of marketing. Images on canvas were copied on to cheap paper and reprinted, and producers began to rely extensively on print and radio, television and merchandising to create awareness about their films.

While marketing has changed dramatically since the early twentieth century, Singh says the industry is in for another great disruption. He points to the use of the Internet and social media, which have turned traditional marketing techniques on their head. 'Digital dominance is changing consumption of content. It's accounting for a larger proportion of the time your target audience is spending on it. Therefore it's no longer about putting a poster up on the wall because they aren't even looking up from their mobiles to notice it,' Singh says.

As a result, studios have had to adopt new models of marketing. According to Singh, 'One opportunity digital offers is the ability to do micro-targeting. It allows you to profile audiences much better and make it a one-to-one relationship. It's very different from the world we lived in where you relied on posters and television. Shikha is very well poised to understand and lead these changes.'

Despite the push towards digital marketing, television remains an incredibly powerful medium simply because of its reach. Television is booming in India, with a viewership of around 780 million, or about 65 per cent of the population.[2] 'It's not something we can do without,' Shikha explains. Television remains a key part of any marketing campaign—and of its budget. Film trailers and songs are staples on television and film stars

---

[1] Madhavankutty Pillai, 'The First Movie', *Open*, 11 May 2013.
[2] According to Broadcast Audience Research Council (BARC) India.

appear regularly on reality TV and comedy shows to plug a film before it
is released.

According to a 2017 KPMG India–FICCI report on the Indian media
and entertainment industry, the marketing budget of movies has steadily
increased over the years.[3] The report says:

> Currently, for a Bollywood movie, it varies from INR 100-250 million
> depending on the size of movie release. Television still takes the
> maximum share of 40 percent, print around 8-10 percent and digital
> comprising 10-15 percent. For a youth oriented movie, marketing
> budget allocation to digital platforms can go up to 20 percent.

Just four years ago, the average film-marketing budget ranged from Rs 80–
120 million, according to the FICCI–KPMG Media and Entertainment
report of 2013. For big-budget films, it went up to Rs 150 million and for
low-budget films, in some cases, it exceeded the production cost.[4]

Shikha markets all kinds of films—big commercial entertainers as
well as art-house indies. Whatever the content, the goal remains the same:
'To challenge the status quo all the time, whether it's an actor, director,
my team, or the CEO. Movies need to be marketed differently. There
is a filter that needs to change with every film.' She gives each film the
individual attention it deserves. 'It isn't a one-glove-fits-all scenario. The
more generic the industry becomes, the more challenging it is to try and
do things differently.'

Always up for a challenge, Shikha thrives on marketing difficult films.
'Not because it's my passion but because my expertise lies there. I like to
market unique films,' she says, her diamond nose pin glistening.

Neerja is a case in point. The 2016 movie was based on the true story
of a twenty-three-year-old Indian flight attendant, Neerja Bhanot, who
died while saving hundreds of passengers during the hijacking of Pan

---

3   KPMG India–FICCI, 'Media for the masses: The promise unfolds', Indian
    Media and Entertainment Industry Report, 2017.
4   FICCI–KPMG, 'The power of a billion. Realizing the Indian dream',
    Indian Media and Industry Report, 2013.

Am Flight 73 in 1986. Actor Sonam Kapoor played the title role. Shikha knew Sonam had delivered a fine performance. The challenge was to get people to believe that the actor, known as a style icon, was Neerja. Shikha wasn't sure if audiences would be able to separate the two. 'Would they be able to cross the divide and see Sonam as Neerja, a gritty, courageous heroine?'

There were other challenges as well. Those who remembered the Pan Am hijacking knew how the story unfolded. 'They knew the outcome—Neerja was going to be killed,' Singh says. 'So how do you build interest in a subject?' In addition, India's youth, which makes up a major chunk of the moviegoing population, did not know who Neerja was. It was up to Fox to find a way to lure this demographic to theatres. They needed a hook.

Shikha immersed herself in the film from its inception. It gave her time to breathe it, to live it, to feel it. When the time came to work on the marketing campaign, she was able to create something authentic. The ethos of her campaign was 'less is more'. To start with she talked about Neerja's story through subtle placements in the media. This piqued the audience's curiosity and created a low-key buzz about the film. Once Shikha felt the audience was ready, she released the film's trailer. Gradually, she amplified the campaign across various platforms but kept the tone subdued.

At its core was one central idea: to keep a laser-sharp focus on the protagonist, Neerja. 'When it came to integrating the film into general entertainment channels, into dance shows, reality shows, we were very sure we didn't want to go on set to sing, dance and judge,' Shikha says. 'It didn't reflect the film we had made.' At the same time, she wanted to reach the people watching those shows. 'We wanted to go there and tell people that this film is coming and that it's an important film.' It required a delicate balancing act.

Eventually, Shikha's team decided that Sonam would go on reality shows and appear on dance competitions on TV but on one condition: they would define the terms. 'We were strict about it. We said, "If you want Sonam to dance, we are not coming. If you want her to chat about her favourite comedy moments, she will not come."' Sonam understood that. 'She knew what she had to do. She would attend the shows, stay a couple of minutes, talk about *Neerja* and leave.' This way, Sonam created curiosity about the film but the team was able to maintain a steadfast focus on the character, Neerja.

The campaign worked. The film's success defied expectations. Critics hailed Sonam's performance in *Neerja* as her best work to date. Made on a modest budget of around Rs 20 crore, the film brought in a 300 per cent return on its investment.

'People are intelligent,' says Ram Madhvani, *Neerja*'s director. 'They can smell dishonest marketing. When there is honest marketing, it reflects the DNA of the film. The nice thing about Shikha is, in the way she marketed *Neerja*, she made no false promises.' Ram says Shikha understands the *sur* (tone) of a film and never looks at it as just a product. Every film she markets is *her* film.

Neerja was well received by audiences, even though marketing films with female leads has traditionally been a struggle in India. But as content is changing, so is the public's taste. 'What has become important is the reason to watch the film,' Shikha says. 'If there is a compelling reason to watch the film, the audience will watch it. It is not about who is in the film, but why I should watch the film. We have graduated from who to why, where and how.'

Neerja was a milestone in Shikha's life, and it came at a time of both triumph and despair, of a professional high but a personal low. Even as her career boomed, Shikha, who had dealt with a broken marriage and a fractured relationship, had slipped into deep depression. 'It was such a contrast. While I was going through depression personally, I delivered my best campaigns, on the films *Neerja* and *M.S. Dhoni: The Untold Story*. Ironically, both were films about courage.'

Shikha had endured many anxious days when she was studying philosophy at the prestigious Lady Shri Ram College for Women in Delhi. She was in love with a young man her parents did not approve of. The couple eloped hours before her final exam. The marriage lasted ten years before unravelling, leading to a messy divorce and an ugly legal battle for the custody of her son.

While she fought her personal battles, Shikha never stopped working. In fact, she says work became her refuge. 'I worship my work because it has always bailed me out. When I have not had the mental strength to come out of a situation, be it a relationship, be it a broken marriage, be it anything, work has helped me come back and attack something with a vengeance. I am happy I do something I love.'

Shikha speaks candidly about her battle with depression. She believes it's important to shine a light on a condition that is often brushed under the carpet. 'It's still a hush-hush topic in India and I don't know why. People worry about what others will say. It's still taboo. If someone says he or she could be depressed, a parent or a friend will tell them it's a phase. I don't see people recommending professional help. But telling a person who is suffering that this is a phase and it will pass can do more damage.'

In 2015 actor Deepika Padukone went public about her struggle with depression, marking the first time a film celebrity had spoken about her vulnerability openly. 'I really respect her for this, and am so proud of her,' Shikha says. 'Your experiences should be able to contribute to society. If you are able to influence even one life positively, it's a life well lived. We are blessed to be in this world. Let's make it count.'

Shikha is in a better place today. She says she doesn't look back except to learn from the past and doesn't seek the future. 'I love the present. It is the only reminder of being alive. Not the past, not the future,' she says. The practice of mindfulness, which believes in being present in the current moment, is a big part of her life. 'Every day there is something new to learn—that's the beauty of mindfulness.'

In an industry where uncertainty is par for the course, Shikha stays centred by meditating. It is the first thing she does in the morning before the routine demands of everyday life distract her. After that, it's time for exercise. Sometimes it's the gym, otherwise a yoga class. She doesn't look at her first email till 10 a.m. 'Until then, it's only me.'

She is a dedicated Headspacer—a fan of the popular mobile meditation and mindfulness app Headspace and derives strength from the inspirational teachings of spiritual author Eckhart Tolle. 'Following his practice changed my perspective on life. He taught me to just accept things the way they are, to not resist them or quiet them. Because they are not going to go away—and in that radical acceptance lies the beauty of meditation.' It is in these moments spent in quiet reflection, in stillness and in silence that Shikha finds peace. 'Meditation heals but it's not easy. The reason I began meditating is that I had no place to go but within.'

She doesn't say much more, except that she is reluctant to talk about a particularly challenging relationship because she doesn't want to give it any more importance in her life. 'But,' she says emphatically, 'sometimes you have to look the devil in the eye to find your courage and move on. Let's just say I met the devil and moved past my personal shortcomings.' She thinks of it as a huge personal victory.

Spending time by herself is the most gratifying part of her life. 'Because it's when you really do that do you discover yourself and connect with a part of you that is otherwise not accessible. It's like spending time with your own thoughts. Let them settle, let the dust settle. Let everything else come above. That's been my journey over the last few years.'

Meditating helped her become comfortable in her own skin. She has no public persona—she is who she is, and in her own words, she is a loner. 'I know that I am shy, an introvert. Our industry is a window-dressing industry. Being seen with the right people, speaking to the right people is important. But over a period of time I realized that this is not me. And I am not going to do anything which is outside the grain of who I am. What speaks is the quality of my work.'

She believes in a simple formula for success—when you are at work, give it your all. When at home, switch off. When her son, Trish, was little, 'it was all work, work, work,' she admits. 'After a point, I realized it's not worth it. That comes with age, it comes with experience and it comes with knowing that there are certain battles to fight and certain battles to just let go.' Today, the single mother is disciplined about separating her professional and personal life. 'When I am at home with my son, you can call me but I won't take your call. When I am at work, my mom can call me but I won't take her call either.'

Shikha and her son engage in friendly banter as Trish, back from a shopping spree ahead of his birthday, pulls out the clothes he has bought to show his mother. 'That's cool,' she says as he shows her a hoodie from Zara. 'Yeah, I like that,' she says. He smiles. The name plaque outside their apartment reads 'Shikha and Trish'. 'She's like my friend,' the fourteen-year-old says thoughtfully. 'I know she went through a really hard time a few years ago but throughout, she has been both my mother and my father.'

With no roots in the industry, Shikha thinks of herself as an outsider. The young girl who loved singing and dancing and dreamt of becoming an actor never actively sought out a career in the movie business. After dropping out of college, she enrolled for a graphic design course at an Aptech centre in New Delhi, which set her up for her first job—as a wedding card designer. A few years later, Shikha and her husband moved to Mumbai, where job opportunities were more promising. She worked in public relations before accepting a job at Subhash Ghai's Mukta Arts as the head of its marketing department. At Mukta, she learned a valuable lesson: Marketing isn't about numbers, it is about trusting one's intuition.

After cutting her teeth at Mukta, Shikha's next job at UTV gave her a chance to really come into her own. UTV Motion Pictures was producing the Aamir Khan starrer, *Rang De Basanti* (2006), which became the first film Shikha worked on. She made a name for herself by introducing several new, innovative strategies to promote the film, which was about India's youth. The apparel brand Provogue created a *Rang De Basanti*–inspired line of clothes, phone maker LG created wallpapers and screen savers from the film, the movie's cast and crew visited campuses to discuss issues facing students. And, in multiple fan-girl moments during several marketing meetings, she found herself in the same room as her teenage crush, Aamir Khan. 'Oh, but it's not the same thing. He's such a taskmaster!' she laughs loudly, a full throaty laugh. 'On a serious note though, he taught me profound business and life lessons. He really respects hard work and preparation.'

That admiration is reciprocated. In those meetings, Shikha clearly impressed the superstar. 'She is someone with a very sharp mind,' Aamir says. 'She's very passionate and committed to what she is doing, very dependable.'

Shikha is serious about her work but doesn't take it too seriously, which means she does not believe marketing is more important that the film itself. 'It's not the nucleus of a film. It is a catalyst.' She compares marketing to a drug. 'The high is what the audience decides. If it is bad marketing, they are not going to get that high and they will abuse the shit out of you.' That has happened, she admits. When confronted with failure, she takes it in her stride.

Her first film at Fox, the big-budget period drama *Bombay Velvet,* performed miserably at the box office, despite a marketing campaign that had created a buzz. The day *Bombay Velvet* released, Shikha was in her office. She knew the film had failed. Although she's not one to burst into tears easily, that day she did. She called Karan Johar who had made his acting debut in the film. She distinctly remembers what he told her. 'Go and have a glass of wine, come back to work in the morning and it will be a fresh day.'

Since then, Shikha has learned the value of detachment. 'It's enough to know I did my best,' she says. 'Even if things go south.'

She's pragmatic. Her home and workspace reflect that. Her office at Fox is tidy, organized and has a corporate look and feel to it except for a pair of flip-flops lying on the carpet. Noticing them, Shikha, who wears heels one day, flats or chappals the next, laughs. 'I like to walk around barefoot at work!' The footwear comes off when she reaches her desk. Framed prints of the films she has worked on are displayed on one wall but it's another, narrow wall in one corner of the room that screams for attention. It's covered with colourful postcards. Each one has a phrase: 'Notice Strangers'; 'Yes Yes Yes'; 'Tension Is a Teacher'; 'Listen Deeply to Others'. And many more. These are mindfulness cards that Shikha bought online. Does she have a favourite? Actually, there are a few, she says. 'Watch the Mind Like TV'; 'There's Always More' and 'Let It Go'.

These are simple ideas; perhaps the only simple ones Shikha embraces.

AMRITA MAHAL NAKAI
THE PRODUCTION DESIGNER

D adasaheb Phalke Chitranagri, better known as Film City, is a sprawling studio complex in Mumbai's Goregaon suburb. On a hot day in early 2018, one of its largest open spaces is a hive of activity. An elaborate set, built to look like Lahore's Heera Mandi in the 1940s, is being erected. Over 200 workers are constructing, carving, welding and moving equipment under the blazing sun. The whirr of drilling, sawing and hammering is everywhere. Arched doorways, elaborately carved windows, intricately decorated three-storey buildings and a maze of alleyways have been propped up with scaffolding. It looks like early twentieth-century, old-town Lahore, but with a beauty and symmetry that suggests artistic licence.

Inside one tent sits a team from the art department, going over the plans in detail. Walls are pasted with photographic references, bulging binders full of historic information lie neatly stacked, and a mock-up of the grand set dominates an enormous centre table. These could be the plans for a major city construction site, but are in fact a blueprint for a film set that will be built in three months. Amid this painstaking preparation and construction frenzy sits Amrita Mahal Nakai, the production designer. She has been dreaming and thinking of this set for more than two-and-a-half years.

Production (or set) designers have one of the most important roles in the movie business. At the 1990 Oscar awards, Hollywood actor Mel Gibson explained that production designers are men and women whose vision and imagination turn a director's dream into reality and everyday reality into fantasy. Setting up the environment is critical when telling a story and without such a creative person, a film would fall flat. Writing in the *New York Times*, cultural journalist Boris Kachka explained, 'An auteur's designer has his ear, and becomes his eyes and hands. Directors might get all the glory, but without production designers they'd be flying blind.'[1]

Amrita's work brings films to life. Critics have called her work 'superb' and 'sumptuous'. Karan Johar, for whose company, Dharma Productions,

---

[1] https://www.nytimes.com/2017/09/13/t-magazine/entertainment/
   production-designers-film-movies.html

Amrita has done some of her best work, says, 'I always noticed her strong sense of aesthetics and her complete ability to work beyond what is expected of her. Her passion supersedes what is required. I love that in any professional, where they go beyond what is expected and just do it because they are so immensely passionate about their craft.'

Since 2008, when she began her career as an independent designer, Amrita's work on films like *Dostana* (2008), *Little Zizou* (2008), *Wake Up Sid* (2009), *No Problem* (2010), *I Hate Luv Stories* (2010), *Jo Hum Chahein* (2011), *Student of the Year* (2012), *Yeh Jawani Hai Deewani* (2013), *Bombay Talkies* (2013), *2 States* (2014), *Shandaar* (2015) and *Ae Dil Hai Mushkil* (2016) has been widely appreciated. When she was interviewed for this book, she was working on two films simultaneously, both for Dharma Productions—Abhishek Varman's *Kalank*, and Ayan Mukerji's *Brahmastra*.

Imagination is critical in setting up a story visually. Props, background and location come under Amrita's remit, and she works closely with the director to realize his or her vision. Sometimes, real outdoor locations fulfil needs, but often, they don't. Remember the cool Miami apartment in *Dostana*, used by Sam (Abhishek Bachchan), Kunal (John Abraham) and Neha (Priyanka Chopra)? It was a set built in Mumbai! Or the wedding scene in *2 States*, which was shot in a beautiful temple? Amrita and director Abhishek Varman had gone to Mahabalipuram to shoot the scene at the iconic Shore Temple. Unfortunately, the restrictions due to the monument's designation as a World Heritage Site made that tricky. They had to come up with an alternative, so they built a similar looking temple on a cliff! The result was a visually impressive backdrop for the climax.

The directors she has worked with agree that Amrita has an instinctive understanding of what a movie requires and that she immediately absorbs the director's vision. Tarun Mansukhani, who hired her for *Dostana*, considered by some to be one of India's most stylish films, says he did so because he had 'confidence in her and the belief that she would give her life to the film. There was that energy and fire that she came with that is still there today. No matter how big a film is, she will handle it.'

Abhishek Varman, who worked with Amrita on *2 States*, says, 'She can interpret a director's visuals and take it a step forward. Sometimes, it is difficult for a production designer to understand what a director is looking for, but Amrita has a knack for understanding that vision. She makes every film she works on very personal.'

Film-maker Sooni Taraporevala, with whom Amrita worked on *Little Zizou*, says, 'She totally got that I wanted the film to be as real as possible, and that meant shooting at locations where we could not alter much and working within those parameters. Amrita had a lot of constraints and she did a marvellous job even within those.'

Amrita got her big break working with Sharmishta Roy, the pioneering production designer who is considered a doyenne of the craft. Roy was a mentor. She says Amrita has an innate sense of design, which she expresses in the most unexpected ways. 'One of her strengths is dressing—the use of colour, props, texture, decor,' Roy says. 'In *Ae Dil Hai Mushkil*, she used a blue chandelier on an off-white background in the song '*Channa Mereya*', which was unexpected in a courtyard scenario and looked beautiful. It's these unexpected touches that stand out in her work.'

Award-winning cinematographer Anil Mehta, who has worked with Amrita from her earliest days in the business, describes her as 'difficult, because she has a definite point of view, stubborn, because she knows what is good for the movie and will insist on it, and opinionated because she has a finely honed aesthetic and a refined sensibility. All these qualities bring a lot of value to the look of a film.' He points to the fact that a production designer is integral to the work of a cinematographer and that the relationship is both vital and tenuous. After *Kabhi Alvida Na Kehna* (2006) wrapped up its filming, Mehta gifted Amrita a book by Screencraft, *Production Design & Art Direction*, and inscribed it with the words, 'For one of the best "workers" on KANK.'

Her husband Vir Nakai calls his wife a perfectionist. 'Everything has to be done to a T—if she plans something, it has to be done exactly like that. Once Amrita sets her mind to something, it is very hard to break what she wants to do.'

Amrita works predominantly with Dharma Productions, which was founded by the late Yash Johar, and is now helmed by his son Karan, whose early movies in the 1990s became famous for their larger-than-life, lavish sets and dramatic stories. Then, at the turn of this century,

Dharma began delivering more realistic urban fare, which required truer-to-life film sets. For that, the company needed a production designer with a contemporary aesthetic. Amrita arrived at the right time, beginning with *Dostana* and following it up with *Wake Up Sid*.

She likes Dharma's collaborative approach. Significantly, the company has a reputation for allocating healthy budgets to production design and pays attention to detail, care and quality. If Hindi movies command higher production values today and look much slicker and more authentic than they did in the past, Dharma deserves major credit for the change.

Dharma has also been an extremely supportive working environment for Amrita. Given the odd and long hours her job demands, the firm has given her a wide berth, actively encouraging her to bring her family along on shoots. Two months after her daughter Gia was born, Vir and the baby were by Amrita's side on the sets of *Student of the Year*. Karan made sure the new mother had whatever assistance she required.

'I feel like I am her professional parent,' jokes Karan. 'Amrita has been schooled and educated by her parents and has been raised by me professionally. I have seen her since she was a young girl, when she was an assistant to Sharmishta, and she completely integrated herself into the Dharma ecosystem. We call her an exceptionally lucky force because she has had a 100 per cent success record—she has worked on all of Dharma's big hits. She is the art and production designer on two of our most ambitious films, *Brahmastra* and *Kalank*.'

'It goes without saying that she's amazing at her work,' says stylist Anaita Shroff Adajania, who is also working on *Brahmastra*. 'But the other quality I admire about her is that she never stops working. Even if a set is ready and it's built, she's always looking for the tiny details to see how to make it better, to make sure the walls are nice, the book on the table is the right one, and those little details that humanize her work.'

Amrita is intuitive. Through her years of experience, she can tell when something looks wrong. For technical assistance, she turns to Munindra D. Jangam, better known as 'Kedar Dada', whom she's known since his days as Sharmishta Roy's chief assistant. He is a fine draughtsman and works closely with Amrita as a supervising art director.

Kedar Dada describes Amrita as detail-oriented. 'She looks at every single tiny requirement. I have learnt the art of detailing and its importance. Earlier, we could get away with putting anything on set without much thought, but it doesn't work like that any more. For example, for a dining set earlier, we'd put any thali, any plate, but not today. Now we have to think ten times about the right spoon to use, the right material of the plate. Since I have started working with Amrita, I have been inspired to look into the details, and the result is evident on screen.'

Their process typically works like this: Amrita lays out references for him, based on which Kedar Dada makes sketches, drawings and models. 'Amrita is very correct in all ways. In our profession, there is no definition of a lot of work or less work—if there's a lot of work for one set, there might be less for another. It all depends on the story and the film. For example, if we're constructing a haveli, one has to look into the interiors, the exteriors, one has to design the whole look of the haveli. This takes a lot of manpower. We need to look at all the detailing required for the inside of the haveli—sofa, interiors, all the upholstery. Leaving aside the costumes, we look into everything else.'

Fifty years ago, Bollywood set design meant elaborate homes with winding staircases and chandeliers. Movies were usually filmed in beautiful outdoor locations around India like Kashmir. From the mid-1980s onwards, Yash Chopra made Switzerland famous for Indian audiences by filming there assiduously. In the twenty-first century, animation and special effects became popular as India made large strides in sophisticated computer-generated technology and began gaining ground as Hollywood's back office for such technical skills. That knowledge spilled over into our moviemaking too. Movies like *Ra.One*, the *Dhoom* series, *Bhaag Milkha Bhaag*, *Om Shanti Om* and *Chennai Express* used special effects, often without the audience realizing it.[2]

'These guys are visual,' Amrita explains about directors like Karan, Ayan Mukerji, Abhishek Varman, Puneet Malhotra and Tarun Mansukhani, who work with Dharma Productions. 'They tell you how they want the

---

2   http://www.maacindia.com/blog/index.php/top-5-bollywood-films-that-
     have-used-vfx-effectively/

film to look even before it goes on the floor. We spend time on references, mapping each section out. Each scene has to have a feel. It's in your brain even before filming begins and even if you don't have a team in place, you know where you want it to go. The costume is imperative and the director of photography plays an important role, so that it all comes together.' Because she knows her directors well, a movie's concept becomes just as real in her head.

In fact, she knows her directors so well that Karan jokes, 'She needs one cabin to do her work and one to do therapy. She has become the private therapist at Dharma Productions, listening to everyone's trials, tribulations and terrors.'

For a production designer, translating a story from concept to reel means thinking about everything, from the colour of a wall to the way a sofa is dressed to how a temple appears on-screen and everything in between. In Hollywood, a production designer is responsible for conceptualizing the overall look, including overseeing locations, colour palette, set design and the like. He or she is responsible for supervising art directors, costume, make-up and hair, because they are in charge of making the production come to life. That hasn't yet happened in India. The term production designer has only recently come into vogue in Bollywood; previously, art directors were responsible for set design and a film's 'look'.

'In Indian films, we are primarily art directors,' Amrita explains. 'Production designer is a credit that has come in more recently. In the past, the costume people did their own thing, the art department did their own thing and if anything looked great, it was because of the director. Nowadays, production design means putting together the entire colour palette and locations, and working closely with the costume folks. It's a fancier-sounding designation but involves essentially set design and construction, identifying locations and making them usable—anything you see visually is what we are responsible for. Slowly, it's becoming more like the overall feel.'

The transition from over-the-top sets that offered audiences an escape happened sometime at the beginning of this century. Amrita believes it is because the stories being told became more realistic and less fantastical. 'Cinema has changed. The newer kids who came in wanted to make films differently and they were more exposed to world cinema. Take the directors

I work with—for them, it is important to understand the significance of a character's bag, what's in the bag, why should that person be carrying a bag? That's the kind of detail we worry about now.'

When asked about her creative prowess, Amrita shrugs. 'It's just something I do, yaar,' she says with a laugh. She finds it embarrassing to talk about herself and dismisses her accomplishments with a casual air. Dressed in her on-location uniform of blue jeans, a black shirt and blue sneakers, her hair tied back, her 'office' look includes kohl-rimmed eyes, a diamond nose ring, big silver hoop earrings and a silver *kada* (bangle). Remarkably relaxed amid the construction chaos around her, she smiles often, revealing an endearing gap tooth.

It's been a thrilling journey since Amrita first worked on *Dostana* as an independent art director. At the time, the twenty-eight-year-old had initially refused the job when Tarun Mansukhani offered it to her. The two had worked together on *Kabhi Alvida Na Kehna,* where Tarun was an associate director and Amrita was working under Sharmishta in the art department. 'She was in shock and there was a moment of silence, and she looked at me like I had gone mad!' Tarun remembers. Amrita was overwhelmed. 'Then she got extremely emotional and started crying.'

Karan Johar recalls that when Tarun told him he wanted Amrita on board as the production designer, 'there was no question of me debating it because I had seen her work as a production designer and I knew she had what it takes in terms of attitude, craftsmanship and the ability to succumb to the director's vision, and also to create a new vision of her own. She had all of that in abundance.'

Amrita spoke to Roy, who told her she was crazy to refuse the assignment. 'She said, if I don't take the plunge now, I never will, so that set me thinking,' Amrita remembers. Overwhelmed by the massive responsibility, she says she felt anxious and on many days, feared she might have a heart attack. 'I was so scared during that film because I had never been in charge like that,' she now says with a laugh. It was extremely challenging. Amrita worked long hours and barely went home, despite the fact that she had recently got married.

Her hard work paid off. As Karan says, 'Amrita went on to give *Dostana* the aesthetic that matched the ethos of Dharma Productions, but also gave it a new synergy and energy. She collaborated completely and so efficiently with Tarun's vision. She gave it the grandeur and gloss that the film warranted.'

So committed is she to her work that Amrita changed her wedding date since it clashed with *Dostana's* shooting schedule. 'The film was too big a deal and honestly, the amount of money you are responsible for as a production designer is a bit daunting; so that weighed on me as a challenge,' she says. Her then-fiancé Vir was supportive. 'What was the big deal?' he says nonchalantly. The two had met at Vivek High School in Chandigarh, when Amrita was sixteen, and had started dating in college. 'We were together for eight years. It's not as though our wedding was going to change the way things were going to be.'

After *Dostana*, there was no looking back. Amrita has worked on some of the most impressive-looking movies to come out of Bollywood in the past decade.

Production designers typically have some art or architectural background. Amrita has a bachelor's degree in fine art from Government College of Art in Chandigarh. She had topped the entrance exam, much to her parents' surprise.

Dismissing any thoughts of innate artistic talent, Amrita says she only chose an art college because she didn't want to study subjects like psychology and economics. 'I used to draw disfigured people, slightly abstract weird stuff which could not be called art,' she jokes, in her typical self-deprecating fashion. Clearly, she is gifted. For the fiftieth anniversary of India's independence, Amrita made a painting in school for which she won a prize. 'Till that time, I never realized she had an artistic streak,' her mother says. But thinking back, her parents remember that on every birthday or anniversary, she would make them cards or beautiful paintings as gifts.

Amrita was born on 14 December 1980 in Bengaluru to Rabina and Wing Commander G.P. Singh. Amrita was the baby of the family, with three older siblings—Surinder, eighteen years older, is a major general in the army, Sabrina, sixteen years older, works in television, and Ramnique, eight years older, lives in the United States. Rabina remembers her youngest as a happy child. 'All the neighbourhood children would come over and play with her,' Rabina says. 'Everyone loved her because she was the youngest and her sisters' friends would shower her with gifts and chocolates.'

The Singhs moved every few years, given G.P.'s air force job. Amrita studied in Mumbai, Noida and eventually in Chandigarh. The family didn't watch many Hindi movies, although Rabina was a big Shashi Kapoor fan. G.P. preferred books. The earliest film Amrita recalls being excited about was *Hum Aapke Hain Kaun*, the 1994 romance starring Salman Khan and Madhuri Dixit. She was fourteen years old and enjoyed the love story.

In 2002, Amrita moved to Mumbai with Rs 20,000 given by her parents, and lived with her sister Sabrina, to whom she is extremely close. She eventually rented a flat with two girls and found work at a jewellery export house.

Her family knew she wasn't happy, though. Her sister Ramnique told her to quit and sent her a monthly stipend from the US while Amrita looked for a job that would be more fulfilling. 'Amrita was always determined she wanted to go into some field to do with the arts,' her mother says. Later, when her sister Sabrina got divorced, Amrita and she moved in together along with Sabrina's daughter Naima. The whole family is enormously supportive and close-knit.

Sabrina worked at Yash Raj Studios, so Amrita started hanging out there. She was good with Photoshop and helped anyone in the office who needed to use the program. One day, Sharmishta Roy walked in to pick up some reference books and randomly asked, 'Does anyone have an assistant? I need one!' Sabrina suggested Amrita.

'We were in the middle of *Bunty Aur Babli* and Sabrina dragged me into her cabin and said there's someone I want you to meet,' Roy remembers. 'Amrita stood with her back to the door. She was a little kid.' When asked what she did, Amrita recalls telling Roy, with characteristic candour, 'Nothing!' Roy ignored her and went off for a four-hour meeting. When she returned, she told Amrita, 'Just come—there's literally no one, and how bad could you be?' That was how Amrita got hired by one of Bollywood's most celebrated and sought-after art designers.

'It never really bothered me that she wasn't formally trained in the field in architecture or interior design,' Roy says. She was looking for someone with discipline, which Amrita had in spades. She was extremely punctual, hard-working, never said no to anything, and had a point of view, qualities that Roy appreciated.

'The way I do my job, the discipline and the way I function is because I trained with Sharmishta ma'am,' Amrita says, always using the respectful term for her former boss. Roy was an architect who could make her own drawings, drafting on AutoCad, the software most architects use. 'She knew exactly where each beam and *patti* was, which is different from how I do it,' Amrita explains, admitting that she herself has little technical knowledge. 'I wasn't trained as an architect and if I know something today, it's because I have built sets.'

Her lack of technical know-how has not hindered Amrita's creative output. As Abhishek Varman, a trained architect himself, says, 'She has a team that helps her execute, but what's more important is her ability to translate what's in a director's head. Whatever I imagine, it comes out far better thanks to her because she has a knack for opening up the space.' He cites the example of *2 States*, where he was constrained by the limitations imposed by the actual temple in Mahabalipuram. Amrita said, 'Why can't we replicate this?' I was sceptical because I knew it would be difficult and I certainly didn't think it would look real. A set is a set, after all. But she got the depth and the importance of the sequence because I told her the film might fail if the sequence doesn't work—it's the culmination of the entire script and the audience has to feel that the characters have worked towards this moment. She made it happen. I still have people come up to me and ask me where that location is, we want to get married there or shoot our film there. And when I say it was a set, they are taken aback.'

Amrita learnt all the tricks of her trade on the job. Her first experience on set was as an assistant on 2005's *Bunty Aur Babli*, starring Abhishek Bachchan and Rani Mukerji. 'Either you love it or are scared by it,' Amrita says. 'Sets are intimidating. Everyone can't handle being on one. Not everyone has the patience to deal with you. For me, I think it just happened.'

Amrita also worked under Roy on *Salaam Namaste* (2005), *Kabhi Alvida Naa Kehna* (2006) and *The Namesake* (2006).

On *Kalank*, her assistant production designer is Kshamata Sachin Gaurav, who describes Amrita as 'easy-going, someone who doesn't panic or shout, and manages well. She knows what she wants—often, people are confused on set, but she is not.'

Sumayya Shaikh is a former assistant who worked with Amrita for five years. She enjoyed the experience. 'Because Amrita is also young, she actually ends up designing a space in a very modern, new way and the atmosphere is fun and innovative. She is not someone who will be superficially present. She is constantly on throughout the job and can be quite a taskmaster.' Shaikh says Amrita thinks hard before putting something on set and creates a scene carefully. If a lamp is required and she can't find it in the market, for example, she will fabricate one herself. 'She's also not one to get frazzled if it's a big set,' Shaikh notes.

Amrita's sensibility is contemporary, but her process is old-fashioned. She draws on paper and shares it with a technically skilled deputy—typically Kedar Dada, who converts it into a technical drawing. 'Sharmishta ma'am was capable of giving a drawing with specifications and it would be just right,' Amrita explains. 'I do it by eye.'

Roy puts it slightly differently. 'Around the world, each production designer interprets things differently. How you communicate a film, how well you do that, is what counts. The audience is willing to believe an environment that you have created—it doesn't matter how you go about it.'

Sooni Taraporevala recalls Amrita's ability to conjure up spaces on *Little Zizou*. 'She created many things. Our production office was in this wonderful building—Parsi Lying In Hospital in Mumbai's Fountain area. Amrita was able to turn those hospital rooms into various other kinds of spaces, like the flight simulator scenes and the principal's office. Boman Irani's character had a newspaper office—Amrita created and dressed that room to make it look like his office when there was nothing there before.'

For *Dostana*, the art department, under Amrita's supervision, made 100 sketches. The slick apartment, the plush Verve office and the set for the '*Desi Girl*' song were built in Mumbai. Director Tarun Mansukhani says he did not provide Amrita with much of a brief for any of the sets. For the house, he wanted a three-bedroom flat, with two of the rooms sharing a bathroom as per the script. Because he had worked with Karan for a little too long, he says he wanted everything on a bigger scale. 'We ended up with a 1,500 square foot living space, three large bedrooms, a kitchen and a balcony with a swimming pool. When the unit and I walked into that house, we were all like "when are we going to have a house like this?"' The finish was fantastic!'

Similarly, for the *Verve* magazine office set, the director didn't provide a brief. They had not had a conversation about decor and how the cabins should look. 'Eventually, when I walked on to that set, I was blown away,' he recalls. 'I thought, "My God, it's like this woman is in my head!" How did she manage that?' Amrita had chosen darker colours, in contrast to the apartment where Priyanka Chopra's character stays. It was a cool, contemporary office that continues to look relevant even a decade after the movie was made. As Mansukhani says, 'If you walk on to a set for the first time and if you don't feel you're there, it's not going to happen, and you're in trouble. What Amrita always brings to the table is the feeling that you are there.'

'We didn't think she had such talent,' Amrita's mother says. 'But we know that she likes to put 100 per cent into her work and won't compromise on anything.' Husband Vir says he never fails to be amazed whenever he sees his wife's work. 'The kind of nonsense she can pull together to erect a brilliant set, I look at it and can't believe that it comes out of her head.'

After getting married, the couple didn't take a vacation for nine years because Amrita was working non-stop. She hardly gets any downtime, and when she does, she likes to paint walls and furniture at home. Vir says their house changes every six months because artistic Amrita likes to constantly try new colours. She also rearranges furniture and paintings regularly. 'If she had her way, we would live on an IKEA set,' he says jokingly, referring to the DIY home furnishings store.

When Amrita started out, Roy was the only woman working as a production designer. The rest were all men. The field has grown exponentially since then. Kedar Dada, who began working in 1995, recalls how there were few women on set at the time. 'There were two or three women working as art directors then, including Sharmishta,' he says. From 2003 onwards, he saw a sea change and today, he estimates that there is a 60/40 divide in favour of women.

Rangarao Choughle, senior vice-president at the Association of Cine & Television Art Directors & Costume Designers, says, 'Earlier, there were very few women in the art department, though this number is increasing slowly. There are more women in the costume department but overall, there are more men than women across all departments—I would say the ratio is 70 to 30.' The union currently has about 2,250 members, including production designers, art directors, set designers, costume designers and assistants.

The merging of the art and costume department unions happened in 1998, according to Choughle. 'R.K. Handa was then president of the art directors' union and felt that it would be better for both costume and art to fall under one union. What happened earlier is that no one knew what the costume and the set were till these were ready and then one had to work together—sometimes it clashed, like the set would be blue and the actors' clothes were also blue. To avoid this and create a holistic palette, the unions were merged as we thought it was better for them all to work with each other. Manish Malhotra became the first costume designer to join us back then.' Today, the coordination between these two departments has helped improve the overall look of Hindi cinema.

Some in the industry, including Amrita, think women bring a different eye to production design. Abhishek Varman feels that women technicians have a certain eye that enhances detail. 'Men are invested in the structural, technical aspect, but not always in the dressing aspect, or the small personal things that are required to make a set come together.'

There's no such thing as a regular day for a production designer. As husband Vir says, 'When she's working, we all live the work. Her work never finishes since there is no 9 to 5.' Karan Johar describes her as 'a super worker'. He also credits Vir with being a progressive husband. 'Vir understands Amrita's passion and respects it, he represents the Husband 2.0 of this country.'

Indeed, working in the movie industry is stressful, and Amrita readily admits that she is terrible at managing hours. It's a 24/7 job that she doesn't leave behind at the office. 'Even when I go home, my brain is constantly on. I look at stuff and think up things all the time. You can't take a break, and a lot of it comes from the fact that you love the person who is putting the film together and it becomes personal. If it's not personal, it won't work.'

SHUBHA RAMACHANDRA
THE SCRIPT SUPERVISOR

Shubha Ramachandra calls herself a watchdog.

Hunched over a monitor on a film set, she watches each scene painstakingly, looking for any errors or slip-ups as the camera rolls. Shubha is a script supervisor, someone who ensures there is continuity between each scene in a film. It's her job to ensure that props, costumes, hair and make-up, set design and actions flow seamlessly from one shot to the next. Script supervisors have been described as 'secret ninjas', people who anticipate and solve problems on set even before they occur. Shubha is one of the most accomplished script supervisors in Hindi cinema today.

In Hollywood, the role of a script supervisor is a given. In Indian cinema, it's not as prevalent, although in the last decade it has become a more recognized job. Shubha was ahead of the curve. She has been a script supervisor for fifteen years, a remarkable tenure given how recently the position has entered Hindi filmdom's lexicon. There was a time when mainstream masala films were completely unfamiliar with script supervisors. They relied on a second assistant director to assume basic continuity duties. That is now changing.

When Hindi films took years to shoot and actors worked on multiple sets, continuity gaps caused some hilarity. Movie stars would unintentionally have different looks at different stages in a film. In the book *First Day, First Show*, film critic and journalist Anupama Chopra writes of one example from the early 1990s where a busy writer 'inadvertently mixed up scenes for two different films that were being shot simultaneously. Bollywood lore has it that both crews shot the wrong scene before realizing it was from another film.'[1] In the 1994 film *Andaz Apna Apna*, actor Salman Khan sported various hair lengths at different points in the film because it took three years to complete. The focus of Hindi films was escapism and fantasy. Continuity was of little consequence.

As Hindi cinema moved into the twenty-first century, production values went up. There was a growing realization that films must have authenticity and flow. Even if a movie is in the realm of make-believe,

---

[1] Anupama Chopra, *First Day, First Show*, New Delhi: Penguin Books, 2011, p. xvii.

it began to dawn on film-makers that audiences will not accept complete absurdity.

At forty-four, Shubha is at the pinnacle of her career. Her CV boasts of critically acclaimed films like *Amu* (2005), *Honeymoon Travels Pvt Ltd.* (2007), *Loins of Punjab Presents* (2007), *Manorama Six Feet Under* (2007), *Luck by Chance* (2009), *Karthik Calling Karthik* (2010), *Game* (2011), *Talaash* (2012) and box-office bonanzas like *Bhaag Milkha Bhaag* (2013), *Dil Dhadakne Do* (2015) and *Gold* (2018). She has also worked as an assistant director on *My Brother Nikhil* and *Jhankaar Beats*.

She has come a long way from her first film, the 2002 *Agnivarsha*, when she knew nothing about script supervision to 2018, when she wrapped up work on Reema Kagti's *Gold*, starring Akshay Kumar. For many years, Shubha found it hard to get jobs and gain recognition. Nowadays, she gets calls from the offices of mainstream movie makers like Rohit Dhawan, asking her to work on commercial comedies and entertainers.

'I really like working with Shubha,' says Zoya Akhtar, the award-winning director. 'She has got a very strong sense of story. I find that she is not intrusive and at the same time she's totally on. I can turn to her at any moment and she knows exactly what I'm thinking and we are really in sync.'

Zoya says a script supervisor is very important for her because she likes having someone on the team who looks at scene coverage. 'As a director I don't really look at my script once I start shooting, because I have written it and just go with it. The story is in me. But it's good for me to have someone who is making sure the script is covered and it really helps me have someone beside the DoP who is looking at eyeline. Because we don't shoot linear, it's important to discuss character, and whether the tone and mood is correct. Shubha checks all the boxes.'

Although she comes across as serious when you first meet her, Shubha is anything but. She's quick to laugh. With her short, cropped hair, she looks younger than her age. When she smiles a big, broad, ear-to-ear smile, her face lights up. She has a no-nonsense, simple attitude towards clothing: it's typically a loose T-shirt and comfortable trousers. A large backpack that she lugs around gives her a college-student air.

Script supervisors are becoming an essential part of a shoot, whether for film or for television. 'A good producer always invests in a good script supervisor today,' says Udayan Bhat, chief operating officer at Anil Kapoor Film Company. Bhat, who worked with Shubha on the Indian version of the American television series *24* in 2013, says the season's first series would not have been as successful without Shubha on board. The show was praised for its crisp storytelling and Bhat gives Shubha credit for that. 'She has the knack for spotting inconsistencies in an instant,' he says. The crew shot for 188 days across twenty-four episodes and Bhat points out that even on the 188th day, if an actor was referring to the first day or episode, Shubha had to make sure the information was accurate and consistent. 'You can trust her,' he says. 'She is very calm on set. She is succinct in what she is presenting. She's very clear in terms of what has been written on which page. She can identify a problem but also has a solution.'

Script supervision is catching on in India, but is yet to be recognized as a specialized field, unlike in Hollywood where 'scripty' keeps track of continuity from scene to scene. In the 1930s and '40s, it was done by 'script girls' who worked behind the scenes and for no personal glory. Doing the job right meant there was nothing to show for it—no errors. Later, the nomenclature changed, and it was no longer gender-specific.

The late Hassan Kutty is thought to be Hindi cinema's first real and lauded script supervisor—he worked on fifty films,[2] including hits such as *Salaam Bombay!*, *Lagaan* and *Taare Zameen Par*. When Shubha started working, she could count the number of script supervisors on the fingers of one hand. These days, she has the numbers of about twenty script supervisors on her phone.

'People recognize that not hiring a script supervisor can save on time and money and their contribution may not be immediately apparent but having them on board means you are getting your creatives right,' she explains. 'On the edit table you are not saying "oh shit, we didn't get this right, we need to reshoot". A good script supervisor fills in those gaps.'

When Shubha came on board for *Agnivarsha*, she was filling in for Hassan Kutty, who was unwell. Because she knew editing, an integral

---

2   Tanul Thakar, 'Written Off : The Unappreciated Work of Bollywood Script Supervisors', *Caravan*, 1 February 2016.

part of the continuity process, she got the job. Shubha had never worked as a script supervisor. To prep, she read and memorized the book *Script Supervising and Film Continuity*, a 250-odd-page industry classic by Pat P. Miller, an American script supervisor, in four days!

Inexperience has its advantages. Shubha credits her first film as her best experience because she didn't berate herself for making mistakes. It was a learning process. Since then, she's plagued by guilt whenever she makes mistakes. 'Forgiveness doesn't come easily to me, so it's hard to be doing a job like this,' she says, again with a laugh. When she realized there was a continuity mistake on *Gold*, Shubha went off into a corner and shed copious tears. Reema Kagti, the director who knows her well, tried to make her feel better—'You can't do that, you're too old to cry,' she said.

She enjoyed working on *Agnivarsha* so much that Shubha decided movies were her future. In October 2001, the twenty-eight-year-old moved from her hometown Bengaluru to Mumbai to follow her dreams. She had no connections to the Mumbai film world and landed up in the big city without a job. The early days of struggle would have broken a weaker person. But not Shubha.

In Mumbai, she stayed at the Good Shepherd Convent, a working women's hostel in Four Bungalows, where all she had was a bed, her clothes and some books. Later, she shared a one-bedroom apartment in bustling, congested Amboli. It was a far cry from the serene and pristine Bengaluru she was used to.

With a laser-sharp focus on finding a job, she would stand in a public phone booth everyday, *Yellow Pages* in hand and cold-call people asking for work. Her pitch was simple. 'I'd say, "I am from Bengaluru. I would like to see if I can meet someone and get work."'

'People rarely took my call, or they would say "call me tomorrow or next week" and then not pick up,' she rues, even after so many years. 'They don't understand that someone's life depends on this "call tomorrow"! If they had said no instead it would have been kinder.'

One of the people she cold-called was the venerated director Shyam Benegal. Benegal told her to come and meet him. Shubha says that meeting gave her hope.

'He chatted with me for forty-five minutes and asked about me: where I came from, what I had done, and then he said, "Look I'm sorry I can't offer you a job because you don't speak Hindi."' Despite the rejection, Shubha was happy. 'Although he said no, he gave me the time, he treated me like royalty! I love that man. He said, "Call me when you get some experience and can speak a bit of Hindi, and we'll see if we can work together."'

It was the encounter Shubha needed. It spurred her to continue hunting for work. Two months later, the moment she was waiting for arrived. She got a call from Pritish Nandy Communications. It was for a film called *Jhankaar Beats*, directed by Sujoy Ghosh. 'By then I had run out of my savings and was penniless,' Shubha remembers. Even though it was a big break, the pay wasn't great. Shubha made Rs 7,000 a month over eight months and worked two jobs—as script supervisor and as assistant director. That meant she did pretty much everything.

'The kind of value and strength a script supervisor brings to a film is incredible,' says Ghosh, who went on to make *Kahaani* and *Kahaani 2*. 'They are the fulcrum and they hold the film together on set. I can forget what dialogue or angle I have taken and I do forget that in the rush of things but the script supervisor reminds you that you forgot this or you are doing this wrong. That's where a script supervisor like Shubha saves your ass.'

That's Shubha, the professional. Those who have worked with her also rave about Shubha, the person. 'There's something very nice about her,' Ghosh says. 'She hasn't changed in all these years. I would love to work with her again.'

After *Jhankaar Beats*, Shubha found herself broke and without work again. She headed home to Bengaluru to do freelance gigs, made a bit of money and returned to Mumbai to look for work. By the end of 2003, she could no longer sustain herself. She thought of leaving again, this time for good. Just then, Highlight Films, a breeding ground for film talent, came calling. Srila Chatterjee, who helmed Highlight for more than twenty-five years, was line-producing a film on the Swaminarayan faith.

The film needed a script supervisor of international calibre. According to Chatterjee, Shubha rose to the occasion. 'The director has to be confident you are on their side, ensuring what they want done is done without interfering too much. It's a very fine line and Shubha walks it very well, because she's not loud and in your face, but works quietly and efficiently.'

In 2004, film-maker Shonali Bose came to India from Los Angeles to make *Amu*, her debut film. She needed a script supervisor. Through her training at film school, she knew this role was critical to moviemaking. Bose thought she would need to bring someone from the US to do this job, but Chatterjee, an old friend from Kolkata, instantly recommended Shubha, whom she considered the best in India. 'I remember asking Srila what if I can't get Shubha, and she replied: if you can't get Shubha get someone from America,' Bose says. Luckily, Shubha was available.

Bose and Shubha got along famously. The director relied on Shubha completely. 'A script supervisor sits at the monitor and is the one you are most in contact with—they are right by you the whole day,' Bose says. 'Shubha became my right-hand person on *Amu*. She is the person I relied on to check if a shot or performance was fine. I could totally count and rely on her judgement. She understood both framing and performance. There were times when I was feeling totally isolated creatively and having a difficult time and Shubha was marvellous. We were completely in sync creatively. I have yet to find someone of Shubha's calibre.'

Bose, who describes Shubha's personality as easy-going and bindas, points out how professional and thorough she is on set, and that Shubha's brain understands the relationship between camera and subject.

Mary Cybulski, an American script supervisor who has worked on major motion pictures like *Life of Pi*, *Eternal Sunshine of the Spotless Mind* and *Syriana* describes the job:

'First, we analyze and supervise the script. Second, we are in charge of continuity. Third, we are technical advisors for the grammar of filmmaking. It is our job to understand the bones and spirit of the story. We imagine all the little bits of the movie we are making.'[3]

A script supervisor is the person who will authoritatively tell you about technical details like eyeline matching, which involves continuity

---

[3] Mary Cybulski, *Beyond Continuity: Script Supervision for the Modern Filmmaker*, Taylor and Francis Group, 2014.

between shots. He or she takes copious, detailed notes. First, there is a shot-by-shot breakdown; then, each shot is broken down by angle and she needs to ensure that continuity matches, which is especially vital for action shots. If an actor picks up a glass, has a sip of water at a particular word, then leans back in her chair—she has to match those actions in the next frame. It can be a lot for the actor to remember. Shubha's job is to distinguish the wood from the trees, to know what matters and what doesn't.

Shubha is a one-woman band, only answerable to the director and to the film. The job requires collaboration—with costuming, with directing, with editing, with sound and props. And it requires tact and deftness with which to speak to movie stars and other talent—especially when corrections need to be made.

When Shubha spends time mentoring emerging script supervisors, she advises them not to behave like chowkidaars. 'Be assertive but be nice. Don't behave in a subservient way but don't have an ego on set. Behave as an equal.'

What about dealing with failure? 'Almost every film has mistakes,' she admits with candour. In Zoya Akhtar's film *Luck by Chance*, Konkona Sen Sharma wore a little necklace with her name, 'Sona', on it. 'When we shot her in the bathroom bathing, on the first day of the shoot, she wore it. About three-and-a-half months later, we shot the sequence of scenes before she is bathing, and I did not notice that she was not wearing the chain. I went to Zoya and told her of the problem. We came up with a solution. Farhan's character was being filmed writing a letter to Sona, so I thought we could place the chain next to the letter at her bedside or something like this and then she wears the chain when she is bathing because she's happy to have the love letter. I think that worked!'

Shubha was born on 14 September 1973 in Chennai and grew up in Bengaluru in a joint family. Her childhood was difficult because her parents had split up when she was a toddler and her sister Sunitha was just a few months old. Her mother and the two girls lived with Shubha's maternal aunt, a primary school principal, and her husband, a marketing executive, and their children, Sachin and Sandhya. At the age of eleven, her mom remarried but Shubha decided to stay on at her aunt's home.

'We were a middle-class family with not much money, but despite that, what we got seems incredible,' Shubha says. 'We had total freedom to choose our life paths, without explanation or fear. That's what my aunt, uncle and my parents gave us. They instilled in us the importance of excelling in whatever we did. If am a sweeper, I better be the best sweeper around!' By the time Shubha finished school, her aunt had passed away and her mother was battling cancer. It was a difficult time.

From an early age, she knew she would have to stand on her own feet as her family's resources were limited. After finishing BSc in physics, chemistry and maths at Mysore Education Society, she worked at an ad agency called Renaissance for a year. It was fun. She then found out she had aced the entrance exams for Hyderabad Central University. Shubha opted for a master's degree in communications.

Shubha remembers her years in Hyderabad with affection. 'I truly enjoyed studying and had brilliant classmates,' she says. She made lifelong friends like Deepika Adhikari and Meghna Haldar. The latter, a Vancouver-based film-maker, describes Shubha as chicken soup for her soul. 'Shubha has a wonderful generosity of spirit in an industry that is largely about self-interest and commerce,' notes Haldar. 'She will give the last cent in her pocket to you if you need it, she will engage with everyone and anyone—autorickshaw drivers to high and mighty producers— earnestly and spiritedly when she believes in something. She has spent years tutoring other script supervisors in the industry without charge and expectations attached. She wasn't fluent in Hindi, she didn't have a lot of savings and she knew only one person there.'

Meghna recalls Shubha telling her that she would sit in total darkness in her apartment because she didn't have money to buy a light bulb. 'But that's Shubha,' says her friend. 'Determined, ambitious and focused. She is entirely self-made—no godfathers, nobody to guide her path—and that in itself is worthy of such deep respect. In a tough, often cruel business, Shubha has managed to retain her deep sense of humanity, justice and artistic integrity. What an achievement!'

After her master's, Shubha headed back to Bengaluru and found herself at Broadcast Media Incorporated (BMI), where she met her mentor, Prem Chawla, who taught her the rigours of editing. Shubha remembers being scared of machines—computers weren't her forte—but Chawla took her under his wing. 'The only way to overcome any fear is to throw oneself wholeheartedly into the thing that frightens you and this is what I encouraged Shubha to do,' Chawla recalls. 'Shubha was bright and enthusiastic and eager to learn.'

Shubha loved editing but hated sitting in one place. She also faced the issue of not wanting to edit for clients when she disagreed with their viewpoint, a tricky issue in a service-oriented business. She decided to move on and quit BMI. This is when the *Agnivarsha* gig came about, in 2001.

On this film, she learned the nitty-gritty of the craft. She realized that waking up at 2 a.m. to dress 1500 extras for a month in exactly the same outfits was a waste of time and effort, because in a crowd of 1500, the audience doesn't notice these details. One didn't need to match shot-for-shot, but use one's wits.

After the film was shot, Shubha was determined to be part of the editing process. 'I went and planted myself in the office for two days and each time I saw the director Arjun Sajnani, I told him I had to work on the edit. I didn't need to be paid I said, but after a few days they gave me a little money. I made the editor Jabeen Merchant's life miserable by acting like a precocious kid, asking why he couldn't edit like this or that, doing backseat driving. She put up with me politely but that's when I also learned what matters and what doesn't in edits. I tell everyone to just sit in an edit studio to understand continuity.'

Shubha says script supervision does not require a laser-sharp memory. On a film set, where there are so many details to note, photographs are an important tool to aid the process. 'When you see a hero walking through the crowds, why is it that your attention is drawn to the hero and not the crowd?' Shubha asks rhetorically. 'There's a filmic language. The viewer is drawn to the hero and this is a function of lensing, sound design and many other elements to keep the audience focused. It's impossible to have everything in continuity, it's like trying to freeze the world, and you can't freeze the world. There will be little things that go wrong, so it is about approximation, and knowing that the editor has options of masking these errors. Editing is in my subconscious.'

When she's not working, Shubha writes scripts, but none have measured up to her satisfaction. She made a short film, called *From Here*, in 2006, about the meaning of home. She's holding on to her directorial ambitions, but till she takes to the floor in that role, she's happy where she is—working as a secret ninja to make cinema seamless.

HETAL DEDHIA
THE GAFFER

Hetal Dedhia holds a bulky light in her hand. It's a 2-kg Par Can, commonly used for theatre and concerts. She rotates it effortlessly, as one would a steering wheel. As she twirls it, a beam of white light makes a dramatic arc on the wall opposite her. She does it again, in the reverse direction. This time, the light is red. This is how Hetal tells a story—with her tool of choice—lights. The white lights indicate a car going forward, the red light, a car braking. As she manages the lighting in the middle of a cavernous set in Mumbai, an army of assistants—all men—hover in the background, ready to help the boss.

'I think lighting is the most important thing for films and commercials,' says Hetal, Hindi cinema's first and only female gaffer. 'Without it, you can't make anything look good.' The head electrician on any film or television production unit she's part of, thirty-two-year-old Hetal is proud of the unique place she holds in Indian cinematic history. 'I love it!' she says, her face melting into a wide grin. 'I don't think there can be anything better than that.'

Hetal has earned a reputation as a top-notch gaffer. 'She is my first choice,' says ad film maker Shashank Chaturvedi, known within the industry as Bob. He has worked with Hetal on over fifty projects. 'She's everyone's first choice. Everyone in the country wants to work with her.'

Lighting is a critical aspect of film-making and getting it right is key to effective storytelling. Jason West, a cinematographer with whom Hetal has been working for the last four years, says: 'A picture is created when light travels through the lens of a camera. That's it. It's the single most important thing in film-making.'

Hetal began her career in 2005, following in the footsteps of her father, Mulchand Dedhia, India's most celebrated gaffer. Among the numerous films she has worked on are the well-known Bollywood hits, *Bluffmaster*, *Karthik Calling Karthik* and *Road, Movie*. She has also assisted her father on multiple international productions shot in India and is particularly proud of her work on *Mission Impossible: The Ghost Protocol* and *Un Plus Une*.

On set, Hetal stands out. Not only because she's a girl handling cables and lights—usually work done by men—but because, as West says, 'She knows her stuff.' He first met Hetal when she was assisting her father on a film set and recalls a bright young girl hanging around, eager to learn the tricks of the trade. 'She's really smart and not scared of anything. That's why I like working with her. She's cool. I have a lot of respect for her.'

The word 'gaffer' was first used in the sixteenth century as a term of respect for an older gentleman.[1] It is believed to be a variation of 'Godfather'. Over time, the use of the word broadened and by the nineteenth century it was used as an informal title for the supervisor of a work crew. This was adopted by the movie industry, which began using the title for the chief supervisor of the lighting team. On Hetal's lighting company's website, a gaffer, sometimes also called the chief lighting technician, is described as 'the key backstage technician involved in the production of the film, managing every single task in lighting'.

Hetal loves gaffing. 'It's fun!' she says, because no two days are ever the same. 'Every lighting set-up is new, every director is new, every DoP's perception is different; so on every job, you do different things and meeting new people,' she says.

Each assignment throws up a new challenge—like lighting up one of the busiest neighbourhoods in the heart of Mumbai for a car-chase sequence at night.

The film was *Mission Impossible: Ghost Protocol*, starring Tom Cruise. Mulchand's team, which included Hetal, was responsible for lighting up Mumbai's historic Victoria Terminus, a UNESCO World Heritage Site, plus the streets around it. Filming took six days but the scene made up just a few seconds of the film.

'Three seconds is also very important for a film,' Hetal explains. 'Anything to make cinema happen in the nicest way possible is worth it.'

A gaffer's job begins well before a movie set is built. When Hetal takes on a new project, she works closely with the director of photography to understand the vision for the movie. It then becomes her job to create it. That usually begins with scouting locations. If it's a day shoot, she will check the position of the sun, which is key, Hetal explains, because sunlight and shadows can often pose a challenge. 'Sometimes, you don't want to use the sun at all,' she says. In such a situation, she has to find a way to block the sun and create an artificial one instead. 'You have to see—how

---

[1] *New Oxford Dictionary of English.*

the character will look better? It's not easy to light each and every kind of face. Faces look very different in different types of light.' For a night shoot, she'll see if there is enough space to set up the lights required.

Once the location is confirmed, she designs a lighting plan. 'That means deciding which lights to use, how many, how to distribute the power, the connection of the generators, daylight tungsten, colour matching, colour correction, all sorts of things,' Hetal says. She does it the old-school way, by drawing the layout on paper.

Next comes the execution stage. Lights are placed, tracks are laid, scaffolding goes up, generators are installed and power lines drawn. Throughout the process, Hetal takes a hands-on approach. Though she has a team of gaffers and light boys working with her, she doesn't think twice before scurrying up a ladder or climbing scaffolding to adjust the lights herself. No job is too small for her or unsuitable for a girl. If someone suggests it is either, Hetal laughs. She is fiercely independent and does what she wants. Is she a rebel? 'That describes me perfectly,' Hetal chuckles. 'Nobody can make decisions for me or tell me what I can and can't do.'

Born in Mumbai on 31 March 1985, Hetal is Mulchand and Chandrika's youngest child. Their firstborn, Keval, was physically and mentally challenged. Two daughters, Jinal and Minal, came before Hetal. The family never looked at Keval with pity or sadness; they celebrated his courage. 'We didn't cry seeing him because we saw him fight so much,' Hetal says. They derived strength from his attitude and applauded the enthusiasm with which he lived. Keval used to bathe and feed himself and go to school. 'What I learned from him was to just be happy,' Hetal says. 'He was unable to fight with this world but he kept smiling. I am sure he did not have the ability to know that he could only be this way—he did not have the option. He was always a happy soul—and he would bring chocolates back for me from his school.'

Hetal would drop Keval off at his special needs school on the way to hers every morning. Sometimes, she would linger at the doorway and watch him for a few minutes. She would think about the life Keval could have led. She'd find herself wondering, 'What if I stood up for my mum and father since he can't? Obviously Keval didn't have that choice. That thought crossed my mind many times.'

The Dedhias are a close-knit bunch and the family bonds are strong. Hetal's mother, Chandrika, is a homemaker. 'I saw my mother working all her life to keep the family going,' Hetal recalls. 'It is a full-time job and shouldn't be considered nothing. I think being a housewife should be a highly paid job.'

Her father is a self-made man. 'Dad has come from rags to riches,' Hetal says. 'He has his own story.' Mulchand, who never got a chance to study, worked as an electrician at weddings and other functions before he became a cable and generator operator. While laying cables on a film set, he would watch the 'lighting dadas' working around him—technicians were not called 'gaffers' back then. By silently observing them, he learned which light went where, what kind of connection each set-up needed, how much wattage each one required. He took it all in and taught himself how to light up a film set. Gradually, he began getting lighting jobs. His first big break came when Mira Nair hired him for *Salaam Bombay!* in 1998.

'We were not rich,' Hetal says, remembering her childhood. And there was added pressure on her father to support his extended family as well—his parents and sister relied on him. The family could not afford a television so the children never watched films. A visit to the cinema hall was out of the question. But they were drawn to the film world. Hetal and her sisters would drop in on the set where their father worked. The hustle and bustle, the chatter about lighting, watching her father give instructions, seeing the effort he put in on each assignment, made an impression on Hetal. She was intrigued. 'It was exciting to see how much of a process one had to go through for even one shoot, you know?'

The wide-eyed child was awed by one set in particular: *Bandit Queen*. 'It's a fantabulous film,' she says, remembering the big lights she saw as a nine-year-old. 'To me, it was mind-blowing.' It was a fancy set-up for the era it was shot in. 'Back then things were not so elaborate, the way they are now. For example, if they had to make a moon box, it would take almost one day of pre-lighting. These days, it can be done in three hours.'

A moon box?

'It's a big light box in the distance. It's used to light up a huge area. It goes up in the air, around 100 feet high on industrial cranes,' Hetal explains. At that time, she couldn't look past the technicalities of the grand set. But when she watched the film again two years ago, she was blown away not only by the sensitive lighting, but by the raw power of its story.

Hetal did not expect to follow in her father's footsteps. But those who know her say they are not surprised by the path she chose. They point to her brother's death as a turning point. Keval passed away in 1999 after a sudden heart attack. He was twenty-two.

It was a huge blow. 'A bad time,' says Ramesh Sadrani, a close family friend and fellow gaffer who has worked with Mulchand for several years. 'Hetal was a small girl but even back then, she thought she should do this, take over as a technician, take the company ahead.'

All three Dedhia girls work for the family-owned company, Light and Grips, founded by Mulchand in 1993. Jinal handles the finances while Minal works in management—thought she is currently taking a break to look after her young family. Hetal, now a director at the company, is the only one who took to the physically intense role of gaffing. 'My sisters would never think of doing what I do!' she laughs. 'Nobody wants to get their hands dirty. They are not one of those chicks.'

Jinal and Minal followed more conventional paths. They went to college, earned BCom degrees, got married and now have families of their own. Those items are not on Hetal's bucket list. 'They're on my Don't Do list!' she says, her eyes crinkle as she lets out a full-throttle laugh.

So what made the sisters choose such diverse paths?

'The difference is that I went to school with the intention of not studying at all and they went to school with the intention of studying a lot.' Hetal dropped out of St Anne's midway through high school and went on to finish the grade 10 privately. Her family was worried about her, Jinal says. 'We thought what good would she do if she failed school?'

Hetal got admission at Wilson College in south Mumbai. Instead of attending classes, she rebelled and played pool and snooker at a local gaming club called Sports and Spirits. Her explanation : 'I obviously had to kill time.'

There was another reason she was drawn to the game. Very few girls played it. 'It made me feel like I should do something that a woman has not really tried. That's why gaffing also attracted me. No woman was doing it.' Eventually Hetal became really good at pool. She started winning tournaments and briefly considered pursuing it professionally. But the thought of doing the same thing every day turned her off. She can't bear monotony.

Plus, it was hard to suppress the lure of the film world. Ever since she had stepped on to a film set as a little girl, Hetal knew she belonged to one. She couldn't ignore that pull any longer. Hetal told her parents that she wanted to follow in her father's footsteps. She was going to become a lighting technician.

Mulchand was not sure whether she would be able to hack it as a gaffer. 'I tried to convince her that this is a man's job because it involves lifting heavy cables and walking on scaffolding to fix the lights,' he says.

Hetal understood her parents scepticism. They did not know a single woman gaffer. It was an unconventional career choice—not just for an Indian woman but for a woman in any part of the world. 'Normally, in the culture we come from, girls get married by the time they are my age,' Hetal says. But she would have none of it. When Mulchand realized she was not going to back down, he simply said, 'This is your choice.'

He didn't ease his daughter's entry into the world of gaffing. Like every other aspiring gaffer who comes to him seeking a job, Hetal worked for the company for six months without pay. Mulchand told everyone on his team not to give her any preferential treatment. 'He wanted me to find my path,' Hetal says. The early days were tough. The learning curve was steep. The equipment were heavy and rigging lights meant climbing ladders and scaffolding. Hetal never thought twice about doing any of the grunt work. She would work out regularly to stay strong. She wanted to prove herself as a gaffer.

Sadrani, who remembers Hetal's early days, says, 'She would not just sit around but work on every front—on the loading, helping out with physical labour, learning how to rig lights, everything. In India, there's this wrong notion that only boys can do hard work or physical labour. For me Hetal is a proper light girl, a gaffer.'

The first film she worked on was *Bluffmaster*. She did that and many early initial jobs for free. It is the way trainees learned.

Hetal's career choice and her success as a gaffer surprised her family who had spent years worrying that a girl with no interest in academics would end up having no future. 'We never thought she would get into the technical side of things, into filming and gaffing,' Jinal says. 'But she took up this profession easily and so far, she has set a benchmark and it is very commendable. She is an example of someone achieving success without studying—an example to the future to show how women can have liberated lives without necessarily focusing on education.'

Hetal's tenacity forced Mulchand to change his opinion. 'She is doing very well. She has a good sense of lighting. I am very proud of her because there are very few female gaffers in the world.'

A woman electrician is an anomaly on a lighting team but Hetal says her gender has never come in the way of her work. The men who work with her agree. 'Just because she is a girl, it doesn't mean she has no knowledge and she can't do it. She knows everything about lights—like if this light is kept at this distance from the set, what the diffusion will be. She does all the rigging work herself. She never says, you set it up, and as head gaffer I'll come later and check. No, she is involved right from the set-up,' Sadrani adds.

Often the only woman in a testosterone-packed world, Hetal doesn't feel the need to downplay her feminine side. At 5'8", with her athletic frame and long dark curls, Hetal is often mistaken for a model. She has been offered several roles in front of the camera but has never considered it. 'I could not build that confidence,' she says, smiling self-consciously.

On a set or in her lighting workshop, she's girly but practical. The focus is on comfort and safety. 'As far as you are doing your work well, nobody is going to say because you have put on nail polish you have forgotten to do something. That's not going to happen.'

Rubber-soled shoes are mandatory for safety, to protect people from getting an electric shock through their feet, so Hetal usually wears sneakers at work. 'Gaffers cannot run around without shoes because the work has got to do with electricity. If I have to teach people what electricity really means, I would say, I can't wear sandals on shoots,' she says.

When she's not on set, it's a different story. When the crew has a wrap-up party to celebrate the end of a film shoot, Hetal wears a dress or a sari. 'And heels. I love heels!' she says. The crew is usually shocked to see her glamorous avatar. 'They say, what? Really!'

Hetal relishes the contrast. 'I think it's amazing to be so feminine and be a gaffer, which are two opposite roles,' she says, adding that being feminine should not be mistaken for being weak.

Jinal says, 'She is aggressive, rebellious in terms of justice—she'll do the right thing no matter what. She's soft with animals and poor and helpless people, she's very kind to them. Her behaviour and appearance on set may seem tomboyish but, she's soft on the inside.'

Hetal is a natural leader. 'I come across as strong,' she says. Despite being one of the youngest people on a set and almost always the only woman in her team, she says she does not have to work harder to command respect. 'I put things across from the beginning very strongly, so they don't have an option but to accept it and do it.'

In a deeply patriarchal society, that isn't always welcome. 'Sometimes it's really obvious that some people don't like it, being told what to do by a woman,' West says. They have filmed over 300 commercials together including the high-profile promotional film for the Indian Premier League. Personally, he loves working with Hetal not only because she is technically sound and creatively astute but because she brings a refreshing sensibility to the job as a woman. 'I'll tell you what doesn't come to the table . . . ego doesn't come to the table,' he says.

'She's like one of the boys,' Chaturvedi says. 'She talks like them. She abuses when needed and always has the right cuss words.' He laughs. In his experience, he says the men on a set have got used to having a female boss and says they respect her, 'Because they get to learn a lot from her.'

Are some men intimidated by Hetal? 'Yeah, they are, they are,' Hetal admits with a chuckle. It makes it that much harder to find a compatible partner. Hetal, who is currently single, says a guy she was dating didn't like the profession she was in. 'He thought it was not correct for a woman to be in a place like that.' The romance didn't last long.

Hetal is surprised that more women are not drawn to the exciting world she inhabits. Although some women are intrigued by what she does—they come and work with her for a few months—they use it as a stepping stone to move on to camera work or editing. Hetal, who assists

Jason with camerawork, loves being behind the lens too but says her goal is not to become a director of photography. 'Being DoP is a nice, well-paying job but I don't think there is that much fun in it, you know?'

Lighting on Indian sets has changed dramatically since *Apradhi*, the first Indian film shot with artificial lights released in 1931. P.C. Barua, an actor and film-maker in pre-independent India, observed the production techniques in a London studio and bought the equipment to take home to India. *Apradhi*, directed by Debaki Bose, was the first film made by Barua's studio.

Digital technology has dramatically changed the landscape since then. Lights are smaller and lighter and newer cameras can shoot at high speeds, requiring much less light. Instead of making a gaffer's work less relevant, Hetal says these technological advancements mean more work for lighting technicians. 'It gives you the liberty to shoot for longer hours. In the evening, if you are running out of bright daylight and you have one big light, you can easily cheat your close-ups into that—you can vouch for that because your cameras can go up to that level. So you can stand up and say OK, we can do a couple of shots even if it's dark. It gives a gaffer more work, not less.'

There is plenty of work—but money is tight.

Given a choice between working on an international production and a domestic one, Hetal will always pick the foreign one. 'There's no comparison. You don't find that much satisfaction when you are working on Indian films.' The reason? Budgets. In India, the primary goal is to save money. And the biggest casualty is safety. 'The moment you are hired for an international job, you are insured for everything. In India, if you are going to work for a Bollywood film, you are not insured for one damn thing. So if anything goes wrong, it's your loss. If you are going to catch fire, it's your loss. Your family gets nothing. It's sickening.'

She says the value of money has deteriorated over the years and experience has shown her that clients don't always honour their promises. 'You don't get paid. As a lighting company we keep struggling for payments.'

The power lies with leading men and ladies. 'I have a problem with the industry being so star-struck,' she says. 'It's not personal, but the system is dysfunctional. Stars are so overpowering that we, or directors or the DoPs, do not get a chance to do our respective creative jobs.' When filming an advertisement that should be spread over three days, an actor will give the shoot just eight hours of his or her time. The technical team has to squeeze in three days of work into those hours. 'That's not right,' Hetal says.

She works hard. When she started training to become a gaffer, she did not allow herself to take time out. 'I was running a race. I was a work machine.' Nowadays, when there is a gap in her schedule, she travels. 'I think I will only work and earn to see different parts of the world. Otherwise I don't need money.' She travels alone, loves to explore new cities and meet different kinds of people. She has seen Europe. Next on her itinerary is America. 'I feel travelling gives you a variety of experiences, which allow you to assess your own life and surroundings because you always feel the grass is greener on the other side, which is mostly not true until you go and see it for yourself.'

No matter where her journey takes her, her home, which she shares with her parents, holds a special place. 'I can't do without coming back home, you know. First thing, I can't even cook Maggi noodles properly. I don't think I will ever be able to live alone!' she laughs.

Plus, she likes going home to her pets. She has a dog, a couple of cats and also had a rescued monkey she adopted while on a shoot with her father in the historical town of Hampi in 2004. Mulchand was working on *The Myth*, starring Jackie Chan. In several interpretations of the Ramayana, Hampi was considered the kingdom of monkeys. They are everywhere. One little monkey would hang around the Dedhias' light truck. 'She was really insecure, she was really tiny. She didn't want to leave the light van, so I just decided to bring her home.' She named the monkey JC, after Jackie Chan. JC shared a room with Hetal for sixteen years before she passed away in 2018, leaving Hetal grief-stricken. 'She was like my child,' Hetal says. 'I don't know if anyone will spend sixteen years in my room with me like JC did.'

In Mumbai, Hetal finds it hard to find time for herself. She manages to snatch a few minutes alone when she goes for walks with her dog. 'Giving space to yourself nowadays is difficult. You are constantly into something. There is so much going on in your life.' Sometimes, she manages to give her mind and body a rest while on a work trip. By going straight back to her hotel room after finishing a shoot, she saves on time that would have otherwise been lost commuting in Mumbai's heavy traffic. 'Those two extra hours give you time to think about what you want to do and what you don't want to do,' she says. Being on her own inspires her.

Part of her plan is to produce high quality advertisements and films. In August 2017, she set up a production house with Jason called DW Films, which will look at making story-centric advertisements. 'Quality and creativity is deteriorating,' she says, referring to the advertising space, 'so obviously I do not like that. We would like to bring a change, make nice films.' That's not the only goal. 'I want to set an example of how simply and easily a shoot can be done. Without complications, without going over budget, without running out of money so that you can't pay people.'

She will continue to be part of her father's company as well. 'I will work there forever. That's my world. And the one hundred light boys and gaffers who work there? They are my family.'

Sitting in the workshop, resplendent in the glare of large lights, this path-breaker says the world of gaffing is ever evolving—it is a field that allows her to pick up new skills. 'My father, who has been a gaffer for four decades, is still learning. I recently worked with a seventy-two-year-old French gaffer who insisted he was still learning. It was amazing to see that people are gaffers for all their lives in other countries.' That's not the case in India. Hetal says people usually stop gaffing after a while because the profession is underpaid and they can earn a better living by shooting or editing.

'Nobody's aim today is to become a gaffer,' Hetal says, the disappointment in her voice is unmistakable. 'No little girl says I want to be a gaffer when I grow up.' After a pause, she adds, 'That's the truth.'

But, for anyone who feels inspired to try their hand at lighting—or any other field that is male-dominated, she has some advice: 'If it challenges you, I say, go for it.'

Acknowledgements

This book would not have been possible without the help of numerous people, but before we thank them, we thank each other. We met twenty years ago at Columbia University's Graduate School of Journalism in New York, two twenty-somethings who didn't know where life would take us. In a happy coincidence, a decade after finishing graduate school, we found ourselves living in the heaving megapolis of Mumbai. Although our work took us in different directions—one pursued broadcast, the other print—we were storytellers who wanted to work together. The push and pull of daily deadlines, travel and business that come with being working parents meant this didn't happen for several years . . . till the idea of this book came upon us. This journey wouldn't have been intellectually engaging or any fun if the two of us hadn't undertaken it together.

It also wouldn't have happened without the twenty wonderful women we have profiled. We approached them as strangers—two nosy reporters with a tall ask. We asked them to open up about their lives to us, to let us into their homes, to tell us about their careers, to talk about their setbacks and comebacks, to introduce us to their families, to discuss their frustrations and hopes and share their life stories with us. All of them did so, generously. They welcomed us with a warmth and openness—sometimes, accompanied by an amazing home-cooked meal—for which we remain grateful. The more we learnt about their journeys, the more excited we became to share them with the world. We remain firmly indebted to these twenty incredible artistes for trusting us to tell their stories.

We are fortunate to have had many cheerleaders who encouraged us to convert an idea for a book into reality. We thank our agent, Kanishka Gupta, for putting up with our crankiness, for giving us courage and for being such a good sounding board; Farah Khan for her unflinching support and for generously sharing her Rolodex with us; Rajeev Masand for brainstorming sessions in person, on the phone or via WhatsApp, wherever in the world he was; Anil Kapoor for his unbridled enthusiasm, knowledge of the industry, and for never letting a single message or call go unanswered. Udayan Bhat for helping us compile our list and his abundant patience; Reshma Shetty and her wonderful team at Matrix Bay, including Grishma; Meghna Ghai Puri for putting our research into context. Our research assistant, Anisha Lalwani, was the goddess of transcription, going through endless interviews—we would have been bereft without her meticulous organization, administrative support and fact checks. And to our brilliant editor, Swati Chopra, and the entire Penguin team led by CEO Gaurav Shrinagesh, thank you for seeing the book through.

We would also like to thank Ambassador T.C.A. Rangachari, Dr Nitya Mohan Khemka, Rahul Jacob, Ravi Agrawal and Priya Iyer for reading early drafts and offering invaluable inputs. In addition, numerous individuals were generous with their time despite their busy schedules. A big, big thanks to Aamir Khan, Ronnie Screwvala, Karan Johar, Katrina Kaif, Priyanka Chopra, Raju Hirani, Vishal Bhardwaj, R. Balki, Hrithik Roshan, Deepika Padukone, Vidya Balan, Siddharth Roy Kapur, Alia Bhatt, Zoya Akhtar, Sooni Taraporevala, Shonali Bose, Kamna and Navin Chandra, Pimmi Seth, Mahesh Mathai, Srila Chatterjee, Tarun Mansukhani, Abhishek Varman, Ayan Mukerji, Raja Krishna Menon, Mozez Singh, Mihir Bose, Farrokh Chothia, Rashmi Uday Singh, Priya Tanna, Ronnie Lahiri, Smriti Kiran, Vishnu Rao, Sharmishta Roy, Shikha Sharma, Gopal Shah, Garima Vohra, Arjun Varain Singh, Udesh Sharma, Stanley Rosario, Jayanti Saha and Karishma Prakash of Kwan. We are also grateful to Boney Kapoor and the late Sridevi Kapoor. A thank you to T.C.A. Srinivisa-Raghavan, who got the ball rolling.

We want to say a special, heartfelt thank you to our friend and award-winning photographer Vijay Bedi, who made multiple trips to Mumbai to take portraits for this book—and refused to be compensated for it. He is content championing the work of a group of women in India. Having known Vijay for years, we know that this is true of the person he is: sensitive, committed and generous of spirit.

We would like to send a big shout out to our friends and family who put up with us as we spent much of the last fifteen months on the phone, commuting to interviews, travelling, WhatsApping, texting, Skyping, researching, reporting, Facetiming and never going anywhere without our laptops. We are grateful for all the support.

There are many people who have influenced us as storytellers and helped shape this book—the list is far too long to share here but each of us owe the following people a great deal of gratitude.

Mallika: A big thank you to my colleagues at CNN and at Bloomberg for giving me the space and support to write a book. To my mentor, Richard Quest, for teaching me to make it out of the gates and to the finish line with grace and rhythm (and manoeuvring those hurdles!). Ramana Nanda, Arjun Punshi and Priyal Gulati for reading early, messy drafts with patience and a smile. Ambika and Anuja for the kind of feedback only sisters can get away with. Rajiv Mehrotra, you remain a tonic for my soul. To Satish and Preeti Kapur, my rocks, for encouraging every dream. Rahil and Saher, thank you for tolerating a distracted mom, putting up with my odd hours and keeping the dog quiet while I recorded hours and hours of interviews. To Sid, my wingman and forever man. You have my love and my thanks.

Gayatri: To Tina Brown, thank you for showing me that when determined women get together, wonderful things can happen. To Kokila and T.C.A. Rangachari, for instilling in me a love of books and for ensuring that I never become a 'lotus eater'. To Toni, thanks for sharing the same sense of the ridiculous. To my extended family, the Zutshis and to my aunts Chandra Chari and Jaya Krishnamachari, for seeing through my inherent indolence and always encouraging me to write a book. Yuvraj and Serena, thank you for patiently bearing with a harried mother, and for giving me the space to work endless hours in my 'office' aka the bedroom! Finally, to Sachin, my beginning, middle and end. Thank you for lighting up my world.

ENDNOTES

Introduction

KATRINA KAIF

All quotes from Katrina Kaif in this Introduction are from an interview of Katrina by Mallika conducted on 19 April 2018.

VIDYA BALAN

All quotes from Vidya Balan in this Introduction are from an interview of Vidya by Gayatri conducted on 6 September 2017.

ANIL KAPOOR

All quotes from Anil Kapoor in this Introduction are from a phone interview of Anil by Mallika conducted on 24 April 2018.

KARAN JOHAR

All quotes from Karan Johar in this chapter are from an interview of Karan by Mallika conducted on 10 August 2018.

Charu Khurana

CHARU KHURANA

All quotes from Charu Khurana in this chapter are from interviews of Charu by Mallika conducted on 9 and 11 June 2017 and by Medhavi Arora on 8 July 2017.

NEELAM KHURANA

All quotes from Neelam Khurana in this chapter are from interviews of Neelam conducted by Mallika on 20 June 2017 and by Medhavi Arora on 8 July 2017.

VIDYA TIKARI

All quotes from Vidya Tikari in this chapter are from an interview of Vidya conducted by Medhavi Arora on 12 November 2017.

NAMRATA SONI

All quotes from Namrata Soni in this chapter are from an interview of Namrata conducted by Mallika on 1 September 2017.

JYOTIKA KALRA

All quotes from Jyotika Kalra in this chapter are from an interview of Jyotika by Medhavi Arora conducted on 30 July 2017.

CCMAA: We tried to reach the association on multiple occasions via phone, text, WhatsApp messages and an email sent on 8 April 2018 but never heard back.

Juhi Chaturvedi

JUHI CHATURVEDI

All quotes from Juhi Chaturvedi in this chapter are from interviews of Juhi by Gayatri conducted on 16 March 2018 and 19 March 2018.

LEKHA CHATURVEDI

All quotes from Lekha Chaturvedi in this chapter are from an interview of Lekha by Gayatri conducted on 2 April 2018.

ASHEESH MALHOTRA

All quotes from Asheesh Malhotra in this chapter are from an interview of Asheesh by Gayatri conducted on 4 April 2018.

RATI BAWA

All quotes from Rati Bawa in this chapter are from an interview of Rati by Gayatri conducted on 9 April 2018.

SONIA SEN

All quotes from Sonia Sen in this chapter are from an interview of Sonia by Gayatri conducted on 5 April 2018.

RONNIE LAHIRI

All quotes from Ronnie Lahiri in this chapter are from an interview of Ronnie by Gayatri conducted on 18 April 2018.

Guneet Monga

GUNEET MONGA

All quotes from Guneet Monga in this chapter are from interviews of Guneet by Mallika conducted on 26 June 2017 and 9 July 2017.

KAMLESH AGARWAL

All quotes from Kamlesh Agarwal in this chapter are from an interview of Kamlesh by Medhavi Arora conducted on 30 July 2017.

MAYANK JHA

All quotes from Mayank Jha in this chapter are from an interview of Mayank by Mallika conducted on 12 September 2017.

PRERNA SAIGAL

All quotes from Prerna Saigal in this chapter are from an interview of Prerna by Mallika conducted on 15 March 2018.

BARADWAJ RANGAN

All quotes from Baradwaj Rangan in this chapter are from an interview of Baradwaj by Mallika conducted on 13 March 2018.

Anaita Shroff Adajania

ANAITA SHROFF ADAJANIA

All quotes from Anaita Adajania Shroff in this chapter are from interviews of Anaita conducted by Gayatri on 20 June 2017 and 15 August 2017.

MAHESH MATHAI

All quotes from Mahesh Mathai in this chapter are from an interview of Mahesh conducted by Gayatri on 26 October 2017.

HOMI ADAJANIA

All quotes from Homi Adajania in this chapter are from an interview of Homi conducted by Gayatri over email on 13 July 2017.

FARROKH CHOTHIA

All quotes from Farrokh Chothia in this chapter are from an interview of Farrokh conducted by Gayatri on 28 October 2017.

HRITHIK ROSHAN

All quotes from Hrithik Rohan in this chapter are from an interview of Hrithik conducted by Gayatri over email on 31 October 2017.

DEEPIKA PADUKONE

All quotes from Deepika Padukone in this chapter are from an interview of Deepika conducted by Gayatri on 6 November 2017.

KARAN JOHAR

All quotes from Karan Johar in this chapter are from an interview of Karan conducted by Gayatri on 23 April 2018.

Deepa Bhatia

DEEPA BHATIA

All quotes from Deepa Bhatia in this chapter are from interviews with Deepa conducted by Mallika on 7 August 2017 and 8 October 2017.

GOVIND NIHALANI

All quotes from Govind Nihalani in this chapter are from an interview of Govind by Mallika conducted on 25 January 2018.

AAMIR KHAN
All quotes from Aamir Khan in this chapter are from an interview of Aamir conducted by Gayatri on 12 May 2018.

AMOLE GUPTE
All quotes from Amole Gupte in this chapter are from an interview of Amole by Mallika conducted on 6 October 2017.

MALA BHATIA
All quotes from Mala Bhatia in this chapter are from an interview of Mala by Mallika conducted on 8 October 2017.

ABHISHEK KAPOOR
All quotes from Abhishek Kapoor in this chapter are from an interview of Abhishek by Mallika conducted on 7 October 2017.

RAJ SURVE
All quotes from Raj Surve in this chapter are from an interview of Raj by Mallika conducted on 21 September 2017.

JEROO MULLA
All quotes from Jeroo Mulla in this chapter are from an interview of Jeroo by Medhavi Arora conducted on 17 August 2017.

Gauri Shinde

GAURI SHINDE
All quotes from Gauri Shinde in this chapter are from interviews of Gauri by Gayatri conducted on 22 August 2017, 5 November 2017 and 11 February 2018.

SRIDEVI KAPOOR
All quotes from Sridevi Kapoor in this chapter are from an interview of Sridevi by Gayatri conducted on 8 January 2018.

KAUSAR MUNIR
All quotes from Kausar Munir in this chapter are from an interview of Kausar by Gayatri conducted on 5 December 2017.

R. BALKI
All quotes from R. Balki in this chapter are from an interview of R. Balki by Gayatri conducted on 12 December 2017.

KAVITA ADVANI
All quotes from Kavita Advani in this chapter are from an interview of Kavita by Gayatri conducted on 14 December 2017.

SHIKHA SHARMA
All quotes from Shikha Sharma in this chapter are from an interview of Shikha by Gayatri conducted on 22 December 2017.

ANIL GUPTA
All quotes from Anil Gupta in this chapter are from an interview of Anil by Gayatri conducted on 14 December 2017.

AMER JALEEL
All quotes from Amer Jaleel in this chapter are from an interview of Amer by Gayatri conducted on 8 January 2018.

ALIA BHATT
All quotes from Alia Bhatt in this chapter are from a recorded voice message of Alia sent to Gayatri on 2 February 2018.

VAISHALI SHINDE
All quotes from Vaishali Shinde in this chapter are from an interview of Vaishali by Gayatri conducted on 9 January 2018.

Geeta Tandon

GEETA TANDON
All quotes from Geeta Tandon in this chapter are from interviews with Geeta by Mallika conducted on 6 August 2017 and Anisha Lalvani on 27 July 2017 and by Gayatri on 7 January 2018 and 7 February 2018.

RESHMA PATHAN
All quotes in this chapter are from an interview of Reshma by Mallika conducted on 14 August 2017.

HARSHA TANDON
All quotes from Harsha Tandon in this chapter are from an interview of Harsha by Mallika conducted on 6 August 2017.

PRATAP TANDON
All quotes from Pratap Tandon in this chapter are from an interview of Pratap by Mallika conducted on 6 August 2017.

AEJAZ GULAB
All quotes from Aejaz Gulab in this chapter are from interviews with Aejaz conducted by Mallika on 30 August 2017, 12 January 2018, 20 January 2018, 24 April 2018, 21 May 2018.

Geeta has spoken to the BBC:
http://www.bbc.com/news/magazine-36924617
To Huffpost—and to many more mags and papers:
https://www.huffingtonpost.in/2016/06/02/geeta-tandon_n_10235460.html
https://www.firstpost.com/living/packing-a-punch-how-geeta-tandon-became-a-leading-bollywood-stuntwoman-2828468.html
She's done an independent Ted talk:
https://www.youtube.com/watch?v=HWmpqatvD6I
Another one:
https://www.youtube.com/watch?v=B5lFmB3Z9Bk

Kiran Rao

KIRAN RAO
All quotes from Kiran Rao in this chapter are from interviews of Kiran conducted by Gayatri on 31 August 2017 and 21 September 2017.

AAMIR KHAN
All quotes from Aamir Khan in this chapter are from an interview of Aamir conducted by Gayatri on 12 May 2018.

ZOYA AKHTAR
All quotes from Zoya Akhtar in this chapter are from an interview of Zoya conducted by Gayatri on 6 March 2018.

SRILA CHATTERJEE

All quotes from Srila Chatterjee in this chapter are from an interview of Srila conducted by Gayatri on 31 October 2017.

ANUPAMA CHOPRA

All quotes from Anupama Chopra in this chapter are from an interview of Anupama conducted by Gayatri on 12 January 2018.

SMRITI KIRAN

All quotes from Smriti Kiran in this chapter are from an interview of Smriti conducted by Gayatri on 19 January 2018.

SHIVANI BHASIN SACHDEVA

All quotes from Shivani Bhasin Sachdeva in this chapter are from an interview of Shivani conducted by Gayatri on 26 January 2018.

UMA AND SATYANARAYAN RAO

All quotes from Kiran's parents, Uma and Satyanarayan Rao, in this chapter are from an interview of her parents conducted by Gayatri on 25 January 2018.

SOPHY V. SIVARAMAN

All quotes from Sophy V. Sivaraman in this chapter are from an interview of Sophy conducted by Gayatri on 9 April 2018.

VISHAL BHARDWAJ

All quotes from Vishal Bhardwaj in this chapter are from an interview of Vishal by Gayatri on 11 November 2017.

Anvita Dutt

ANVITA DUTT

All quotes from Anvita Dutt in this chapter are from an interview of Anvita by Mallika conducted on 8 August 2017.

MAYANK DUTT

All quotes from Mayank Dutt in this chapter are from an interview of Mayank by Mallika conducted on 26 October 2017.

AMIT TRIVEDI
All quotes from Amit Trivedi in this chapter are from an interview of Amit by Mallika conducted on 15 February 2018.

JATIN VERMA
All quotes from Jatin Verma in this chapter are from an interview of Jatin by Medhavi Arora conducted on 24 October 2017.

VISHAL DADLANI
All quotes from Vishal Dadlani in this chapter are from an interview of Vishal by Mallika conducted on 26 October 2017.

GAURI DHANALAKSHMI
All quotes from Gauri Dhanalakshmi in this chapter are from an interview of Gauri by Mallika conducted on 14 February 2018.

MRS RAGHUVIR
All quotes from Mrs Raghuvir in this chapter are recalled by Anvita.

Anupama Chopra

ANUPAMA CHOPRA
All quotes from Anupama Chopra in this chapter are from interviews of Anupama by Gayatri conducted on 19 June 2017, 19 August 2017 and 1 January 2018.

EUNICE DE SOUZA
All quotes from Eunice De Souza in this chapter are from an interview of Eunice by Gayatri conducted on 6 July 2017.

ABE PECK
All quotes from Abe Peck in this chapter are from an interview of Abe by Gayatri conducted on 28 June 2017.

KAMNA AND NAVIN CHANDRA
All quotes from Kamna and Navin Chandra in this chapter are from interviews of Kamna and Navin by Gayatri conducted on 31 August 2017.

KOMAL NAHTA

All quotes from Komal Nahta in this chapter are from an interview of Komal by Mallika on 19 November 2017.

BILL MCDOWELL

All quotes from Bill McDowell in this chapter are from an interview of Bill by Abe Peck as told to Gayatri during an email interview of Abe on 28 June 2017.

Shanoo Sharma

SHANOO SHARMA

All quotes from Shanoo Sharma in this chapter are from interviews with Shanoo by Mallika conducted on 6 August 2017, 9 November 2017, 14 November 2017, 7 April 2018.

ARJUN KAPOOR

All quotes from Arjun Kapoor in this chapter are from an interview of Arjun by Mallika conducted on 4 November 2017.

HONEY TREHAN

All quotes from Honey Trehan in this chapter are from an interview of Honey by Mallika conducted on 4 November 2017.

UDESH SHARMA

All quotes from Udesh Sharma in this chapter are from an interview of Udesh by Mallika conducted on 6 August 2017.

SUDHIR MISHRA

All quotes from Sudhir Mishra in this chapter are from an interview of Sudhir by Mallika conducted on 24 March 2017.

CHARMI GONDALIA

All quotes from Charmi Gondalia in this chapter are from an interview of Charmi by Mallika conducted on 4 November 2017.

KARAN JOHAR

All quotes from Karan Johar in this chapter are from an interview of Karan by Mallika conducted on 10 August 2018.

AMIT BEHL

All quotes from Amit Behl in this chapter are from an interview of Amit done by Anisha Lalvani on 16 December 2017.

Priya Seth

PRIYA SETH

All quotes from Priya Seth in this chapter are from interviews of Priya conducted by Gayatri on 12 June 2017, 7 July 2017 and 31 January 2018.

RAJA KRISHNA MENON

All quotes from Raja Krishna Menon in this chapter are from an interview of Raja conducted by Gayatri on 4 August 2017.

SAJID SANWARI

All quotes from Sajid Sanwari in this chapter are from an interview of Sajid conducted by Gayatri on 21 August 2017.

VISHNU RAO

All quotes from Vishnu Rao in this chapter are from an interview of Vishnu conducted by Gayatri on 23 August 2017.

PIMMI SETH

All quotes from Pimmi Seth in this chapter are from an interview of Pimmi conducted by Gayatri on 13 July 2017.

SHIMONA SHAHI RANA

All quotes from Shimona Shahi Rana in this chapter are from an interview of Shimona via Facebook Messenger conducted by Gayatri on 20 September 2017.

GOPAL SHAH

All quotes from Gopal Shah in this chapter are from an interview of Gopal conducted by Gayatri on 25 October 2017.

MEGHNA GHAI PURI

All quotes from Meghna Ghai Puri in this chapter are from an interview of Meghna conducted by Mallika on 7 August 2017.

Rohini Iyer

ROHINI IYER

All quotes from Rohini Iyer in this chapter are from interviews of Rohini by Mallika on conducted on 6 August 2017 and 9 March 2018.

KATRINA KAIF

All quotes from Katrina Kaif in this chapter are from an interview of Katrina by Mallika conducted on 19 April 2018.

SUSHANT SINGH RAJPUT

All quotes from Sushant Singh Rajput in this chapter are from email comments by Sushant Singh Rajput to Mallika on 1 February 2018.

PRIYANKA CHOPRA

All quotes from Priyanka Chopra in this chapter are from a recorded voice message sent to Mallika on 20 April 2018.

RAHILA MIRZA

All quotes from Rahila Mirza in this chapter are from an interview of Rahila by Mallika conducted on 9 March 2018.

VIDYA BALAN

All quotes from Vidya Balan in this chapter are from an interview of Vidya by Gayatri on 6 September 2017.

BHAWANA SOMAAYA

All quotes from Bhawana Somaaya in this chapter are from email comments by Bhawana sent to Medhavi Arora on 1 October 2017.

FARAH KHAN

All quotes from Farah Khan in this chapter are from an interview of Farah by Mallika and Gayatri on 5 August 2017.

Geeta Kapur

GEETA KAPUR

All quotes from Geeta Kapur in this chapter are from interviews with Geeta conducted by Gayatri on 4 July 2017 and 12 September 2017.

HEMA MALINI CHARI

All quotes from Hema Malini Chari in this chapter are from an interview with Hema conducted by Anisha Lalvani on 24 October 2017.

FARAH KHAN

All quotes from Farah Khan in this chapter are from an interview with Farah conducted by Gayatri on 5 August 2017.

KEN GHOSH

All quotes from Ken Ghosh in this chapter are from an interview with Ken conducted by Anisha Lalvani on 29 October 2017.

FAISAL KHAN

All quotes from Faisal Khan in this chapter are from an interview with Faisal conducted by Anisha Lalvani on 29 October 2017.

RUEL DAUSAN VARIDANI

All quotes from Ruel Dausan Varidani in this chapter are from an interview with Ruel conducted by Anisha Lalvani on 30 October 2017.

TARUN MANSUKHANI

All quotes from Tarun Mansukhani in this chapter are from an interview of Tarun conducted by Gayatri on 26 February 2018.

SHILPA SHETTY

All quotes from Shilpa Shetty in this chapter are from an interview of Shilpa conducted by Gayatri on 16 February 2018.

RICK ROY

All quotes from Rick Roy in this chapter are from an interview of Rick conducted by Gayatri on 4 July 2017.

Sneha Khanwalkar

SNEHA KHANWALKAR

All quotes from Sneha Khanwalkar in this chapter are from interviews with Sneha conducted by Mallika on 13 November 2017 and 7 April 2018.

RUCHI BAKSHI SHARMA

All quotes from Ruchi Bakshi Sharma in this chapter are from an interview of Ruchi by Mallika conducted on 28 January 2018.

SUBHASH KHANWALKAR

All quotes from Subhash Khanwalkar in this chapter are from an interview of Subhash by Mallika conducted on 19 January 2018.

AMIT GURBAXANI

All quotes from Amit Gurbaxani in this chapter are from an interview of Amit by Mallika conducted on 23 March 2018.

DIBAKAR BANERJEE

All quotes from Dibakar Banerjee in this chapter are from an interview of Dibakar by Mallika conducted on 18 January 2018.

KOMAL NAHTA

All quotes from Komal Nahta in this chapter are from an interview of Komal by Mallika conducted on 19 November 2017.

VISHAL BHARDWAJ

All quotes from Vishal Bhardwaj in this chapter are from an interview of Vishal by Gayatri on 11 November 2017.

Amrita Pandey

AMRITA PANDEY

All quotes from Amrita Pandey in this chapter are from interviews of Amrita conducted by Gayatri on 28 June 2017, 3 July 2017, 21 July 2017, 31 July 2017 and 13 February 2018.

SIDDHARTH ROY KAPUR

All quotes from Siddharth Roy Kapur in this chapter are from an interview of Siddharth conducted by Gayatri on 25 July 2017.

RONNIE SCREWVALA

All quotes from Ronnie Screwvala in this chapter are from an interview of Ronnie conducted by Gayatri on 9 July 2017.

AAMIR KHAN

All quotes from Aamir Khan in this chapter are from an interview of Aamir conducted by Gayatri on 12 May 2018.

RAJU HIRANI

All quotes from Raju Hirani in this chapter are from an interview of Raju conducted by Gayatri on 25 October 2017.

KARAN JOHAR

All quotes from Karan Johar in this chapter are from an interview of Karan conducted by Gayatri on 23 April 2018.

MAHESH SAMAT

All quotes from Mahesh Samat in this chapter are from an interview of Mahesh conducted by Gayatri on 9 April 2018.

VISHAL BHARDWAJ

All quotes from Vishal Bhardwaj in this chapter are from an interview of Vishal by Gayatri on 11 November 2017.

FARAH KHAN

All quotes from Farah Khan in this chapter are from an interview of Farah by Mallika and Gayatri on 5 August 2017.

SUJATA CHANDA

All quotes from Sujata Chanda in this chapter are from an interview of Sujata conducted by Gayatri on 28 June 2017.

Shikha Kapur

SHIKHA KAPUR

All quotes from Shikha Kapur in this chapter are from interviews of Shikha conducted by Mallika on 31 July 2017 and 5 August 2017.

RAM MADHVANI

All quotes from Ram Madhvani in this chapter are from an interview with Ram conducted by Mallika on 15 November 2017.

TRISH KAPUR

All quotes from Trish Kapur in this chapter are from an interview of Trish by Mallika conducted on 14 November 2017.

PASHAN JAL

All quotes from Pashan Jal in this chapter are from an interview of Pashan by Mallika conducted on 15 November 2017.

AAMIR KHAN
All quotes from Aamir Khan in this chapter are from an interview of Aamir conducted by Gayatri on 12 May 2018.

VIJAY SINGH
All quotes from Vijay Singh in this chapter are from an interview of Vijay by Mallika conducted on 19 January 2018.

SIDDHARTH ROY KAPUR
All quotes from Siddharth Roy Kapur in this chapter are from an interview of Siddharth by Gayatri conducted on 25 July 2017.

SAVITA KHANNA
All quotes from Savita Khanna in this chapter are from an interview of Savita by Mallika conducted on 5 August 2017.

Amrita Mahal Nakai

AMRITA MAHAL NAKAI
All quotes from Amrita Mahal Nakai in this chapter are from interviews of Amrita conducted by Mallika on 26 June 2017 and by Gayatri on 6 February 2018 and 13 February 2018.

KSHAMATA SACHIN GAURAV
All quotes from Kshamata Sachin Gaurav in this chapter are from an interview of Kshamata conducted by Anisha Lalvani on 9 February 2018.

VIR NAKAI
All quotes from Vir Nakai in this chapter are from an interview of Vir conducted by Gayatri on 14 February 2018.

SOONI TARAPOREVALA
All quotes from Sooni Taraporevala in this chapter are from an interview of Sooni conducted by Gayatri on 15 February 2018.

ABHISHEK VARMAN

All quotes from Abhishek Varman in this chapter are from an interview of Abhishek conducted by Gayatri on 26 February 2018.

TARUN MANSUKHANI

All quotes from Tarun Mansukhani in this chapter are from an interview of Tarun conducted by Gayatri on 26 February 2018.

MUNINDRA D. JANGAM

All quotes from Munindra D. Jangam in this chapter are from an interview of Munindra conducted by Anisha Lalvani on 7 March 2018.

SUMAYYA SHAIKH

All quotes from Sumayya Shaikh in this chapter are from an interview of Sumayya conducted by Anisha Lalvani on 5 March 2018.

ANAITA SHROFF ADAJANIA

All quotes from Anaita Shroff Adajania in this chapter are from an interview of Anaita conducted by Gayatri on 5 March 2018.

RABINA MAHAL

All quotes from Rabina Mahal in this chapter are from an interview of Rabina conducted by Gayatri on 7 March 2018.

RANGARAO CHOUGHLE

All quotes from Rangarao Choughle in this chapter are from an interview of Rangarao conducted by Anisha Lalvani on 30 March 2018.

SHARMISHTA ROY

All quotes from Sharmishta Roy in this chapter are from an interview of Sharmishta conducted by Gayatri on 23 April 2018.

KARAN JOHAR

All quotes from Karan Johar in this chapter are from an interview of Karan conducted by Gayatri on 11 April 2018.

ANIL MEHTA

All quotes from Anil Mehta in this chapter are from an interview of Anil conducted by Gayatri on 1 March 2018.

Shubha Ramachandra

SHUBHA RAMACHANDRA

All quotes from Shubha Ramachandra in this chapter are from interviews of Shubha conducted by Gayatri on 13 June 2017, 14 July 2017 and 11 February 2018.

UDAYAN BHAT

All quotes from Udayan Bhat in this chapter are from an interview of Udayan conducted by Gayatri on 24 October 2018.

ZOYA AKHTAR

All quotes from Zoya Akhtar in this chapter are from an interview of Zoya conducted by Gayatri on 6 March 2018.

SRILA CHATTERJEE

All quotes from Srila Chatterjee in this chapter are from an interview of Srila conducted by Gayatri on 31 October 2017.

PREM CHAWLA

All quotes from Prem Chawla in this chapter are from an interview of Prem conducted by Anisha Lalvani on 30 October 2017.

SUJOY GHOSH

All quotes from Sujoy Ghosh in this chapter are from an interview of Sujoy conducted by Gayatri on 30 October 2017.

SHONALI BOSE

All quotes from Shonali Bose in this chapter are from an interview of Shonali conducted by Gayatri on 30 October 2017.

MEGHNA HALDAR
All quote from Meghna Haldar in this chapter are from an interview of Meghna conducted by Gayatri on 28 October 2017.

Hetal Dedhia

HETAL DEDHIA
All quotes from Hetal Dedhia in this chapter are from interviews of Hetal by Mallika conducted on 8 November 2017, 20 November 2017, 17 February 2018 and by Anisha Lalvani on 8 January 2018.

MULCHAND DEDHIA
All quotes from Mulchand Dedhia in this chapter are from an interview of Mulchand by Mallika conducted on 6 December 2017.

JINAL DEDHIA
All quotes from Jinal Dedhia in this chapter are from an interview of Jinal by Anisha Lalvani conducted on 8 January 2018.

RAMESH SADRANI
All quotes from Ramesh Sadrani in this chapter are from an interview of Ramesh by Anisha Lalvani conducted on 8 January 2018.

JASON WEST
All quotes from Jason West in this chapter are from an interview of Jason by Mallika conducted on 22 January 2018.

SHASHANK CHATURVEDI
All quotes from Shashank Chaturvedi in this chapter are from an interview of Shashank by Mallika conducted on 15 March 2018.